# Where Liberty Dwells, There Is My Country

## American Civil War Letters, Photographs and News Reports

*Suzanne Meredithh*

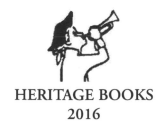

**HERITAGE BOOKS**
2016

# HERITAGE BOOKS

*AN IMPRINT OF HERITAGE BOOKS, INC.*

## Books, CDs, and more—Worldwide

For our listing of thousands of titles see our website at
www.HeritageBooks.com

Published 2016 by
HERITAGE BOOKS, INC.
Publishing Division
5810 Ruatan Street
Berwyn Heights, Md. 20740

Heritage Books by the author:

*Town of Union, New York: Civil War Enrollment & Troop Records*

*Where Liberty Dwells, There Is My Country:*
*American Civil War Letters, Photographs and News Reports*

*With a True God Bless: Civil War Letters*

International Standard Book Numbers
Paperbound: 978-0-7884-5728-9
Clothbound: 978-0-7884-6470-6

## DEDICATION and Acknowledgments:

George Quon – editing
Ron Katchuk
Allen Sweet
Carol Bills
Bruce Stuart Clark family
Dave Pickering
Chuck Howard
Carol Poirier
Pearl Webb
Rev. Dave
Garry & Becky Meyers
Hal & Lolita White
Library of Congress
    Photo Collections
Robbie Noles – R & R
    Collectables, S.C.

Unattributed photos and documents were obtained as single pages with no sources noted.

Without the assistance of the above people this book would not have been possible. Each contributed valuable information. Due to a love of history these moments in time from the lives of people who lived and died during the American Civil War were preserved.

A CALL TO ARMS
"Rallying the Line" – printed by C.D. Graves for
"The Civil War Through the Camera" – 1912

# "Where Liberty Dwells, There is my Country"

## *CONTENTS*

**PART ONE – Personal letters to and from the sutler from Candor, William C. Gridley, and his friend and future wife, F. A. Keeler, are interspersed throughout the chapters.**

**PART TWO – Letters from Family & Friends**

# INTRODUCTION

The United States, we were many in one, until our states were cruelly divided into opponents in government, homes and on battlefields. The American Civil War developed from a conflagration of ideologies, state rights, secession and slavery. The war ripped through the fabric of loyalty of friends and families and more than a century later mending the rift is still ongoing.

The letters contained in this volume are the words of the average citizen voicing courage and anguish. Many missives are between a sutler from upstate New York and his loved ones in Candor, and others from friends on the front lines. These echoes from the past are vibrant with life, hardship and death; on farms desperate for workers, and villages struggling to meet draft quotas. These are words from people whose lives are our history. In 1861 through 1865 the music of war could be heard resonating across the continent, to encourage recruits, boost morale and keep cadence on marches. Songs of patriotism, faith and love illustrating the beliefs of both North and South, are a recurring theme in this volume....the notes resonating through time as the soul of our nation was warped by war.

The Great American Conflict was the most thoroughly documented war in history. Thousands of camera images made from glass negatives and on site drawings of soldiers and combat filled the pages of newspapers. A significant number of photographs are included to illustrate the letters. Each document portrays the struggle to preserve the union through battlefields drenched crimson with the blood of patriots.

Ordinance that once reigned supreme havoc on brothers at war today rest on the lawns of municipal buildings, parade grounds and in memorial parks. Mounds of cannon balls and blackened cannons stand as sentinels in memory of a war fought for a new version of liberty.

*NOTE: Francis Augusta Keeler had several nicknames; Gus, Gussie, and Frank. Wm. Cadwell Gridley also was known as; Will, or Cad or Willie but the letters are all between the same people.*

**Frank Leslie's Illustrated Newspaper** – January 14, 1861
Of premonitions of war we have had a plenty any time during the
past three weeks, and what these premonitions have resulted in
the telegraph has, of course long ere this made you aware, WAR is
actually upon us; war, always deplorable, but now bringing with it
a train of horrors beside which the carnage and rapine engendered
by the quarrels of nations in all the world's history, must sink into
insignificance. For this is a war of kinsmen; a war of brothers and
of father against son. In short, a civil war – the bloodiest of all
wars, to end Heaven only knows when.
Written in the "Republic of South Carolina" by W.F. correspondent
of **Leslie's illustrated**


## WAS THE AMERICAN CIVIL WAR INEVITABLE?

*A division of the United States seems to have been considered from
its inception…….*


**The New York Times** – December 6, 1863
**New-York, April 5, 1790**
The following letter, written by R.B. LEE, purported to be the
grandfather of the present Commander-in-Chief of the rebel army,
was found in the dwelling-house of Gen. STUART, in Virginia:
**A Curious Revelation of the War**
*(This is only the last paragraph from a lengthy letter…that may, or
may not be, the grandfather of Robert E. Lee)*
"……I confess that I feel myself often chagrined by the taunts
against ancient dominions, but disunion at this time would be the
worst of calamities. The Southern States are too weak at present to
stand by themselves, and a General Government will certainly be
advantageous to us, as it produces no other effect than protection
from hostilities and uniform commercial regulations. And when we
shall attain our natural degree of population, I flatter myself that
we shall have the power to do ourselves justice, with dissolving the
bond which binds us together. It is better to put up with these little
inconveniences than to run the hazard of greater calamities."
Adieu, R.B. LEE.

**The American Civil War**
A patriotic view of war from the 1865 publication
**"The Tribute Book,"** by Frank B. Goodrich:
"..........In the first month after the fall of Sumter, the people of
the United States spent a million dollars for flags, and half as much
more for badges, emblems, cockades, rosettes and other patriotic
devices. For one flag torn down, thousands upon thousands were
thrown to the wind. In cities they floated not only from liberty
pole, flag staff, and casement, not only from ropes and halliards,
but from steeple, spire and belfry......The streets were gorgeous
with the loyal colors; and when the wind blew at right angles with
the grand thoroughfares of the larger cities the sky seemed heavy
with massive red and blue, and stars could be seen at mid-day........
there may be a certain beauty, fantastic and weird, in a feast of
lanterns; but there is more than beauty, there is grandeur, inspiration,
sublimity, in a carnival of flags."

**Gate City Guardian,** Atlanta – February 25, 1861
War feeling in Louisiana
A dispatch from Baton Rouge states that since Mr. Lincoln's late
speech, foreshadowing a Coercion Policy, war is deemed inevitable.
No apprehensions are felt of the conflict in the South. On the
first demonstration by the Lincoln Government the Provisional
Government will send immediately a large army to the North. The
South will never wait to be invaded. One hundred thousand dollars
were asked for on the 20th, in the legislature, to put the forts on the
Mississippi in complete defense. An appropriation bill amounting to
$1,500,000 has passed the house.

**Harper's Weekly** – January 5, 1861
The Birth of the Confederate States of America began with the
secession of South Carolina in December, 1860
South Carolina Proclaims Independence
Governor Pikins has, agreeably to the ordinance of secession
issued a proclamation proclaiming to the World South Carolina a
Sovereign, free & independent state and as such has a right to levy
war, conclude peace, negotiate treaties, or covenants, and do all
acts whatever that rightly pertain to a free and independent state.
Frequent violations of the Constitution of the United States by the
Federal Government and encroachments upon reserved rights of the
states: Right of the state to govern itself and the right of the people

to abolish a government when it becomes destructive of the ends for which it was instituted. South Carolina will resume her position among the nations of the world.

*Politics has not really changed much, as illustrated by the following editorial in the **Southern Confederacy** newspaper.*

**Southern Confederacy** – March 1861
The Last President of the United States of America
The term of four years, commencing the 4th of March 1857, for which James Buchanan, ("The Old Public Functionary") expired Today; and with his term has expired the last President of the United States of America.
An imbecilic official is succeeded by a stupid Rail Splitter from Illinois, elevated to a position of Agrarianism and Fanaticism, resulting in the overflow of the best government that ever existed.

*In England there were doubts about which side of our Civil War to support, if either. As illustrated by this poem published in a British newspaper in 1862*

"Though with the North we sympathize,
    It must not be forgotten
That with the South we've stronger ties
    Which are composed of cotton,
Whereof our imports mount unto
    A sum of many figures;
And where would be our calico
    Without the toil of Ni.......s?
The South enslaves their fellow man,
    Whom we love all so dearly,
The North keeps commerce bound again,
    Which touches us more nearly.
Thus a divided duty we
    Perceive in this hard matter –
Free trade or sable brothers free?
    O, will we choose the latter?"

**Southern Confederacy** – March 1861

The Great Funeral Day

What a day of thick gloom and foreboding this will be in Washington City. In the past history of the American People, an inauguration day was, to the majority, one of the grand days of the calendar......All this was true a few short months ago, and now how changed!

If one single man today in Washington can be glad he is either insensible to havoc and ruin, or he must be a Bedlamite. A once mighty league of states is riven and scattered; a once united and invincible brotherhood are divided to be no more of one household again................

A Black Republican should of all men, be the most wretched, for had he the will to commit a treason against Liberty heinous enough to damn a world.........As Lincoln and his crowd today look upon the wreck and ruin that are strewed all around, they will ask in vain, for whose good is it? ............Would to God that a remorse as hopeless and unappeasable as gnawed at Judas, vitals would dive the Black Republican to Judas' fate. But of this we have no hope, since the last Baltimore races. Lincoln may be hung yet, probably will be, but we cannot promise any such thing from his pluck.

**CENSUS OF 1860**

There are 19 free states consisting of 18,950,759 citizens
There are 15 slave states equaling 12,433,409 of whom 3,999,283 are slaves.

Abraham Lincoln and Hannibal Hamlin
    Campaign ribbon – 1860
Newspapers of the day stated that the election of Abraham Lincoln
was the true prelude to war.

**PART ONE**
*Personal letters to and from the sutler from Candor,
William C. Gridley, and his friend and future wife F.A.
Keeler are interspersed throughout the chapters*

## 1   THE CADENCE OF WAR

**"His drums is silent"**

The youngest soldiers who served during the American Civil War were the Drummer Boys. Many were as young as ten or eleven years old. The tin photo of this boy was bought at a flea market with no indication of name or location....however when the old photo holder was dismantled a very tiny scrap of paper was found rolled into a corner containing only the tearful words **"War is broken hearts The boy is dead, his drums is silent."** He was one of many who lost their lives beating the cadence of war.

A soldier's life was regulated by the tap of the drum, the haunting notes of a bugle, and the wailing fife. The musical instruments were essential means of communication and inspiration. From Reveille through Taps, the life of a soldier was managed by music. Thunderous feet marched to drums, their treads through marsh and fields encouraged by the repetitious thrum. Discipline and cohesion were evident in Grand Reviews of the troops. An important facet of a drummers duties was transmission of commands. It was crucial for orders to be relayed quickly, clearly and easily recognizable with the rap of a drum. Retreat, charge or rest could be signaled by the bugle....and at the end of a day, a life, or a battle, the mournful notes of Taps could be heard throughout the camps. Music was also important on the home front to encourage military fervor for recruiting, patriotism, entertainment, and social commentary. Some of America's most enduring music resounded from home, street and stage during the Great War of the Rebellion.

"The Battle Hymn of the Republic" was probably the most beloved song during the long American Civil War, and when bullets were not renting the air with death, the music of soldier voices alleviated their despair, expressing courage and longing for home.

Patriotic images and songs embellished Civil War stationery and envelopes.

**Moore's Rural New-Yorker** – August 9, 1862
The United States Congress has disbanded all regimental bands.

John Brown's Last Moments.

*Music galvanized abolitionists and the nation during the Civil War era with songs such as: "John Brown's Body."*

*John Brown, born in 1800, was a militant abolitionist who believed blood and arms were the only way to end slavery in America. His failed raid on the armory at Harpers Ferry led to his capture, conviction for treason, and death by hanging. The photo shows Brown in the last few moments of his life in 1859.*

**New York Times** – July 6, 1861 – **NEW PATRIOTIC MUSIC PUBLISHED** By Horace Waters, agent store, No. 481 Broadway
"Where Liberty Dwells, There is my Country"
"Our Country Now & Ever"
"God Save our Land"
"Three Cheers for Our Banner"
"Freemen's Gathering"
"Madman Spare that Flag"
"Hail Columbia"
"Star Spangled Banner"
"Yankee Doodle"
"My Country 'Tis of Thee"
Price 25 cents each, Patriotic Song Book of 64 pages words and music 10 cents each….a pianist in attendance will try new music for customers.

**Moore's Rural New-Yorker** – June 14, 1862
"OLD HUNDRED" IN CAMP
On Saturday evening a few hours after sunset, with several other "specials," one of our number, laying his hand upon our knee suddenly said to us, "Hark, what is that!" In a second all had ceased talking, and every ear endeavored to catch the sound which had attracted the attention of his comrade. There was a silence for a moment and then there was wafted across the air the music of that glorious anthem, "Old Hundred," in which it seemed ten thousand voices were participating. All of us immediately sought the open air, until the last note died away upon the ear. Never before have we heard anything so magnificently grand as that same "Old Hundred" sung by the soldiers of the Union Army on the plains of Yorktown. The air was made vocal with the music and the woods around reverberated with the mighty strain. Beneath the canopy of Heaven the soldier gazed up into the starlight sky and sung unto God "From whom all blessings flow," an anthem that stirred in the heart of man the best and holiest emotions. The incident was a sublime one either for the poet or the artist.

## 2   THE MUCH MALIGNED SUTLER AND HIS GOODS

*The Sutler from Candor, New York, William C. Gridley, in his*
*own words claimed to be a great patriot, providing necessities*
*for the troops, at a hopefully large return on his investments, and*
*risking his life, liberty and goods to do so.*

*Most sutlers, purveyors of merchandise and victuals, were*
*inspired only by profit, the greatest motivation to head, almost, to*
*the front lines. News articles praising these mobile shopkeepers are*
*nearly nonexistent; whereas tales of their perfidy abound. However,*
*they were often the only source for the soldier of groceries and*
*personal supplies not provided by the military. Local newspapers*
*and mail was occasionally delivered in care of the sutler attached to*
*each unit.*

*In 1896 W.C. Hibbs wrote about sutlers as part of his "Tales*
*of the Civil War." Even from a distance of three decades attitudes*
*toward this group of unenlisted camp followers had not improved.*

*News reports from both North and South during the years of*
*1861 through 1865 referred to sutlers as profiteers and parasites*
*who often sold shoddy or spoiled goods at usury prices.....although*
*the US Commissaries often could not provide even spoiled meals*
*for the soldiers. Graft, corruption, shinplasters, and sutler tokens*
*added to the confusion surrounding the sutler shanty. Sutlers served*
*the military under military orders but were civilians.....thus making*
*their status murky to soldiers and officers.*

### GENERAL ORDER 11-182

General U.S. Grant issued an order that all Jewish sutlers and
traders be expelled from military areas to stop the black market.
President Lincoln objected to the blanket order and it was reversed.
Thus the onerous duty of controlling the sutlers was given to local
commanders.

### THE SUTLER – from "Tales of the Civil War" – 1896
### By Waldo Campbell Hibbs

Sutler!  What a world of reminiscence that title, brings to mind
of the volunteer soldier of the American Civil War.  All attempts to
find his like have failed.  The Sutler of to-day is not he.  The Sutler
of the Revolution had not even the prerequisite of sex; for in her we
find also the camp washerwoman; and no woman could have ever

5

risen to the dizzy heights of inglorious eminence in such a vocation, or shall we call it art? To which he aspired and reached. He was sui generis; his species is extinct.

Of any nationality was he, yet no nation acknowledged him. What was his status? He was a volunteer; no sutler was ever drafted. He entered into the cause of Mammon, with an eagerness to serve which, had it been one tenth as intense in some other causem must have won him laurels such as would have sunk into oblivion the deeds of all heroes in times before or after. But for need of praise, crown of fame, honorable scar or storied bust, he cared not; nay despised. He professed no patriotism, though among patriots; he pretended to no bravery, though brave men surrounded him; he cherished no warlike ambitions, though he existed only in time of war. Of money he risked all he had; for money he suffered or rejoiced.

**Subject to military discipline, he ranked a trifle higher than corporal, a fraction lower than an army mule.** In theory, his position was impregnable, secured by official mandate; in practice, kicks, curses, and wanton spoilation were his dues; yet his revenge was keen.

Men's food is their spirit, their nature – within limitations. Who shall not say that upon his shoulders rests much of the responsibility for battles lost, for inglorious retreats, for disaffection among generals, for ignominious guard-house incarcerations, for untimely sojourns in gloomy hospital? Would not the sum total of the ills devolving upon the warrior have been less but for the insidious presence of a sutler? A glance at the stock in trade of any one of him forces one irresistibly to this sad conclusion, or at best grave doubt must arise. Such fare as rancid sardines and petrified bologna, gall tasting pickles, cough candy, potatoes hardened to a leaden consistency, and soft bread six months old, topped off with exiled bourbon, streak lightning in liquid form, and Havana onion leaves for smoking purposes, was not calculated to produce heroes. These and a hundred other prime necessaries of luxurious military existence were here, side by side with such articles of the toilet as wooden combs, wrinkled pocket mirrors, eyeless needles, pointless pins, lip salve, razor soap and plasters.

With more or less capital and credit, usually the possession of some mistaken and always unknown personage who secured his right to exist as sutler, he set forth on his mission of extortion. His vocation was indeed one of vicissitudes. The end of a campaign might find him with a balance sheet that would not balance, a tattered tent, a battered wagon, hundreds of pounds of scorned "sundries," and a leger full of charges against the killed and mortally wounded and missing of the great host that he followed and who were his largest "customers." But again, his venture successful, the bloated bondholder, at whose head so much vituperation has been hurled, were but a groveling worker compared to this Prince of Mammon.

And yet it has been said that the Sutler was greatest at a "charge." His was indeed always a post of danger. In the rear during an advance, in front while on retreat, encompassed about with perils, his deeds in defending his traveling treasure house of perishables were marvels of intrepidity and generalship. A rallying point in battle was his vehicle, a position contended for by friend and foe alike when the vicissitudes of combat left it between them. But he was not in the midst of carnage; not he. From some point without the beleaguered citadel he anxiously watched the desperate contest over things despised yet loath of relinquishment by those who struggled. Not until his armed companions, victorious, would turn upon and rend his treasures with mouths made hungry by the mortal conflict, did his smile of "trust" give way to the horror which spread o'er his once gloating visage. If ever a volunteer warrior fell upon the neck of his regimental sutler and embraced him, history does not record it. Suspicion, not affection, was the sole sentiment that distinguished their intercourse. Always was the stock in trade of the sutler suspected and sneered at, yet it was coveted and bought. And when payday came, Suspicion again made her appearance, stalking ominously at the elbow of the dispenser of depreciated greenbacks. The motto, "Base is the slave that pays" though mayhap written in the heart of many a soldier-boy, ne'er found utterance. With wisdom born of close study of military human nature, the Sutler made himself thoroughly "in it" with the regimental pay master, and he who had revealed in the effete luxuries of the Sutler's stock found himself in possession of a bill to settle with a dispatch that ill comported military dignity.

Not only have we seen cavalrymen strapped on their horse, but infantrymen "strapped" on the ground. The one who furnished the material for the strapping was the suttler, and he who paid for it was the individual soldier.

The preparatory command was not "Prepare to strap on" but "prepare to be strapped." The feat was common and not very difficult of accomplishment, for when one received greenbacks with gold at 240, he was pretty well "strapped" already. All that was necessary to complete the job was to walk up to the Sutler's tent or wagon, always placed in an easily seen or convenient spot, square up arrangements, and order "erplugertobacker" or "ercaneroysters." There was grim humor about the Sutler, his ways and his means. Time mars our bliss, yet soothes our sorrows, and to say "Sutler" in any gathering of old soldiers is now almost certain to set the story-telling mill going. Many good ones are related at the expense of both sutler and his victim.

One sutler, the purveyor to a New York regiment, kept in his stock a barrel of really very fine whiskey. The price of it was a little high for patriots wearing corkscrew caps and getting (on the books) $13 a month, but they wanted some of that whiskey. A smooth-faced boyish young fellow proposed a plan. A crowd of his companions in wickedness got into the shanty and kept the sutler busy. Even that usually respectable personage, the orderly sergeant, sat on the barrel and joked and laughed in his loudest key. Into the cellar under the shanty went a few of the boys with camp kettles. The instigator of the plot had an auger, and the orderly sergeant's voice above told him where to locate the cask. It was work of a few moments to bore through the floor and into the keg, and draw all the precious fluid into the kettles. As the thieves sneaked back into quarters they could hear the other folks quarreling with the sutler about some mistake in giving change to one of them the day before. And it was several hours later, when a darky brought a flask from the colonel to be filled, that this time victim discovered the outrage. It was too late then, but doubtless he "got back on 'em" before he was through with that regiment. Incidentally, I may say that the chief robber on this occasion is now the much loved pastor of a church out in Iowa.

While located at forts or other permanent garrisons, the Sutler had things much to his own way, but while campaigning he was compelled to "look a leetle oudt." It happened one day that a New York Battery attached to the Third Corps turned from the road into a meadow to feed their teams, and while waiting the men disposed of the few fragments in their haversacks and called them dinner. There was still, as was often the case, considerable air space left under the belt, and some of the men, seeking what they might devour, spied a sutler's tent, and at once made tracks for it. But they had no money; and when they joined the crowd round the tent and witnessed the things there set forth in appetizing array they groaned in spirit. Cans of lobster and condensed milk and gingersnaps tempted the hungry palate. But the afore said impecunious volunteers soon discovered something in the wind. Going around the back of the tent they saw about a hundred men engaged in quietly watching the gathering of a cyclone destined to sweep down upon and envelop the unsuspecting sutler. Some of the ropes of the tent had been loosened; men held them taut, awaiting the signal for catastrophe. Suddenly, with a wild yell, the crowd surged against the side of the canvas, the ropes were let go and over it went with a rush. The sutler, oh, where was he? Before the bewildered individual could extricate himself from the hopeless entanglement in which he found himself the crowd had dispersed, and with it the treasures he so dearly prized.

And so "going through the sutler," was a favorite pastime indulged in with enthusiasm and dexterity by all within reach, upon the slightest pretext that promised success. But here again the suave dispenser of inedibles enjoyed revenge. After successful wrestle with and consumption of stolen toothsome morsels many a doughty private was fain to lie down in his rubber blanket and wish he might even die unhonored and unsung could he be rid of the direful agony that possessed him. But enough. The Sutler is no more. Of all the unique characters upon the stage in the great drama of the Civil War none played their part so well as he nor became so intimately woven into the lives (and stomachs) of the soldiers whom he fed and bled. He came from no one knows where; he departed without a sign into the misty vale of the past.

**War Department** – General Orders – Washington, March 1862
The following acts and resolution of Congress are published for the information and government of all concerned: An act to make an additional Article of War.

Be it enacted by the Senate and House of Representatives of the United States of America in Congress assembled, that hereafter the following:

No person shall be permitted to act as a **sutler** unless appointed according to the provisions of this act; nor shall any person be sutler for more than one regiment; nor shall any sutler farm out or underlet the business of sutling or the privileges granted to him by this appointment; nor shall any officer of the Army receive from any sutler any money or other presents; nor be interested in any way in the stock, trade or business of any sutler; and any officer receiving such presents, or being thus interested, directly or indirectly, shall be punished at the discretion of a court-martial. No sutler shall sell to an enlisted man on credit to a sum exceeding one-fourth of his monthly pay within the same month; nor shall the regimental quartermasters allow the use of Army wagons for sutlers purposes; nor shall the quarter master conveyances be used for the transportation of sutlers supplies.

### The Philadelphia Inquirer – August 1861
"The State and National Administrations are now using every available means to support the best Government that Providence ever permitted man to organize therefore let all aid in this grand effort to sustain our glorious institutions, until Jeff Davis and his treacherous aids shall find a home in the bosoms of Judas Iscariot and Benedict Arnold."

### New York Times – Washington – February 1864
ARMY OF THE POTOMAC; REBEL DESERTERS
CONFISCATED SUTLER'S GOODS

A large lot of confiscated sutlers' goods were sold at Brandy Station yesterday by Captain Clinton, of General Patrick's Staff. Notwithstanding an apparent combination of sutlers to get them at nominal rates, they netted the average Washington rates. The articles were generally in excess of the manifests and officers' orders. The liquors composing part of the seizures, were turned over to the Medical Department and the proceeds of the sale, about $1,500, placed in General Patrick's hands to be applied to the relief of our sick and wounded.

### New York Times – April 1864
Preparation for the approaching Campaign – Issued from Headquarters of the Army of the Potomac–General Order #17, Sutlers, Civilians & Superfluous baggage ordered to the Rear In view of the near approaching of the time when this Army may be expected to resume active operations…..all sutlers and their employees will leave this Army by the 16th inst., and should sutlers be found with the Army after that date their goods will be

confiscated for the benefit of the hospitals, and their employees be placed by the Provost-Marshall at hard labor.

**New York Times** – January 1862 – **regarding sutlers**
How the Expenses of War are to be Met – A Proposed tax of one hundred & fifty millions

The Committee of Ways and Means have concluded to provide by taxation for a hundred and fifty millions during the current year. The Committee of Ways and Means should not fail to impose a monthly Tax on those who perform the office of **sutlers** to our armies. It is an exclusive privilege and a very valuable one. Merchants in civil life always pay a license. Those who sell in the camps should do likewise, and the funds go into the government treasury. The average value of a sutlership to a regiment is said to be $6,000 a year. If we have 600 regiments in service, the furnishing of sutler's goods to them yields a profit of nearly four millions annually. Why should not a fair per cent of this sum go to the government that furnishes the customers and the money they buy with? Senator Hale's bill to protect the government treasury from swindling contracts comes none too soon. Its introduction today was marked by a severe speech from the senator.

**New York Times** – June 30, 1862
**White House to be used for Hospital Purposes, Women as Nurses, Sutlers a Nuisance**

An order came from General McClellan directing the Medical Director of Transportation to occupy the White House for Hospital purposes – it will not be used for the reception of invalids, but as an office for the Director and a home for the Sisters of Charity. There are sixty-five now on board the steamer "C. Vanderbilt" who will be transferred to the house.

One woman as a nurse is worth ten men. Here we have had able bodied soldiers acting as nurses when they are needed so much at the front, but through mismanagement and the gross incompetency of some of the doctors here in charge, they loaf around the White House acting as aids to the SUTLERS, instead of the army. Let us have women nurses and an order for all idle soldiers at this depot to return to their respective regiments.

The **Sanitary Committee** or the Medical Board, if they value health, ought to take measures immediately to have the **SUTLERS** removed; make an order imperative for them to join their regiments, or refuse them landing, and stop all clearances of their vessels bound here. The health of the soldiers demand it. There are innumerable tents extending from the railroad up to the end of the White House farm, filled with rotten fruits, decayed meats, molded bread, bad whisky and a concoction called ale, and other stuff in damaged condition. These articles are sold to soldiers without any limit, and are rapidly filling the hospitals with unnecessary patients. The filth created by this horde of SUTLERS is perfectly sickening, yet the Provost Marshall, the health officers or whoever else has charge of this depot, suffers this state of affairs to exist without seeking to remedy it. All kinds of liquor are sold here, doing more injury to the health of the troops than all the malaria of the Chickahominy swamps.

It is to be hoped that General McClellan will stop all traffic in SUTLERS stores hereafter, and that he will not allow one to land at the White House. For some time past forage has been very scarce in our army, owing to the railroad bringing up SUTLERS supplies – horses and men were suffering for food while government trains were employed in bringing stuff belonging to private individuals.

**New York Times** – December 1863 News of the Day –
The Rebellion
The holidays are bare of news of a belligerent character. All the armies are quiet. The Army of the Potomac is paying more attention to sutlers supplies, fresh oysters, milk, &c, than to the enemy. General Grant's army is building bridges and railroads. General Foster is quiet at Knoxville. From all quarters there is scarce a ripple to disturb the serene enjoyment of the holidays.

*The Following items were in great demand by the Union Army. Many Sutlers saw the chance for huge profits by conducting a business close to the troops, selling the goods listed, and other items of Questionable value.*

**The Philadelphia Inquirer** – August 1, 1861 – **Proposals**
Army Supplies – Quartermaster-General's Office
Harrisburg, July 26, 1861
Sealed proposals will be received at this office until 12 o'clock on Friday, the second day of August 1861, for the following ARMY supplies deliverable at the State Military Store, Harrisburg, in

quantities as required.  Said proposals to be publicly opened at the time and place named, and the successful bidders to be announced as soon thereafter as convenient – the right being reserved by the state to increase or diminish the number and quantity of said articles:

Ten hospital tents, with flies, poles, pins, etc., complete

Sixteen hundred and Fifty Common Tents, poles, pins, etc. complete

Two hundred and Fifty Wall tents with flies, poles pins, etc., complete

One hundred drums, with sticks, slings, carriages, cases, complete

Two hundred (200) Drum Heads – batter

Two hundred (200) Drum Heads – snare

One hundred Cocoa bites

Ten Thousand Three-pint Canteens, covered and strapped, cotton

Ten Thousand Haversacks, army standard

Ten Thousand Haversacks, enameled cloth

Ten Thousand Knapsacks, straps, &c., complete, enameled cloth

Ten Thousand Knapsacks, straps, &c., complete, Army standard

Six hundred shovels, 6 hundred spades, 6 hundred hatchets, handled, 6 hundred picks, handled

Ten thousand Tin Cups, Three thousand Mess Pans, One thousand Camp Kettles

Ten thousand Blouses, woolen lined

One thousand yards sky blue Tape for chevrons

Ten thousand blankets, wool grey 7 feet by 5 feet 6 inches, weighing 5 pounds each, with black letters, "PV" in center, 4 inches long.

Ten thousand Great Coats

Ten thousand sets Infantry Accoutrements

Twenty thousand pairs of Drawers

Ten thousand pair Trousers, footmen

Twenty thousand white Domet Flannel shirts

Twenty thousand pairs Stockings, One thousand pairs Cavalry Boots, Ten thousand pairs Bootees

Ten thousand Forage Caps

Twelve thousand Double numbers 39 to 50 inclusive

Twelve thousand letters A to K inclusive

One hundred and thirty Sergeants' Sashes

Forty Ambulance Wagons, of the pattern of the United States Army, of four wheels and two wheels

Forty Hospital or Medical Transport Carts, United States Army pattern; also sets of Harness for horses of the above

The Ambulance Wagons, Carts and Harness subject to the inspection and approval in quality and finish of the Surgeon-General of Pennsylvania, whose decision shall be final and conclusive. It is desirable that all the above articles be *of domestic manufacture*, and when any of them are furnished by the United States, the same must conform in all respects to the sealed standard patterns in the United States Quartermaster's office and military store, Philadelphia. Ten per cent of the amount of each delivery to be retained as a forfeiture until the contract is completed. Contractors to state in their proposals the time when the goods can be delivered, and the speedy delivery of such articles as are needed will be considered in awarding the contract. Successful bidders to give bonds with two approved securities. Every proposal to be endorsed, Proposal for Army Supplies, August 2d, 1861. All supplies contracted for under these proposals to be delivered at the Military Storehouse in the city of Harrisburg, unless otherwise directed, free of all charge for freight, boxing or drayage, unless freight to place of delivery is greater than to Harrisburg, in which case the difference will be allowed – All packages so delivered to be marked on the outside with number and description of articles therein, and name of party furnishing same, together with an invoice of contents, enclosed, embracing, in addition to above, notice of what special supply it is a part.

R. C. Hale – Q.M. Gen. PM

INVOICE OF SUBSISTENCE STORES *turned over at Camp near Sharattenville this 23rd day of October 1862, by Lieut. Capt. George R. Meyers* ..................... *N.S.*
*to Lieut. Geml L. Hurley 3d Brigade* .................... A. C. S., *United States Army, viz:*

|  |  | Dols. | Cts. |
|---|---|---|---|
| 5 barrels of Pork, | per barrel. |  |  |
| pounds of Bacon, | per pound. |  |  |
| pounds of Ham, | do. |  |  |
| 3 barrels of Salt Beef, | per barrel. |  |  |
| barrels of Flour, | do. |  |  |
| 3600 pounds of Hard Bread, | per pound. |  |  |
| bushels of Beans, | per bushel. |  |  |
| bushels of Peas, | do. |  |  |
| pounds of Rice, | per pound. |  |  |
| pounds of Hominy, | do. |  |  |
| pounds of Rio Coffee, green, | do. |  |  |
| 121 pounds of Rio Coffee, roasted and ground, | do. |  |  |
| pounds of Tea, | do. |  |  |
| 570 pounds of Brown Sugar, | do. |  |  |
| pounds of White Sugar, | do. |  |  |
| gallons of Vinegar, | per gallon. |  |  |
| pounds of Sperm Candles | per pound. |  |  |
| pounds of Adamantine Candles | do. |  |  |
| pounds of Soap, | do. |  |  |
| 1½ bushels of Salt, | per bushel. |  |  |
| gallons of Molasses, | per gallon |  |  |

(SIGNED IN DUPLICATE.)

*George F. Meyers*

NOTE—Price of stores should always be inserted in this invoice and one copy of such invoice should accompany monthly "Return of Provisions."

*Capt.*, C. S.

1862 – Military Invoice

LOC Sutler camp

## SUTLER GOODS

Items offered by Civil War sutlers varied according to season and availability, and the cash flow of the sutler. Often the goods were poor quality resulting in great anger by the soldiers who had no other option to purchase things not provided by the army.

*Some of the traditional goods in stock included: forks, spoons, tin cups and pans, bedding, arms and bullets, canteens, preserved and, supposedly, fresh food, tools, knives, axes, boots and other clothing items, tobacco, pipes soap, eye glasses (one prescription for all usually just magnifying lenses), sewing kits, bone buttons, suspenders, coffee, Bordens' Cans of milk, soap, cheese, sardines, ginger cakes, games such as checkers, and writing supplies.*
*Alcohol could only be sold for medicinal purposes...unless caught. Liquor, playing cards and dice were forbidden by some commanders and accepted by others...smuggling of these items into camps was constant and often creatively accomplished.*

*Games of chance, marbles, and perhaps a harmonica were entertainment while waiting in camp for deployment to the fighting fields.*

*Tobacco was scarce and expensive in the north but was, even for the very young soldiers, a life-long habit and many became fierce if their addiction was not fed. At the time the weed was believed to be medicinal. When available tobacco was often sold in ropes called "pig tails."*

*There was some opposition to tobacco as reported in an article sent home by Wm. Gridley....*

**"Tobacco is a noxious weed,**
**Davy Crockett sowed the seed**
**It robs your pocket and soils your clothes**
**And makes a chimney of your nose"**

*The sutler often provided banned items soldiers wanted. These goods commanded the most profit so the black market continued, although the Provost Marshal Department tried to confiscate obscene literature, alcohol and cheap merchandise. General Butler was said to intercept all sutler boats on the James River to force sutlers into paying tax on goods.....something that was ordered to be done by law but was often "forgotten" by the sutler. Difficulties in regulating sutlers in any respect continued throughout the war.*

**New York Times** – December 30, 1863
News from Washington – Passenger trains of the Army
It has been ordered that but one passenger train shall hereafter leave Washington daily for the Army of the Potomac namely at 9:45 in the forenoon. Other trains are exclusively for freight. SUTLERS

can accompany their goods provided their passes have been countersigned the previous day.

**New York Times** – April 1864
Washington – Army of the Potomac
A Swarm of Sutlers and Camp Followers sent to the Rear
The recent order of General Grant banishing sutlers from the army, rids it of over twenty-eight hundred supernumeraries.

**The Chicago Times** – August 1862 – The Luxuries of Life.
Soldiers do not want for the luxuries of life so long as they have money. The sutlers deal in everything, and, by due pertinacity in searching, anybody's wants can be satisfied. If the principle applied which rules in some classes of society, viz.: that what costs the most is most luxurious, then soldiers would be the most luxurious people in the world, for they pay immense prices for everything they buy. To begin with the primary luxury, whisky, costs a dollar a pint. A barrel brings the sutler from three to five hundred dollars, which may be reckoned a nice profit. They are allowed to sell to commissioned officers only, but the restriction merely necessitates the operation of passing the bottle and the money through a commissioned officer's hands. Under this arrangement the liquor does not become the curse it is at home. It is too costly and precious to squander, and men cannot afford to get drunk on it. Taken moderately, as a consequence, it braces them up, and answers a good medicinal purpose. Other luxuries are to be had in the shape of sugar, cheese, candles, lemons, and preserved fruits of all kinds. Sugar can be got at twenty cents a pound, cheese at forty cents, lemons at fifteen cents apiece, and pint cans of fruit at a dollar. The soldiers generally affect the sweets, being destitute of them in their regular food. I have seen them buy a pound of sugar and eat it without delay, and, in the purchase of dollar cans of fruit, they are quite zealous. In this line I must plead a fellow feeling for, after living on camp diet for weeks, I became so ravenous for something fresh and sweet that I rushed one morning to a sutler's wagon and bought a can of fresh pineapple, which I straightway ate with great gusto – feeling the while somewhat guilty, for one of the rules of the camp is that no member of a mess shall appropriate to his individual enjoyment any rare eatables which come into his possession. Reasoning that I could not buy enough for all without a run on my funds, I silenced conscience and ate my dainty with an ineffable

relish. Soldiers are denied even these costly luxuries a large portion of the time, for the deepest purse would soon give out with their rash expenditures, and they consequently have a keen appetite when the pay day comes around.

**The Chicago Times** – August 1862 – The Sutler's Tent
The locality of this institution may be ascertained at any time by the crowd which surrounds it. Soldiers have an irresistible longing to look upon the good things of earth, and they congregate about the **sutler's** quarters as little neighborhoods sometimes convene at the village grocery. When they cannot buy, they derive pleasure from witnessing the transactions of others; and all day long, when off duty, they linger about this place of charmed associations. They are allowed, after spending all their cash, to go in debt to the extent of one-third of their pay. The temptation of seeing others buy is beyond their power of resistance, and, one after another, they clamor for something to buy. The sutler puts down the man's name for a dollar, and he begins to buy. He gets tobacco first, and then matches. Then he thinks he will indulge in a cigar, and he buys one for his chum. This proceeding is not only of interest to himself, but in matter of eager consideration to the bystanders, who discuss the merits of each purchase, and inwardly resolve to become equally blessed the first time the sutler's heart relents towards them. In the meantime the buyer has become confused at the field which opens before him, and he looks around in perplexity, not knowing which to choose. He thinks he will take a lemon, with lemonade in prospect. Then he decides on another box of matches and half a pound of cheese. Still lost in a sea of enticements, he demands in an absent way some more smoking tobacco, which in turn necessitates another box of matches. Then in a desperate way he calls for a pound of butter, but, finding that it costs half a dollar, he relinquishes the fond hope, and takes another lemon and some more tobacco. Sugar suggests itself in a moment of lucid thought, and a pound is speedily transferred to his haversack, followed, in the most natural connection, by some candy. The dollar is nearly expended by this time, and, as a last resort, he takes some more tobacco and matches, and goes off to sit on the ground and look over his purchases. The great end attained in all this is that the sutler makes three and four times the first cost of his goods, and is sure of his pay, for Uncle Sam sees that he is paid before the men are. Many of them have ten

and fifteen thousand dollars due when pay-day comes, besides the cash they have taken in. There are some risks, however, as in the case of the battle of Shiloh, where the enemy took our camps and, with them, all the sutlers' goods. Some of these traders lost three or four thousand dollars on that occasion.

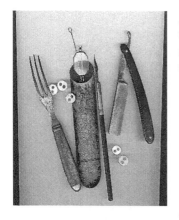

Although food and drink were staples of the sutler tent, other camp necessities, such as forks, buttons, razors, glasses and pens were available.

An ax was as important to a soldier as a gun. Its uses were many for survival in camps. The tool added to the weight of the packs carried by each soldier. Other heavy items the soldier needed were devices for making bullets, such as the iron pot and ladle pictured.

*Miscellaneous:*
*Sutler stores were transported in wagons, by rail and by river.*
*Sutler wagons were sometimes called "cracker outfits."*

*The Elmira, New York Prison for Confederate Soldier, in place from 1864 to 1865, included a SUTLER'S store, located close to the dead house. The prison was named "Hellmira" by the inmates.*

19

Borden's Condensery, located in Deposit, NY was one of the first businesses to produce canned milk. It was a staple of the sutler inventory.

## FINAL STATEMENT

OF

*Pvt. Alexander Wolf*

*11ᵗʰ Reg't of Pennsylvania*

### VOLUNTEERS.

When mustering out of the military **Note 3** in the important Final Statement form reads: **the amount due the SUTLER and laundress must be deducted from final payment.**

NOTE 1.— *Two* of these certificates (or duplicates) are to be given to each volunteer soldier who may be discharged previously to the discharge of his company, that he may at once receive from the Paymaster the pay, &c., due him, and the captain or other officer commanding the company will certify to the act of the delivery of the duplicate certificates; on these certificates the Soldier is "entitled to" his *discharge*, and should also present his discharge to the Paymaster to have the payment endorsed on it. The discharge is to be given back to the Soldier by the Paymaster; the latter only retaining as his voucher the duplicate certificates.

NOTE 2.—If the Soldier is entitled to pay for the use of his horse, the Company Commander will certify to that fact, and also to the time he has pay due for having been so mounted on his own horse.

NOTE 3.—Amounts due the Sutler and Laundress must be entered on the Muster Roll on which the death, desertion, &c., is reported, as well as on the final statement, otherwise the amount cannot be collected from the United States.

NOTE 4.— This blank will be used for deceased volunteers as well as others.

20

Gambling: *Playing cards, bone dice, clay marbles, and dominoes were used by soldiers for entertainment and gambling. All these items were available at the Sutler tent, along with alcohol. Often these goods were creatively smuggled into camp. Not all commanders approved of this form of distraction.... many condemned cards as devil's tools...one general devised a punishment for gamblers, shown below in this Library of Congress drawing.*

**Harper's Weekly** – How General Patrick deals with gambling we discover from the picture above. Mr. Maud, (the artist who sketched the punishment), writes: Some inveterate players, belonging to the Ninety-third New York, were provided with a table, dice, and a tin cup for a dice box, and under charge of a guard, were kept at their favorite amusement all day, playing for beans, with boards slung on their shoulders with the word GAMBLER written upon them. They did not seem to enjoy it, an attempt to make the most of their time and play for greenbacks being nipped in the bud. Dinner was also denied them, on the plea that gamblers have no time for meals.

Much harm, no doubt, results from gambling; but it is useless to punish the men while it is so prevalent a vice with the officers and gambling has always been, more or less, prevalent in armies.

## Playing CARD SMUGGLING – September 28, 1863
## General Orders #327 – War Department

During The Civil War nearly all items were considered contraband and prohibited from being exported from the United States into the Confederate lands. Even though a deck of cards seems innocuous, it was still illegal to provide them to the South, as Col. James A. Tait learned when he was formally charged with Neglect of Duty.
Col Tait was serving in the First District of Columbia Volunteers as Provost Marshall, General Defenses South of the Potomac …when he "did while acting in his official capacity, approve a certificate of goods in the hands of one W.A. Stewart, to pass said goods into the enemy's country, which certificate reads as follows…..four trunks containing articles of merchandise not contraband, and which have been examined"…..Signed, J. A. Tait, Provost Marshall General, Feb. 14, 1863. Which trunks were subsequently seized and found to contain about four thousand packs of playing cards, as well as tea, sugar and coffee. "…these items would whereby provide aid, comfort, and relief to the enemy." James A. Tait did while acting in his official capacity and in disobedience of orders, grant a pass enabling Stewart to pass the line of pickets into enemy country. Col. Tait was found not guilty by his friends in the local trial, but the findings were disapproved by the Major General commanding the Department of Washington, on the grounds that "the evidence adduced shows each charge and specification conclusively proved." The case was than transmitted to the War department and the President of the United States for action, who directed that Colonel James Tait be dismissed from the service of the United States.

## Harpers Weekly – 1864 – Notes from the FRONT & REAR

There is an interesting sketch which we give our readers this week representing a curious but saddening feature, of the battle field. Look at the pictures of the battle field at the front where our poor soldiers, battling for the country, theirs and ours, are risking precious lives, are suffering from severe if not mortal wounds, and their blood stains the contested field. Turn then from this picture and look to what is going on in the rear. Here, under shelter of heavy wagons, are teamsters and SUTLERS, and other noncombatants, playing cards, as regardless of what is going on a few rods distant at the front what games contested or what problems solved as if they were congregated together at a fair. Between the mimic strife in the rear and the exciting game at the front how short a space, but a contrast of what opposites.

## Sutler Wagon Trains Robbed by MOSBY Guerillas
**Harper's Weekly** – September 1863
John Mosby's Guerilla Warfare on Sutler Trains
Instead of "Stonewall Jackson" with his dashing achievements, the rebel cavalry in Virginia have nothing better to show than the performance of Mosby and his guerillas, "citizen by day and soldiers by night." Aided by a perfect knowledge of the country and by information furnished by their sympathizers, they have succeeded in capturing quite a number of sutlers' trains and escaping with a portion of their booty. These guerilla enterprises, while they exert no influence upon the issue of the war, are annoying and must be prevented. They are only possible through the connivance of the inhabitance of the region where they take place and these should be held accountable for all the damage done by their friends. If this rule is strongly enforced the aiders and abettors of these marauding gangs will find that they are carrying on a losing business.

## The Philadelphia Inquirer – August 1, 1861 – BAD BEEF
Since the stringent orders which have been issued by Gen. McClellan requiring the field and like officers to stay in their camps instead of the city, it has been discovered that the fresh beef which is furnished to the soldiers is not fit to eat. The security entered is ample, and Gen. Meigs, Lieut. Beckwith, or some responsible party in the Commissaries' Department should see that the contract is strictly carried out. No man should be enriched at the expense of the gallant volunteers

**General store in Candor, Tioga County, New York** cr. 1870

Sutler William C. Gridley was born and lived most of his life in
Tioga County, NY. Instead of volunteering for the Union Army,
Gridley chose to become a sutler. At first he worked for a registered
stuler, and traveled with the 76th Regiment NYV. Later in the war he
opened his own business.

Many of the letters are from Gridley to his friend, and future wife,
Frances A. Keeler and her replies from Tioga locations. Both
families were among the earliest to settle the area.

The second part of this volume contains war year letters to and
from soldiers and civilian friends. The war behind the scenes, in
homes, farms and businesses of a ravaged land is poignantly penned
by those who lived and died in the American Civil War.

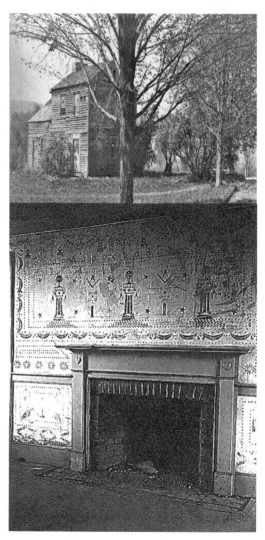

*Sutler William C. Gridley was from a strong Masonic family. His ancestor Selah Gridley settled on the Old Road to Spencer on the North side of Catatonk Creek. In 1802 he constructed the first frame house in the area...this became Gridleyville in West Candor. Selah was one of George Washington's bodyguards during the American Revolutionary War, and he is credited with bringing Masonry to Candor. Masonic meetings were held in this home as early at 1804. The building for decades was considered the birthplace of Free Masons in the Southern Tier of New York, an important destination, for Masons to visit if at all possible. The old Gridley Homestead, and one of its rooms, on the second floor of the home, covered with Masonic symbols of the Craft, are shown in the photos. In 1925 an article appeared in* **the Candor Courier***, courtesy of the* **Syracuse Post Standard***. It declared the building "Ancient Shrine of Free Masonry, and a rare Masonic find" that was finally rediscovered near the "old turnpike road."*

26

*Meetings were held in secret in the 1800's as membership was not a safe thing to admit. By 1925 the site was considered the Masonic equivalent of King Tut's Tomb, the holiest of holies for all Masons.*

**October 4, 1861**
Dearest Gussie, I will meet you at the corner step tomorrow eve, at, eight o'clock by the grace of god permitting. I am in hopes these few lines will find you enjoying as good health as I. And now I am not trifling with you if you think it is so I wish you to tell me so. And as for me I very well know your disposition and relation to matters and things generally

One thing more and that is Folks may talk but you Gussie must learn by observation and not depend upon others sayings. I wood say more but I haven't time to spend. Remember time flies swift. Precious gems are hidden for thee
Willie       (There is a coded note added to this letter....ZYQLFI)

*(Written October 1861, in Candor when both Willie and Augusta are home)*
Willie the young people are going up to Danby to Mr. Fortners this eve & Lau Williams wished me to send you an invite, if you can be there at five this afternoon, I mean at the village, I think of going, if you cannot shall I?

Frank, I received your note at 4o'clock, had just been making arrangements to go to the Cor...when the boys brot in your note. I have not been able to go out of the house since I saw you but had mustered courage enough to go to C......tonight to the P.O. I would be glad to go but under the circumstances I cannot. Since you have a way to go it is my wish that you improve it. I am very sorry that I can't enjoy the company. My heart be with you.
Yours truly Willie       Say to Miss Lau that I am unwell

**February 9, 1862** – Meridian Hill, Washington, D.C.
Dear Augustie, Perhaps you may think that I have forgotten you but that can never come. When I left home I did not Expect to go further than New York but when I arrived there, I learned by the commandant of the Park Barracks that the Reg't was to leave the next day for Washington. We left Rikers Island on Thursday & arrived here on Friday (after a long & tideous ride)

It has stormed Every day since I left home either snow or rain.

27

The mud is from four inches to six feet deep. But to day has been very pleasant but some what cold.

As far as I am concerned, I never was more disappointed than at the sight of this place. I anticipated much more than I have Participated. **There is no end to the martial mania. Bands are heard from every quarter. The hills are crossed with white tents as far as the Eye can observe. I guess you will have your match to read this for it is written on the head of a barrel in my sutlers tent as the boys say.**

I hope you are enjoying yourself up there in the snow if I can't here in the mud. I also wish this may find you in good health.

You must excuse me for not writing before for it was impossible to do so. I saw Fred Pampily today. He is well as usual. This is the third time I have commenced a letter to you and some one has called me off but I think this will go through if the head of this barrel don't fall in before I get it finished. I must close this for I am almost asleep, one foot is asleep, but no one to sleep with.

Please write very soon. My love to all of the folks, but the greatest share to yourself. Hoping to heare from you immediately I remain Yours Ever, A True friend, Cad

My address is Camp Casey Washington, D.C.     76th Reg't NYSV

**The Philadelphia Inquirer** – August 1, 1861
FLAG RAISING AT PENN STATION
Soon after the arrival of the news of the battle of Bull Run at Penn Station, on the Philadelphia and Baltimore Central Railroad, several patriotic ladies, among whom were, Mrs. M. Kelton, Mrs. Charleton, Mrs. Nelson and Mrs. Woodside, determined upon flinging another thirty-four starred banner to the breeze, in order that the hearts of the Union-loving people of that vicinity should be strengthened thoroughly. That feat having been accomplished successfully, the Hon. J. C. Dickey was called upon to address the assemblage. The Hon. Gentleman, in a brief speech most eloquently portrayed the crisis through which the country is now passing, and plainly impressed the necessity of every man defining his position so unmistakably that there need be no doubt as to which banner he stands beside – the one which floated in triumph over Washington, Lafayette, and innumerable hosts of worthies of the Past, or the Rebel rag now floating over slavery both black and white, and so plainly emblematical of ignorance, treason and cowardice, coupled

with an usurpation of the natural rights of the whole human family. How humiliating the truth that there is no freedom of speech either in the press or at the ballot box, wherever the traitorous banner of rebellion now floats.

**March 2, 1862**, Sunday – **Fort Totten** – Washington, D.C.
To: Miss F. A. Keeler Candor, Tioga Co. NY
From: W. C. Gridley
Dearest Friend, Yours of the 13th came to hand about the 20th on a/c of the delays on the Rail Road as they do not run regularly. We have moved from the Hill as you will see from the above on account of the same I have been unable to write you before.

**Our Reg't has been split up and placed in 5 different Forts which makes it very inconvenient for me in Selling goods as I have to set up two shanties in different places**. I think as to banishing of my letter that it is well for you that you have changed your mind.

I hope that you will not stay in the house so much & so long that you will forget how to write. I suppose by what I can learn that the sleighing is as good as when I left. The weather here has been of the worst kind all of the time, although yesterday & today have been very pleasant & the mud is drying up fast.

I am very sorry to learn that your Sister Mary has been sick. Both on you're a/c and hers. I don't know how bright you are but think Bright enough to scold right smart. You may think Sis rather poor company but I don't. I think it is some the way with John Trusdall as others. "They say that change of pasture makes fat calves" all is quiet.

I rather guess that you are mistaken as to that letter not being sealed, for I am sure that it was sealed when it left me. Although open when you rec'd it. You are well aware that a letter can be opened with but little trouble & not have them show. I am very sorry that it happened on you're a/c but as for me I don't care a damn, there was nothing in it that I care anything about.

My brother came out to help me but was taken sick the next day after he got here and staid one more & left for home. I have not heard from him since he left, don't know how he is. Asa Sackett, your coz, is at work for me. Dick Clark is at Hunts. I have seen Barager once since I came here. I am glad that there is one that can appreciate my worth. A trewer friend you never had I own I love

29

thee much. I hope you will not delay in writing to one you own as a friend. I can not write more. Direct your letter to the 76th Reg't NYSV Washington, D.C. and it will come all right. Give my news to all of the friends in Candor. I wish I could be there a short time. I may I can't tell. Asa & myself are going to the City this afternoon & I must shorten this up now. I am in good health now & hope this will find you so. I remain yours as Ever. Wm C. Gridley, PS: be not afraid to tell the news in Candor rumors & c. in haste do not look at mistakes

*(Fort Totten served the Civil War a few miles north of Washington on the road to Silver Springs. It was an impressive facility when sutler Will Gridley was stationed at the site. Protected by a deep moat, high dirt walls and cannons, it was named in honor of General J.G. Totten.)* LOC photo

**February 13, 1862**
From: Augusta Keeler – Candor Tioga Co. NY
To: Wm. Gridley, Camp Casey, Washington, D.C. 76th regt. NYSV
My dear Friend, your welcome epistle arrived yesterday eve. I had a mind to banish yur letter with a look, taking a girls privelage I changed my mind & am not sorry for with it came the assurance that I had a friend to love. Though far away, you laugh if you dare.

I have been out side the gates 4 times since you left Candor. My sister Mary has been very sick for five days & nights. Mother & Augusta did not sleep over two hours in 24. Mary is better we think she will recover (a fevor). I do not think I am very bright, think sis would be poor company at present. Pa & LeGrand have been home since last Thursday, Sarah writes she graduated in full this term & next term goes in The Sub Senior. She inquired if you had gone with the Regiment. You speak of not finding it as you expected, it is seldom we do, you must not accept disappointments but look straight ahead. (this is enough)

Lucia & Julia Hart called yesterday, last Thursday eve most of the young people went to Spencer to a dance. I heard they had high times, will you listen & keep dark, John Trusdell's wife was gone to Ithica visiting & he invited Mary Marshall & she went. They went in the load. THAT WAS NICE, last eve there was a donation for Mr. Arnold, I did not go. Nant Smith's girl Eliza has been very sick. Miss Goodwin was buried Tuesday.

It is good sleighing, not mud, & I wish for a ride, if wishes were horses we might all ride. I cannot imagine how you do there but am thankful that barrel head was not soft, I guess, for I received a letter that had never been sealed. To cheat prying eyes please seal the next. I am so sleepy since I have not slept over night all night, this is uninteresting & I will not write any more, yes I will. I must tell you I received a letter from O. B. Preston, he went in the Candor military company & has just remembered to write. Mother says I shall not answer but I must. It was so sentimental & full of, (shall I say) love that I must politely inform him that it comes to late & to cheap. I pity such. I have had so many such I am sick of the insanity of this world. There is but little lasting truth & friendship & to much gass. Write often as you can for I wish you to. Loved one I miss you so much. Yours as ever, Augusta.

Saturday. This has been written some time. I heard this morning your brother has gone to WDC. Mary is getting better & that makes me better. I have been up so much I can not hold the pen steady. Take good care of your health. I am ashamed of this letter & would not send it if I had time to write another, excuse mistakes & believe me your friend as ever. F.A.K.

**March 1862**
From: F. A.Keeler – Candor, NY
To: A Confidents, Mr. Wm. C. Gridley – 76 regt NYSV
Washington, D.C.
Dearest Friend, I received your welcome epistle & it was most welcome which you will believe when you have read this, it is Sunday afternoon & I will endeavor to write a few lines which I hope you can read. First I am sick or lazy as you please. Last Sunday I came from church & was not very smart. I have not been up & dressed since, but think by another Sunday to be around the

house and at church. I am so much better Ma says I may write to you, do not worry I shall be all right soon. Have not much news to write this time. The Literary Society or Lyceum is moving again. Cad you say Coz Asa Sackett is with you. What you tell him comes straight back to Ans Booth.

The sleighing is nearly gone, five of the girls was here to see Sue yesterday. Your letter came last Wednesday which was acceptable. I often wished you were here & hope to see you dear one. You know that love is confidence. Why do you not write about yourself & business. If the army moves on the Potomack do you expect to go? I heard yesterday that your brother was back & I thought by what was said he was well. I can not write my love for you, it is the same as ever. I am very tired & can not write more this time from one that thinks of you ever. Yours as ever.

F A Keeler

Frances Augusta Keeler, age 15, and a lock of her strawberry blond hair

## March 16, 1862
From: W. C. Gridley – Fort Totten – Washington, D.C.
Dearest Frank, You are well aware that some days has elapsed since the rec't of that much looked for epistle which now lies before me showing its collers ever true. But not was I expecting to hear of your illness. But Gus cheer up that lovely mind of yours & say

32

to yourself there is better days coming, don't you be afraid of Asa learning anything by me for I never saw that Sackett which or who could pump from a griddle fresh gravy (may I use the expression) I am getting allmost home sick for the want of female society. Make that out if you can. **I have not seen any calico in so long a time almost forgot how it would appear,** Especially away back here in the country four or five miles from civilization. Nothing to be seen except the second groth of oak & now & then an old farm house such as are very uncommon to me, & now & then a yellow gal. (excuse me for saying I had not seen any calico. I had forgotten the yellow gals did use that article of aperril, with red white & blue/ rather most of the red lavished upon her person with the few of them that belong to sesech.

There is one (farm house) within less than half a mile of us has a stone pen to keep the infantry quartered in. I do not mean infantry for the service of war I mean live stock.

When I left home I was afraid you would worry & make yourself sick. I know to well the sensation of such. I ever feel it with Sis. I know how to pity such. I cant half write the sentinels are talking & singing all kinds of songs & Asa is sweeping out the store & fixing to go to bed, he has just finished a letter to his dear little wife. How often do I wish I had one too.

**You wanted to know what my business was. It is selling goods to the officers & privates of the 76th. Articles consist of every thing in the line of grocery, we are selling a good many goods & still the boys have not got any money. It may be a mystery to you how we do it. We take orders on the Paymaster & ishew *(issue)* tickets. What the boys call shin plasters. I will send you one if you will keep it dark.**

The army has moved on the Potomack & we stand still & no prospect of moving soon. I am quite under the wether today. I was out all day in the rain yesterday & got very wet & cold.

Dearest Frank fret not my love for you is unchanged you know I love thee. Do I not write as often as you like. If so you must write as soon as you get this & I will as often as I can get time to. We are busy Sundays as well as other days, "view it not with critical eye, but pass its imperfections by." From a friend Ever True Willie

PS Your love is returned meny fold. I have hopes to meet you soon but perhaps not. I hope that this will find you enjoying better health. Frank I believe through out, ever faithful.

*In his letter of March 16, 1862 Will Gridley mentions missing the sight of women in calico. This photo is labeled "cousin" wearing calico.*

**March 21, 1862**
To: Wm. C. Gridley 76th Regt NYSV
Washington, D.C.
From: A. Keeler – Candor, Tioga Co. NY

Dearest Willie, Yours of the 16th has arrived & was very welcome since you could not come in place of it. I am very thin in flesh but up and around, as the girls said they was going up Harris's & get some paint. Lua Williams says I ought to be ashamed to be sick just when all the parties are. The girls have had a great time about their being jelous of each other. I am out of that & sit here in the front room by the window. There goes someone by but not thee one. The snow is falling but not much sleighing and very good walking so I do not get as lonesome since I cannot go out.

The next Tuesday after I wrote to you, Mary Kelsey came up here, she did not know but we were all well. She said they had all been sick, but her Father, with the scarlet fever, she did not look very well rather thin. Your brother was very sick after he came home with the scarlet fever & your father has been sick so she said. Your father went down yesterday & Mary E. went up home with him. Mary said your brother W has gone west. Mary said your people were better. I have not written this to have you worry but thought you might like to know how they had been.

Ward was here to supper with LeGrand (Keeler) yesterday. LeGrand has got home, Sarah writes she is well & gets along very well with her studies. Mary & Norman are getting along fine. I shall not tell how much she has talked about a certain Gent. I laughed at her at first. She seemed to prefer to talk rather in earnest, did not a certain one watch & try to find out something here, I had to lay there and laugh in my sleeves. She will not should she ever know like me, for not making a confident of her as she does me, but not a word was said, although she talked of you.

Mr. Dunbar of Ithaca called last evening. He said when he was down to the Hotel Trusdall they told him he better not come here as you would be after him. I told him to ask John Trusdall who sent

34

him to report. He did not know what to make of John's coming out on him so before the boys as he does not know any of them. His call was nothing only as a friend as he was going to stay at the Hotel that night. I can tell you I am sick of such talk. A pity that I can not have any of my friends call without their medling, now you laugh if you dare & I shall not care. I have had **four teeth taken out & five filled yesterday** & today which does not make me very smart tonight. I have not been out the door. I think of going over to Doc McKeys tomorrow. I am not going to worry one bit so there. You know I would not. You take good care & not get sick & I am & have enough to care for me in sickness, but we will hope you may have that great blessing of health ever. Now love, may every blessing be thine. You write to me to cheer up I dare not hope too much, you know what I often told you. Perhaps you have forgotten if so I can tell you again when I see you again which I hope to do some day. There is a party at Trusdalls for Ella this eve. I am not going, the girls are all going. I doubt your reading this for it is most dark & I can scarcly see to write. My love is with you & I think of you ever. You know I would like to hear from you or see you every day. Since that cannot be, write when you can or wish to, do please yourself. LeGrand says he is lonesome here. It is time I closed this nonsence for you will tire of reading it. Ever Your, Frank
PS as soon as I get out again I am going **to Owego** to Harrison Keeler's & stay a week or so. I wish if you come you would let me know but no, you will come when least looked for, one of your old tricks I believe. Augusta

*(George LeGrand Keeler was Augusta's brother, born in 1842, he most often used his middle name)*

*Letters to and from Civil War participants were treasured items, to be read and reread by the entire family....but some of their more private thoughts William Cadwell and Francis Augusta wished to keep on "the down low" thus the code words in each missive.*

*(An envelope was enclosed with this letter with a copy of the poem Augusta's sister Sarah had sent to her in a letter dated Feb. 24, 1862. On the back of this was the key to the code Augusta & Will often used.)*

Personal codes and letter with private salutation

**Moore's Rural New-Yorker**
**The News Condenser**
March 1, 1862
*Drafting has commenced in Virginia
*Liquor is now entirely prohibited in the Army of the Potomac
*The sale of rebel property at St. Louis yielded the sum of $4,000
*A railroad is now in operation between Alexandria and Washington
*A large number of mail robberies have been brought to light within a few days
*The great Sawyer gun, at Newport News, burst on the 11th inst, killing two men
*The Louisville Journal states that the smugglers are doing a heavy trade along the Ohio river, below Henderson
*Large numbers of counterfeit $5 bills on the American Bank of Providence were discovered in New York on Tuesday week
*General Hallack has issued an order that at all future elections in Missouri all voters will be required to take **the oath of allegiance**
*The steel vests concerning which so much has been said as affording protection to the soldiers, have been tested and proved failures
*The legislature of Delaware has adjourned. A resolution denouncing any move for the abolition of slavery in the state was adopted.
*Envelopes are scarce in the South and the Memphis Appeal recommends turning old ones wrong side out and using them after pasting them

**Moore's Rural New-Yorker** – May 24, 1862
The News Condenser
In Arkansas Union feeling is growing, and numerous secessionists are taking the **oath of allegiance**

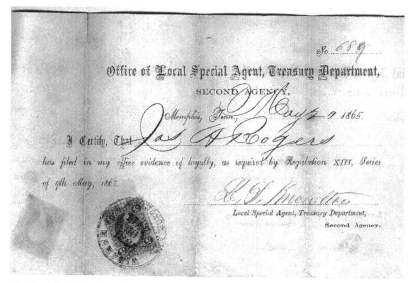

Typical OATH OF ALLEGIANCE used during and after the Civil War era

**The New York Times** – December 9, 1863 – REBEL PRISONERS ENLISTING.
The rebel prisoners at Fort Norfolk are daily offering to take **the oath of allegiance**, and to bear arms in the National service. Three enlisted last Monday in the new regiment raising here, and fifteen or twenty more have applied for permission to join various Northern regiments. Col. MURRAY thinks he could enlist fifty a month, if desirable.

**The New York Times** – December 9, 1863 – TAKING the OATH.
Either because Gen. BUTLER has such a winning way about him, or for some other good reason, several of the most prominent Secessionists in Norfolk have recently gone up to the Custom-house, and taken the **oath of allegiance** required of loyal citizens. Among these new converts are JOHN R. HATHAWAY, formerly editor of the notorious Day Book, and a wealthy Jew named OBENDORFER, who built at his own expense a gunboat for the rebel navy. The former has been made the foreman of the Government job printing-office here by Gen. BARNES.

**Harper's Weekly** – November 1864 – The Tennessee Test Oath

In his Augusta speech Jefferson Davis says; "we must beat Sherman, we must march into Tennessee…there we will draw from twenty thousand to thirty thousand to our standard."

It is to prevent these very persons from voting that the "Tennessee test oath" is proposed. The loyal citizens of that State intend that the rebels shall not regain at the polls what they lose in the field, and shall or obtain possession of the State either by arts or arms. Does any truly faithful citizen of this country object to any **stringency of oath** which secures that result, and defeats Davis's purposes?

**New York Times**
**Richmond Daily Dispatch** – March 1864
Fredericksburg, Virginia
The Yankees are selling commissary stores to the people of the overrun country without requiring their **hands of allegiance**.

*Confederates often objected to swearing an oath of allegiance to the Union even after wars end. The following letter and obituary give testament to the feelings of many southern loyalists.*
Information courtesy of R. Katchuk.

**August 25, 1864** – Richmond, Virginia
Miss Tempie E. Hamilton, Dear Sister, I am happy to state to you that your letter to Joe of July 13th came safely through which makes three we have received from you lately. This is the 3rd that I have written to you lately. I am not overly well at present. Joe is quite well. Jack was also when we last heard from him. Joe was slightly wounded on the 18th inst. Only contused in left breast by a piece of shell. All the boys are doing finely. Tell Lolly that John Powell was wounded in the left hand I received a letter from Dick Seaborn last evening. He was well and in fine spirits, he did not exactly confirm the report of Moses W & John W being prisoners. He says that it was a voluntary act on their part. Very much as I have expected for some time past. We had heard of N.P.H.'s leap some time before we rec'd your letter. Van W. & Joe were a little disconcerted at the news but I am really glad that it is so. I hope Mac & Missie P. will not be so hasty. I have not heard from Ben G. in a long while. He was in Florida and in very ill health. Crisp was well when last I saw him, looked better than he ever did before in his life, said tell

Mollie he had become quite a moral boy. I think of home often, & you all much but I don't expect to see home or you till this sanguine war shall be closed. I hope you will ever be mindful of me in your supplication before the Omnipotent Father. Inclosed you will find some C.S. stamps. Give my love to Mother & Pa. Tell Pusss to write my good wishes to Mrs Waller & enquiring friends. I should like to see sister Beckie. Why don't you prevail on her to write. I will close for the present. Good bye, D.D. Hamilton, Co(H) 7th Tenn Regt – Archers Brigade – Fifth Division, A.N. Va.

## CONFEDERATE VETERAN OBITUARY (a rebel to the end)

After a brief illness, David Dickerson Hamilton died at his home in Nashville, Tenn., on May 11, 1922, the fifty-seventh anniversary of his return from the war of the sixties.

"Dick" Hamilton, as he was affectionately known by his friends was born in Davidson County, July 24, 1842. He was one of twelve children of Eleazer and Emily Perry Hamilton of whom only the youngest brother, Tolbert F. Hamilton, of Mt. Juliet, Tenn., survives him.

He enlisted in Sumner County, Tenn., May 22, 1861, with three of his brothers – Joseph Porter, Eleazer Dent and John Hall Hamilton – as members of Company H, 7th Tennessee Regiment, Archer's brigade, and all fought through the entire four years except Dent Hamilton who was transferred to another company, was taken prisoner, and died in Camp Chase.

**Dick Hamilton was severely wounded in the head and shoulder at the battle of Seven Pines, and again at Petersburg, Va. He was mustered out at Augusta, Ga., May 1, 1865, and made his way home on crutches, walking part of the way, being told that all who came to Nashville were to be forced to take the oath of Allegiance, he slipped from the train at Lavergne, borrowed a horse from a friend, and went across the country to his home near Stewart's Ferry, twelve miles east of Nashville, where he found his family mourning for him as dead. For several years after the war he used crutches.**

He was for thirty years or more a teacher in the schools of Davidson County, Tennessee. In 1870 he was married to Miss Margaret Amanda Page, who survives him, with two daughters and four sons. His friendliness and good humor won for him a place in the hearts of all who knew him. He had a vivid recollection of his war experiences and delighted in narrating amusing incidents of soldier life. For fifty-five years he was a member of the Christian Church.

**The Chicago Times** – 1862 – The Oath of Allegiance at Memphis. The Memphis Avalanche finds serious fault with the form of the oath of allegiance prescribed by Gen. Grant. It says it has been taken by but comparatively few of the old merchants, citizens, and property-holders. The objections are thus stated:

"The uncertainty of the results of war, with the changes and vicissitudes of fortune, in such contests, constitute, with many, grave objections to taking the oath as prescribed; and, with many other peculiar circumstances connected with their affairs and business, it presents to them almost insuperable objections. One objection offered to our people is, that the oath compels persons to swear to certain political views as to the nature of the relations of the States to the Federal government which the great mass of our people do not believe to be correct. To them, under the circumstances, the oath seems to contain false tenets. Now, a person may not believe in the right of a State to seceded, yet, at the same time, he does not believe that the Federal authority is *paramount*. He may believe that the Federal authority is only paramount to the extent of its *delegated* powers. This has been from the foundation of the government up to the present revolution and war, the construction placed by a large majority of the people of the United States on the Federal constitution. Not only this, the adjudication of State and Federal have given the same construction to the powers of the Federal government; yet the oath as prescribed requires the citizen to swear irrespective of this distinction. It does seem to press the conscience a little too much where such political convictions be honestly entertained.

"If it were not for the required oath, we are satisfied that a considerable trade would spring up with the back country. Many little lots of cotton would come in, if the planters were permitted to ship it without having the oath put to them. They would cheerfully give their *parole of honor*, and observe it with punctilious fidelity not to carry information to the hostile forces, if they were permitted to **escape the oath**. We learn that Gen. Grant, to accommodate the objection stated, has determined to modify or change the oath. We will lay it before our readers as soon as we may procure a copy of it."

**August 1864** – Elmira, NY – Camp records – Prison for Confederate soldiers – This day five prisoners were released on taking the oath of allegiance

**New York Times** – June 1862
Governor Johnson Among Nashville Clergymen
Nashville, Saturday June 28
At the special second Conference of Clergymen before Governor Johnson, all declined to take the Oath of Allegiance. Most of them were sent to the Penitentiary, prior to their removal to General Halleck, for the purpose of being exchanged for Tennessee prisoners. Many Nashville churches will be without pastors tomorrow.

**March 30, 1862**
Head-Quarters of Seventy-sixth Regiment, NYSV – Col. N. W. Green, commanding
To: F. A. Keeler
From: W. C. Gridley – Fort Slocum, Washington, D.C.

Dearest Frank, You are well that yours of 21 came to hand in dew time & without delay.

Yesterday the snow fell to the depth of one inch. Today was all gone & it thunders & raines "right smart" (a southern phrase) You will perhaps understand it. It has been very dry here for some days. The dust did fly worse than you ever saw it do in Candor. The dirt and sand is just like traveling in a bin of meal or bran & then when it is mudy it is the mudiest mud & wettest water you ever saw.

I had a good time playing Eucre last eve, the first I have had since I left Candor (Keep dark) I am glad to hear that you are gaining so finely, & think it not necessary to take any paint as it is not intended for disease. Perhaps Miss Lua Williams would not feel so bad if I was up there & she thought there was any possibility of my running her around to parties which you are well aware that I would not do. I do not see the necesity of the girls getting jelious of each other for there are but few that are worth being jelious of.

I rather guess that Mary & Norman will soon leave the status of single blessedness for one that proves to be much better (by the experience of others). I am satisfide that it would suit this child quite well, perhaps you know full as well if not better, that is for you to decide & not for me. I am glad if I have found one girl that can keep her own secrets. She would not think of me when that other gent is about. I think you are very smart. Who are you going to eat with. I won't laugh but smile a little for I know how to pity you.

I am feeling very well with the Exception of a hard cold. The weather is so changeable that one can hardly keep from being sick. You can laugh at the strangeness of this writing, it is so dark that I have to guess at the lines. I hope you will do as you say and not worry one bit, but I am afraid you will forget some time.

Was there or has there been any remarks made about that letter which you said was not sealed, anything to make you think that it had been read? I have forgotten wheather I had written my name in letters or caracters. Let me know in your next if you can find out anything. I can't tell when I can come home for Pay day is comming soon & I must be at my post to receive **what concerns mens pockets. (not womens at all)**

Worthy love, I do not feel smart enough to write much of a letter tonight. I feel as though if I were there I would seat myself in that old rocking chair & take that Bravest friend in my armes and sleep one short hour. Write soon is the earnest wish of a friend. Yours ever Willie, To: F.A.K  Candor, Tioga County, NY

**April 10, 1862**
From: A. F. Keeler Sackett Mansion, Catatonk, NY
To: W. Gridley, 76th NYSV, Washington, D.C.

Dear Willie, I received your letter yesterday & was very glad for Asa wrote that it was very sickly out there & it is two weeks since I wrote & I feared you was sick. I have been here a week today. I am to stay a day or so & as Uncle is gone away Aunty said I must stay with her & Carrie. We three are here alone. You will excuse this paper & pen but it is the best the house affords just now. If you are like me you will not care for the paper, if only you can read what is written for you. You must not try to read this after dark as it will be impossible. It is written so poor. I am sorry that this paper should be the bearer of sad news. Mr. Russell Gridley is dead and was buried on Tuesday. We did not hear that he was sick until Sunday. Aunt Sackett & I went up to see Elizabeth & Mrs. W. told us. Mr. Hubbard was buried on Monday, Mr. George Bacon of Owego last Saturday. Last Monday Mary Ward, daughter of Hiram Ward, was married to Mr. Bose a Methodist Minister, a widower with three children. They were married in church.

You say the girls have but few that is worth being jealous of, that is the reason for their envy, they know very well & what do you think. Asa was down and stayed with Frank Sackett over Sunday. Monday morning **he went up on the cars**, he was at the wedding & after the funeral, in the afternoon Lucia Hart & Lua Williams went & took him up home. The last party he treated Sate VanKleek very cool & from what we see & his going with Lucia, shows to anyone that know him what he is trying to do. You must not tell but Lucia told me that she thought that Sate thought he would have her, & Lute says that she (Sate) is making lots of clothes. I shall not tell what, but Lute thinks she may get her eyes open soon. He has been with her over two years. I am sorry for her and wish that he may get such a one as he ought to have, me for instance or Lua, you know we are such friends.

I can not write all I would say for you to know I lack confidence, not in you but others, you understand, precious one I wish I could just look in on you in your splendid home out there, not that I envy you, for that would not do, since I am quite comfortable here even if we do have snow the 7th of April. The roads are not very bad. I am miss lazy, mother says I am lazy but I tell her I am not & that if she will find me a nice old widower with three children I will see if I am not as smart as Mary Ward. She says if she does a certain Gent would be seen round these quarters very soon so I told her to try it. But no go, she won't, as for Mary and Norman I have not seen either lately. If she does not tell me when she leaves I never will let her know when I leave this single state, If I ever do.

By the way, that makes me think what your opinion on that subject is. I do not know whether to be surprised or not, you off there & I hear & you never tell me any plans or what you intend to do. I for one do not wish to be a burden, but you know best about that little pocket book. I can wait one or two or three years or suit yourself. Think twice then write & tell me all you think on the subject. You have got to say, then I will if this applyes in any way to that hint in your letter as concerns our leaving the state together you have my answer. It would be my hearts desire to call you my own. You did not write your name only Cad in that first letter.

I do not see any of the boys but if I get to laughing about going they ask what will Cad say & I tell them he has gone to war. Charly Baragar asked me the other day when I heard from you last. I told him it had been some time & perhaps you had forgotten me. He said do you think so, I said Charly you must write and find out. I should feel very sorry if you had. He acted as if he would have to go away just about as wise as he came. I have done one thing that Asa does not know of & he is trying to find out about us, do you think he will?

The hints we girls give is enough to kill one........? I do not know how to take them. It is very convenient to be innocent when it would be folly to be wise. I am very weak & cannot write very nice, my hand numbs. You will be very careful & not get sick. I believe I should fly if you should, unless you was where someone would take care of you.

Willie dear what I have written in this letter I would have no one but yourself know, since it is for no one else & can do no one any good. Perhaps you better destroy it & then it will be safe. With you off there if anything should happen there might be some that would see your papers & you know it is best to be safe. With much love & hoping the day not far distant when I shall see you. I must bid you good night, yours ever Frank

*The address "Sackett Mansion" in Catatonk, was Frances Augusta Keeler's mother's family. Her full name was Sarah Warren SACKETT Keeler. Sarah's mother's maiden name was Warren.*

**Moore's Rural New-Yorker** – February 8, 1862
*The Rebs are said to be making large quantities of Powder at Raleigh, North Carolina
*Large amounts of counterfeit money is in circulation about the camp on the Potomac
*Two thirds of the slaves have left Missouri since the war commenced, only about 36,000 left behind
*A gang of counterfeit coiners with extensive "facilities" for the manufacture of quarters and halves, has been broken up
*Nineteen newspaper correspondents accompany the Mississippi expedition. Seven of them represent the New York Press
*The Virginia Assembly has passed a resolution begging her volunteers to re-enlist when their term expires
*The "Great Eastern" the grand mogul of sailing crafts is to be converted into a bath house or floating hospital
*The American residents of Vancouver Island have generously forwarded $1,000 to the Sanitary Commission at Washington

**New York Times** – March 25, 1862

**"The Paris Patrie"** asserts that a member of the English cabinet recently declared to a deputation from the manufacturing districts that, according to information from Washington an amicable separation between North and South will take place about June, and that the basics of the treaty will be as follows:

Missouri, Kentucky and Tennessee are to return to the Union

The two republics are to have no land – customs line

Search for slaves is to be prohibited in all the states

Slavery must disappear within 30 years

**April 20, 1862**

From: W. Gridley – Washington, D.C. – Fort Slocum

To: Miss F. A. Keeler, Candor, Tioga Co, NY

Dearest Frank, You are well aware your letter of the 10th has reached its destination before this although but a short time since. I see by the tone of your letter that you have been writing to your Uncle Dick. By the way I saw R. H. Sackett just before I got your letter. He has come up to see Asa. I learned by Fred P.....that Mary Ward was married before I rec'd yours. I think perhaps she thinks more of large children better than small ones. (lisp not one word as I trust you will not) or I trust she never would have married him. If that certain person who is so inquisitive finds out any thing I guess it will be after this. If Lute don't look out first she knows she will be making up clothes for the same purpose (marriage). Say to her to be aware of what she is doing. I have some feelings for Lute for she is a cousin of mine & a dear one too. I dislike to see any one placed in misery. The best thing for him is to return to the one he has deserted (Lute). I can not tell you anything about him for you know him best in your phrase. I suppose Lute thinks it is fun to get him from Sate.

You need not be afraid to wish any thing as you can avoid your name by printing it. I wish you could enjoy the scene of camp life. We had snow about the same time as you but none since. It has been very pleasant some times. The peach trees are out or nearly so in full blossom. The fields of grain and grass are very green, but a more disagreeable climate I have not seen tho. Inhabitants are forever being sick. I have not been sick but one or two days as yet although I have a cold nearly as bad as the one I had when I left home, it does not seem to get any better. I have been flattering myself that I would go home this week but I see no prospect of it now, when I start or before I will send you a line that you may know as you wished too. Charlie Barager was in this city a few days ago but has gone to **Alexandria** with George. Dick Clark is quite smart. The rest of the friends are all well.

Dearest one I have no occasion to think twice upon that subject for my mind has been made up for some time that you dear one & no one else can fill that place for me, as to that time, it will come at a future time not yet agreed upon. Be constant & true to me & some day you shall become the wife of the one you now love. I long to realize the dreams of love away down in sunny south. They seem like far off visions which I never expected to realize upon the face of this gloomy land. How glad I am that there is one that can appreciate my worth Dearest Frank, you know not the depth of love here concealed for you, as to your request you say that I must say that is just what I expected to do. I did not think nor would not have you think by what was said in that letter that I wanted to have you ask me to join with you in that loving bands of matrimony. I did it only to see what would be the reply. It was settled in my mind what I should do before I left you dear one. The little pocket book remains still in my pocket & wastrels could not drive it from me. I am going to get some photographs taken for Mother soon and I will send you one. As for what you have got there I feel ashamed of it every time I think of it, it is such an awkward looking thing.

I expect to come home before long & then I can talk with you about the subject. I have but little time to write but I can take time to write to you when other friends must wait for them. You must excuse this risible for it is done in haste. I had learned of the death of Grand Father but late to come home. I would have come if heard in time. Here is hoping that this will find you in good health. Yours forever with much love. Willie

**April 24, 1862**
To: Wm. C. Gridley – 76th Regt NYSV – Washington, D.C.
From: Miss Augusta Keeler, Candor, NY

My Dear Willie, Once more I am seated here at the table with your ever welcome epistle open before me & what will I say, I cannot express myself on paper, but when you come I will tell you. Your letter came last eve, I returned from Catatonk (Tuesday) Uncle

Richard came home Sunday. If I had staid till today (Thursday) I would have been gone three weeks. I have heard no news since my return.

As for Lute she would scorn to try to get him away from Sate if she thought they were engaged, she has had some experience. You wish I could enjoy the scene of **Camp life,** perhaps I might, that would depend on who was with me. I must say I should like just to look in & see how you all get along.

The grass just begins to look green, everything is backward this spring. Yesterday & today has been very cold but nice going most to pleasant to stay in the house. You say your cold is not any better, it pains me to hear it for it can lead to no good & our Camp life subject as you are to all kinds of weather is not going to better you. While I was at Catatonk Mrs. Hubbard & her two daughters from Conn. & Mr. Norton of Ohio came there & to all their friends. I like the young ladies very much, they seemed to enjoy their visit. I cannot tell you all about them but when I see you I will, they said your brother was at home & Mary Kelsey was up there when they were.

I have not seen Mary yet, will soon as I can. Uncle Richard tried to get the start of me about you, but it could not take. Now dear one you say your mind has been made up for some time, wish I could have known it before, perhaps it is just as well, time will tell. You never doubt do you that I would not be true? I never doubted you & think I never will have cause to do so. Was you satisfied with my answer? I did not think you would have me say, I thought it might be about half if not more jokeing about Mary. I could not tell, you say everything so funny sometimes.

I shall be only to happy to see you at any time. Do not idolize that pocket book. I want some of those little thoughts & affection from you. I cannot give without return, which I know I have, you say you may come soon, come soon, tonight, now & let me print a kiss upon those lips that would & have said the very wish of my heart.

It is pleasant to have an object, some one to live for, that I am no longer going with this & that one. Once it was, I had no one, I would go & do as I please, thinking those I loved did not love me & they must not know what I thought of them till it was almost second nature to me. You have always known me, I need not tell you. Now precious one if you love me more than I do you I will be getting the best of one. I look with longing eyes for the time to come when you will be all my own when I can sit & look into those eyes & feel that they look only for me. I think of you as you said I would, sitting here & in this room constantly, every thing is changed to me.

It is six months that I have worn that you gave me, never once looking at it without wishing you were here, you have been gone three months & the time seems long.

It is nearly time for the rail cars so I can not write more this time, hoping you are coming soon I shall leave just now. Write, I hope your cough will be better. Do not stay if your health is not good there. Yours ever, Augusta      To a friend

## April 29, 1862
To: Miss Augusta Keeler, Candor, Tioga Co. NY
From: Mr. Wm. C. Gridley  76th Regt NYSV  Washington, D.C.
        Fort Slocum, Washington, D.C.

My own dear Augusta, In due time did your much welcome message reach me & somewhat unexpected to me for it came last eve, just one week ahead of time. But glad indeed to rec'v it, & hope the next one will be as prompt. I do not say this to make you think you have not been prompt for I think you have, more so than I, since last night I rec'd yours & this eve I return it & so intend to do while I stay here.

There is joy in my heart, if my body suffers from pains & fatigue of labor. I long to enjoy your company once more feeling that thare is one whose affections are more than equal to mine. Dare I presume to say to you that the first time that I saw you, which was not less than eight or nine years ago, I thought I loved thee yet neither did you nor any other chick know it, until within the last four or six months. I have had that feeling within me which that there was to be the object of my care & none other, may it prove so. I say that thou art my first & only true love.

I have loved others it is true, but not that pure love which was first created in my heart & if once broken on others can make it good. Yet she may be the Queen on her throne with her Millions, what was first created can never be made second. Perhaps this will be interesting to you to know that while you were going with Sammy there was much love & I deeply pined for you. There was a time when that love was growing cold by means of some trifling things which seemed to work against me. But now we are to the

49

very point for which I sought, & hoping that we may ever remain so. You are well aware that I say but very little about such things unless there is a meaning to it or them, & now dear one, you ask if your answer suited. I thought that I would try and see if I could make you own up. Girls never intend to say that they love one until the last hours. I thought that might perhaps be the case & I was bound to see.

I knew that I had told you that I loved you & no answer returned but now I think I have it. Can I help but worship that book no, without that I should be miserable indeed, & the ring on my finger recalls many a pleasant sweet old time & bro't to my recollection at times when without it would perhaps cancel the silenced thought.

Love thee, so I do with my whole hart. I have now to share your hour the whole, I think you are worthy of it for you have worked hard to gain it in your mind. I think Frank I am so near asleep that I must close this spinning. Write me soon. I don't see the time to come home.        Ever yours most devoted,   Willie

**May 1, 1862**
To: Mr. Wm. C. Gridley   76th Regt NYSV   Washington, D.C.
From: Miss Augusta Keeler   Candor, Tioga Co. NY

My Dearest Willie, I will be prompt just to tease you & write to night instead of tomorrow as you did. Your welcome epistle came this afternoon, also one from Sarah. I have been trying to get Rosa to go to bed, for she keeps talking & saying if I am writing to you just tell you, you had better come home, or some secesh will hit you before you know it. If so I would wish to stand behind him when he looked through the sight….I would try to help him, for you know I am a friend to all such, a good ways off, if close by **I would want some of them pickles that those men at Alexandria was smuggling south. If you had not heard the story just call & I will read it for you.**

The paper came from Washington. You may be glad you was not here tonight when I read the letter where you said that, Girls never would tell till the last hour, for you would have had to prove it, just be a little careful for you may know I have not forgotten how to tease yet. I am only waiting,

Do you say that I tried hard in my own mind to be worthy of you. If I am the only one that has tried, when you come you will see how much you will have to own up to, joy in thy heart may it ever be so, for I am happy. You remember the time of Miss Ina Wards party that was the first that I ever said much to you, what I thought when Mary Eliza called me to come there you & your brother sat there with her. I never told, but may sometime.

Knowing nothing of where you went I concluded not to think of you only as any other, you say when I was going with so many there was that hidden for me, what I was ever looking for, one to love that I knew loved me. I gave mind but it was not returned so I drive that thought back & became what some have kindly termed a flirt, you called me so once. Two years from now I should have finished going as I do now, provided I had lived, then there is not one that could have claimed the privilege of this letter for you know what I once told you. This may not please you but no secrets now you know as for what you call some trifiling thing that was against you, if you have reference to Weed that is one of my conquests & I pray that it may be the last of the kind, we think & stand where you have wished, so be it.

I am surprised when I look over this paper to think I ever dare say so much, but time makes changes. I dream of you, do be careful of your health for we can not enjoy life without health. You write you are no better than when you were here, you must try & have it better.

LeGrands roommate Mr. Brown is here visiting. Sarah Ward is his pet just now. You may hear of him for there is talk as there always is, because he comes & stays with LeGrand. I wish you would get out of that business, it does not seem as if you need to be there.

Do you like it there? I hope you will get out of that soon & come home. Mr. Brown & Miss Bacon has gone out riding this afternoon. Mother is gone to bed, the girls at school, so I am alone.

Norman & Mary was at Church Sunday evening. Mary does not say one word to me. Her or Ward every time I see them say something about you but I do not hear. I wish you was ever coming home. I rather talk than write.

**Pa wants me, about June, when the going gets good to go down to Towanda & around the route with him. He says it will do me good, what do you say?** I would not go if you are coming. I would like to go, you know I thought of going last fall, but for you I should have gone. You know I would not go while you staid. The

51

reason that I write is if you are going to stay there, if so, you will not care if I go.

You understand me dear one better than others do. There is seldom one that does except Mother. Did I not tell you that I loved you? You say I must learn to judge by actions not by what people say, do you? I must not write more you will get tired of reading. From one ever true, Augusta

*Frances A. Keeler's father was IRA KEELER, born in NY in 1810. He had a route as a "candy peddler." One of his children often accompanied him on his route around the county.*

### ..........15, 1862
To: Miss Augusta Keeler, Candor  NY
From: Willie    West Candor
Dearest A I shall leave for Washington today. I do not expect to be gone over 8 or 10 days but perhaps so. I will write as soon as I get there. You will remain at home until you get a letter from me. This is written in haste. I rec'd a letter last night calling for me to go again & so I have not the time to call.   Yours ever true  Willie

THE SEAT OF MILITARY OPERATIONS IN AUGUST AND SEPTEMBER, 1862

*Alexandria, where the pickle smuggling ring was centered, is located at the far right center of this map....just south of Washington, D.C.*
*Also indicated on the map is Culpepper Court House, Virginia. Gridley mentions the battles in two of his letters.*
*Culpepper was occupied at various times by both the North and South. It was the site of fierce fighting.*

*Newspaper clipping of a poem that was included with an 1862 letter to Gridley:*

**By Frances L. Keeler**

**THAT SOUTHERN PLAIN** – Five Corners, NY, December 1861
I am gazing, watching, eager now,/ and my eyes in the twilight strain
To catch a glimpse of those I love–/ Away on that Southern Plain
My soul sighs deep, and my weary heart/ is filled with care and pain
For that concourse vast now gathered there–/Away on that Southern plain
Oh! Hearts will sigh, and eyes shall watch,/ but ah! They will watch in vain
For the ones we love will ne'er return/ From the war on that Southern plain
Oh! Long will it take the blood to dry,/So thee will be left no stain,
Where the brave young heroes nobly die–/Away on that Southern plain.
And long shall we mourn for dear ones gone,/That are numbered with the slain;
But God will avenge the blood that's spilt/ Away on that Southern Plain
But Father, there are some, I know, That Thou will let remain,
To Come, when the battle songs are o'er, Ne'er come to us again,
Should the ones we hold most dear / Ne'er come to us again, –
Should they wrap the banner round them there, / And fall on that Southern plain,–
We'll meet them all in heaven at last, / Where they will ever reign;
For the captain – Death – will march them there, / And camp on that starry plain.

**Moore's Rural New-Yorker** – July 26, 1862
The News Condenser
*The mint is preparing to issue nickel cents in large quantities
*The small pox is carrying off large numbers of Indians in the North West
*Ninety-two different kinds of shinplasters are already circulating in New York City
*It is reported that the President will proclaim amnesty to all repentant Rebels

*Fall River, Mass., has sent six hundred volunteers already and paid bounties of $18,200, she more than doubled her quotas
*Five brothers of the name of Clayton and belonging to the Fifth Vermont Regiment are reported killed during the late battles in Virginia
*Counterfeit fives on the Hampden Bank of North Castle Creek NY are afloat. They are a photograph of the genuine, and are neatly executed

**Moore's Rural New-Yorker** – May 24, 1862
The News Condenser
*Gold is pouring into the treasury by millions in exchange for 7.80 bonds
*Jeff Davis complains that the fall of New Orleans interferes with his plans
*Gov. Pickens, of South Carolina, proclaimed martial law in Charleston on the fifth instant
*The most furious speculators in Wall Street stocks are said to be some lady capitalists
*The "Wheeling Intelligencer" says that in Western Virginia there are only two avowedly pro slavery papers
*The Western Sanitary Commission reports that there are 6,000 sick and wounded Federal soldiers in the St. Louis hospitals
*The "Richmond Dispatch" mentions two instances when the rebels in that city have buried their sick soldiers before they were dead
*Many of the Maryland newspapers are beginning to favor the acceptance of compensatory emancipation for riding their state of slavery
*Governor Letcher, of Virginia, has declared the conscript law to be unconstitutional
*South Carolina has now in the field 39,274 soldiers, 12,000 of whom are in the war. The excess at this time over the State's quota is 4,064
*John Brown Jr., writes that his company has liberated seventeen hundred slaves in the last four months. They operate in Western Missouri

**Moore's Rural New-Yorker** – June 14, 1862

The News Condenser

*It is estimated that over 300,000 troops offered their services to the Secretary of War On the recent call

*About 20 thousand Enfield rifles have recently been captured by our Navy, together with the vessels containing them

*A slab at the head of a grave on the Pittsburg field where four Illinois men are buried bears the laconic inscription "Four Heroes"

*The Albany Journal says nine Sisters of Charity left that city on the 4th inst for national hospitals near the seat of war in Virginia

*It is reported that 5,000 contrabands have reached the Government quarters in Washington and that from 20 to 30 now come daily

*Fourteen hundred Union prisoners many of whom have languished for over half a year in Rebel prisons have been released at Salisbury, N.C.

*The Senate has passed a joint resolution giving $2 to every recruit enlisted in the regular army, and paying recruits advance pay for one month

*Cincinnati daily papers have advanced their **prices one cent per copy per week**, in view of the anticipated government tax on paper, ink, income, etc.

## August 15, 1862

To: Miss Frank Keeler – Candor, Tioga Co. NY

From: Willie Gridley WDC

My Dear Frank, You well remember that I told you that I would write to you as soon as I reached my place of destination but one day has passed and the letter has not gone. I am boarding at a **boarding house on Pa. Av.** This may not reach you until the first of the week, if not, I hope you will not despare, for it would wory me to it. (here I have to go to Ten) you may think you are lonely but it is not so, so long as I am in the U.S. for I am with you with a full heart (not a gizzard as some folks say) I trust Frankie that you may find it so. You dearest did not know how much I dreaded to leave you there, if I had known how I should have been situated you might have come with me but it may not be so yet. Indeed I would love to have you here, female society of the right kind is very scarce in this city. I do not mean to say that there are no fine ladies for there are, but they are the mighty reserve of the other class. The streets are crowded. It was very warm here the day I

56

arrived, from 95 to 110 degrees. Today has been very comfortable.
I only now & then see a musketoe that will quarter like an ox. It is
uncertain what I shall do here & how long I may stay. Frank when
you feel lonesome strike up some of those old pastorate tunes &
think yours are for me. I fancy that I can here those sweet sounds at
this moment. With the news of Candor, have any of the boys come
home on furlo? How do the folks there feel about drafting? As for
my part I don't think that it will come straight. Nothing more at
preasent as I am about to retire to my couch. I'll bid you goodnight.
Yours ever a dear friend, May God bless you,   Willie

*A Grand review of the great armies of Grant and Sherman was*
*held at Washington, on the 23d and 24th May, 1865. After the*
*Grand Review many of the soldiers took out their frustration in*
*dealing with sutlers by raiding all the sutler shops on and near*
*Pennsylvania Avenue. This street is where W. Gridley lived in a*
*boarding house in 1862. He was continuing his sutler business at*
*that time.*

## August 16, 1862
To: Miss Augusta Keeler, Candor, Tioga Co., New York
From: Willie Gridley, Washington, D.C.

Frankie Dear, As it is Sunday & I have nothing to do & thinking
that you would be happy to hear from me, as I am about to leave
Washington tomorrow for Culpepper, Court House. To find the
Reg't & thinking that I might not receive your letter until I return to
W. again. **I am going to view the battle ground near Culpepper**,
one of the most bloody battles ever fought.

My partner came up from there on Friday very sick & I have
been siting up with him & taking care of him since he came until I
feel some what the worse for ware, but not to amount to anything
as I said before I expected to go to Culpepper tomorrow, he being
sick I have to go & see to his sutler matters there. **I obtained a**
**pass from the Provost yesterday**. I can not tell how long I may
remain there, proberly not longer than a week, if so I will let you
know as soon as possible. Yesterday & today have been very
comfortable here, not near as warm as there when I left, all is quiet
in Washington now with the exc'ption to what little stir there has
been when a Regiment is coming in.

There has arrived here four or six, I don't know which & more is expected every hour. Have the Boys left Binghamton yet? Are they enlisting there as fast as ever? There is one thing I am certain of, that is that there will be no drafting in Candor for they must have raised more men than the full quotas for the 600,000 men.

I have seen W.R. & George Sturges here, they have a store here, by the by, they want me to work for them but I han't decided to yet. Tell your father that biz is not so very good here now as it will be by & by, **that it is almost impossible to rent a store in a good locality, but if biz is as good as last winter any where will do.** Tell him that I will write him as soon as I get back from Cullpepper. Here I stop to see a Reg't coming in & I learned that one had passed before.

Dear one, I will try and write to you much oftener than before & hoping that you may be able to do the same. It is of no use to express the feelings of my hart for you know them too well. W.C. Gridley    I have no more to say now, give my love to Sarah your father & mother. Say to LeGrand that he must take you up to the spring for me. **Frank I have been talking of renting a store here and fill it with goods but not as yet.** Yours ever, Willie

**August 17, 1862**
To: Wm. C. Gridley – Washington, D.C.
From: Augusta Keeler – Candor, Tioga Co. NY

My own dear Willie, Your kind epistle arrived safe last night, & was very welcome, for leaving as you did I feared you might not arrive safe, so you may know how much better I feel about you today. It is Sunday & this afternoon I attended the Methodist & heard the funeral sermon of Lieut. Leroy Hewith. The house was crowded & many had to go away. The boys are all home today and go back tomorrow Kelsey says they may go Wednesday & they may stay there 4 or 5 weeks. The boys came back rather sober. It is realy to bad to see them go, but the country must be saved. May they go & return safe. There has got to be 52 more men from this town & there is great excitment as they say they cannot be raised without a draft. There is to be a war meeting tomorrow night, to try & raise volunteers if possible.

**Eugene Smith has run away, & the officer is after him. He said he would not fight, no way. I am ashamed of him & hope justice will be done with such men.** There are some taken in

Owego we heard yesterday. As for you Willie I can not think, as perhaps you would wish, about your going & joining the army, but if you want to go or must go I will try cheerfuly to wait your return. I know you will not shrink from duty let it cost what it may & that you will ever think of me. Nor do I think you will have to go, still I will hope you may not have to go. Enough of this for I am one that tryes to take things as they come & not look ahead for sorrow for each has there own without. It is pleasant, rather cool. Pa has not come home yet. Kelsey & Trumen was here last evening. Kel said it was hard to go from his parents but he could not stay & he did not want anyone to say he ought to. He inquired if I had heard from you & I told him yes & you was at Washington when you wrote. He wished to be remembered to you when I wrote to you.

Willie you will let me know when you have decided what you will do, for if you stay there & should want me to come I will have to do some thing that I did not intend to just now & not get such things ready that I should have to if I stayed here or we should live by ourselves. You know what was talked of before you thought of going to Washington, you will do as you think best. Talk to me about being lonely, how can I help it sometimes. That is nature. When the object of our thoughts is away perhaps you will remember that it is "home where the heart is."

This will be a long Sunday evening as there is no church. I have heard that Ans did not have Sate, that she told him as he did not say for certain either way & she would not go with him unless there was something more decided so there has been a partial engagement. Then, he did not say nor would he say whether he intended to have her so she told him to leave. Good for Sate. What she ought to have said long ago, & he is served just as he deserves. One thing I am sorry to see Sate grow poor which shows what it cost her. Ester Mix is going to be married. That is why she is in Candor getting ready. I spoke to Kelsey about Lutes going with A, he said he had talked to her & told her & she knew what was her bis, if she did as he told her she would be all right, but he rather she did not go with him.

Willie write soon & know there is one ever thinking of thee & waiting, take good care of your health. Rosa says to give her love. It is getting dark I can scarcly see to write. Hope you will enjoy yourself & return safe. May God watch over you & keep you from harm, from your Frank

This letter is long enough for two. Hope you will not get tired of reading. Sarah says if it is very warm you must use a fan, she does when it is warm here. Fannie did Goodrich another – – – – – & will Ellis has been up to the springs staying the past four days.

**Monday. The boys has gone, they do not expect to stay in Binghamton long. They felt worse today than before. Mary Eliza has not come home yet. Norman was down to church last night. There is going to be a war meeting tonight at the Methodist to try & raise part of the 62 if they can to save the draft.** Asa was to see Lau last night.

Willie do not get lonesome & today is worse than blue Monday for I did feel bad to see our boys go. They would not be cheerful. Write often & all the news. Hope you will not be home sick, hope you may have good luck & return safe for there is one waiting, for thee ever wishing Gods blessings to go with you, from one ever yours    Frank

**August 22, 1862**
To:  Willie C. Gridley – Washington, D.C.
(there has been 465 volunteered since Monday)
From:  Frank – Candor, NY

Willie here I am safe, but very tired. Pa went away this morning. I was going for a ride to Catatonk but kept on to Owego. Went down to the store & Peter wanted me to go up to town & see his wife. He said it was only a little way but it was a long ways for me. I did not get back time for the Buss so had to walk to the depot.

**I intended to write yesterday but did not. Shall not have time to write much. Pa has got Bakers team & Baker has gone in the store. They think with what men they may get to night that they will get the 52 volunteers. Mr. Roberts is getting up the company, the talk is that there is going to be a draft of 100,000 more men. The boys expect to leave Binghamton Tuesday if the pay master comes which they have been waiting for the bounties to be paid.**

Willie I hope you are safe back in Washington & are well, do you like that Sturges tribe? Mary Eliza came home Tuesday. Your brother did not come with her only to NY  she stayed here till after ten then went down home, yesterday I was up to your fathers. Sue Marshall & Loen Chidsey is married, she went up to Binghamton Tuesday. They were married & she came back the next day. I cannot like that very much, she is only 17. As for the rest all are quiet, the boys all gone.

You see if Sate is not going to deceive us about Ans. Things look strange if there is nothing but what I wrote. I have not seen one of your people since you left. Fannie has returned from **the springs**, I rather think I shall not go up there. I rather wait till a certain person can go with me. Willie it is lonesome without you although it has not been long since you left. Do you think you will come back to Candor or stay there? I hope that Gent will recover his health & you will have to stay there with the Regiment. Sarah & all send love to Willie. It rains so I cannot get to the store & this ink & paper is not worth sending but I am not going to wait longer.

Most of the young people think so strange you have gone down there, they look as if they expected to see me to feel bad. I will, for there benefit sometime but Willie you know if we both live I expect to see you again & with that hope I bid you good night, for it is most time for the cars. I have got two papers. Thank you from one that thinks of thee often dear one. Frank

*In the 1850's & 60's, a very popular place for young people to visit was Nanticoke Springs. An article in the **Union News** gave the following report of amenities that included the health giving waters containing Sulphur and iron. The "springs" are often mentioned in the Gridley/Keeler letters.*

UNION NEWS – NANTICOKE SPRINGS – 1852
We have made a visit of a few hours at this domestic watering place recently. It has been open to the public as a place of resort for at least 20 years, and is distant about 20 miles from Binghamton. Though the situation is not remarkable for its natural beauty, it combines the advantages of health and retiracy, and offers an attractive retreat to those who wish to "lay off" on its green hills and amid its romantic groves to chew the cud of fancy.

**August 24, 1862**
To: Miss Frank Keeler – Candor, Tioga Co. NY
From: W. C. Gridley – Washington, D.C.

With that pleasure which words cannot express did I receive your thrilling epistle, and though a court martial, the result of which would be death could not have stoped me from reading it. I wrote to you in my last that I expected to go to CULPEPPER,va. the next day but have not gone yet. Neither do I know when I shall now. As the army is on a backward move and a Battle is expected every day. **I had a pass to Culpepper which is today, eight miles within the lines of the Stonewall Jackson army, and our men were at that time at the foot of SLAUGHTER Mountain which is about ten miles from Culpepper C.H.** we cannot get any goods to the regm't as the prospect is not for 6 or 8 days and of corse shall stay in Washington for the present. Then Lieut Hewitt has been buried. You say the boys were all home on Sunday. You dear one can't tell me how they feel, for I have been in the same situation myself while they were at home thinking that no such thing would have to fall into their tracks, but it has come at last and again the Rebbles threaten WASHINGTON stronger than ever before.

The boys are just in time to do their COUNTRY good, for all of these new Reg't are under marching orders and all expect to have to fight **JACKSON on the Rappahannock.**

The newes here last eve at 9 p.m. was JACKSON had tried to cross the Riv. & had been repulsed every time. Yet after all a small force had crossed at **WARRENTON Va.** & was marching up river. McCLELLEN has left the James Riv. & come to **FREDRICKSBURG & ALEXANDRIA** and is marching on to Manassas &c a battle soon which will darken the pages of history to a deeper gloom than ever before, & there will **be many a fair one wearing black crape & weeping over lost ones**. But our country must & shall be saved, let it cost loved ones, husbands & others, together with the countries Treasure. I see in the paper that the Bingh't Reg't was to leave on the 20th & so I have been watching every Reg't that comes hoping to find them. It is time they were here. I learn by my Brother that the 52 men are nearly filled up & that there is no danger of draft.

62

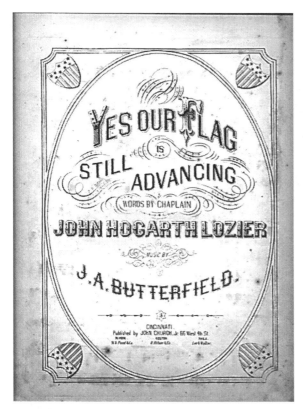

You may think it strange that I do not want to go under the last call but I DO. Yet there is a feeling which the rest have not gotten that is, I spent my time & money at an early hour & also endangered my health & I feel now as though its time for the rest to act as well as talk.

Write me who have enlisted that I know as to your coming out here perhaps it would not be as pleasant here as there for you would have to stay in W and the bulk of my biz would be in the army & I could not be with you but a part of the time, so I think it best to remain there unless I should change my business. (I think I shall return soon) 5 or 6 weeks. At least you would need no extry things as I should Board & it would require but few things for that only Money.

When you see Sate remember me to her. I am afraid the Spring is getting to be just Old. Say I heard yesterday that Dick Clark has gone home sick. Have you seen or heard of him?

Rosa sends her love so I shall have to send her something, you will find it enclosed in this, perhaps it will please her. My love to all. I had almost forgot to say that I was feeling quite well, hoping that this may find you so, Read if you can from one ever yours to Eternity. (write soon)    Willie

*Willie, in his letter of August 24, gives his news about Rappahannock Station. The Rebel forces under General Jackson advanced upon the Rappahannock Station at the river – National batteries replying to the Rebel artillery, August 23, being the commencement of the battles between Gens. Pope and Lee and Jackson, ending at Bull Run, August 30*

*Also mentioned in this August letter was Will's prediction that there would be many women wearing black crape....full mourning clothing.*

**New York Times – 1861**
MOURNING GOODS – A CHOICE STOCK OF MOURNING DRESS GOODS
Just received, will be offered at Retail on Monday, 30th inst., by Arnold Constable & Co. Canal St.
*Mourning stationery private collection and a woman in mourning.*

The length of mourning varied greatly, depending if you were male or female, and also on the degree of relationship. Six months was considered average, some mourned much longer. Flora Stewart, widow of Confederate General J.E.B. Stewart wore widow's weeds till her death, for 59 years after her husband was killed.

Major General A. E. Burnside 1862, left, and General Robert E.
Lee, right picture, at Fredericksburg, Va. 1862
*Note: Fredericksburg was one of the bloodiest battles of the
American Civil War. One newspaper reported that "......the whole
town is a cemetery and every building a hospital." There were at
least 12,653 Union and more than 5,000 Confederate casualties.*

**Harper's Weekly** – December 27, 1862 – The Retreat
During the storm and darkness of Monday night General Burnside
succeeded in making good his retreat across the Rappahannock
without attracting the attention of the enemy. The artillery was first
moved over, the infantry bringing up the rear, and reaching the north
bank safely a short time after daylight. The pontoon bridges were
then removed and the communication between the two shores was
effectually cut off.

**Harper's Weekly** – December 27, 1862 – The Reverse at
Fredericksburg
We have again to report a disastrous reverse to our arms. Defeated
with great slaughter in the battle of the 13th Gen. Burnside has
now withdrawn the army of the Potomac to the north side of the
Rappahannock, where the people congratulate themselves that it
is at least in safety. And now, who is responsible for this terrible
repulse?
.......We are indulging in no hyperbole when we say these events
are rapidly filling the heart of the loyal North with sickness, disgust,
and despair. Party lines are becoming effaced by such unequivocal

evidences of administrative imbecility; it is the men who have given and trusted the most, who now feel most keenly that the Government is unfit for its office, and that the most gallant efforts ever made by a cruelly tried people are being neutralized by the obstinacy and incapacity of their leaders. Where this will all end no one can see. But it must end soon. The people have shown a patience, during the past year, quite unexampled in history. They have borne, silently and grimly, imbecility, treachery, failure, privation, loss of friends and means, almost every suffering which can afflict a brave people. But they cannot be expected to suffer that massacres as this at Fredericksburg shall be repeated. Matters are rapidly ripening for a military dictatorship.

**Harper's Weekly** – December 1862 – A Battle as seen by the Reserve
We publish a drawing that represents a general view of the battle field as seen by the reserve, the line of battle off in the distance, next the artillery and second line of infantry. To the right there is a battery planted on a little hill. Across the road fresh troops are seen rapidly marching into the woods toward the front to reinforce our worn-out-soldiers. Near the center are the generals, with their staffs, watching the fate of the day. The road is blocked up with cavalry, infantry, artillery, and ambulances going to and fro, carrying their burden of wounded to the rear. On the house seen near the center are stationed officers with signal flags. To the left is a house used as a hospital, and still further are a batch of prisoners taken off by a file of our men.
All this and more is seen by the reserve, patiently waiting until their turn shall come to take part in the struggle of the day. The wounded are brought past them, carried so that their injuries are terribly apparent to those who are forced to stand still and coolly view their sufferings, not knowing how soon the same fate may be theirs. The air resounds with shrieks of agony, and the ground near the surgeon's table is strewed with amputated limbs. Such sights as these make some hearts sicken and sink despairingly; while in others it makes the desire to be avenged burn only the more fiercely, especially whenever and anon passes by the familiar form of a late comrade in arms, fearfully mutilated or crippled for life, or perhaps dying. One poor soldier is born along who, in spite of his pain,

renders his last tribute of respect to his commander and cheers him as he passes.

Out of the ambulance and supply-wagon, nearest the hospital, the wounded are lifted one after another, and laid side by side to wail wearily until the surgeon can attend to them. One loyal soldier, who has charge of the prisoners, has captured a rebel flag, and is significantly trailing it in the dust as he walks along.

## August 29, 1862

From: Miss Frank Keeler – Candor, Tioga Co. NY
To: Mr. Wm. C. Gridley – 76th Regt NYSV Washington, D.C.

Dearest Willie. Your welcome letter arrived safe, being four days on the roads. I was so very glad to hear you was still in Washington & very well.

We heard it was very sickly in the army & I thought of you. Has your friend recovered his health? Willie you do not know how lonesome Candor is. Herbert Barenger, Fred Parmalee & Mant S. is all that is left. Henry Smith & Rosa Way expect to belong to the Union this fall if there is a minister to be found.

Mr. Baff had a musical exhibition last eve at TRUSDALL's HALL. Ans was with Lute. The hall was full, had a very nice time. They was going to have a dance after but could not get enough young people together.

The boys did not leave Bing. Last week as Kelsey, Truman N., Judson A., & L Chidsey came home over Sunday. They could not get their uniforms for the Regt. Mr. North said that they were to leave today (Friday) for Elmira to get their arms. Then they would go to WDC. Hiram Scott has gone. Lon Robinson, & others that you might know but I cannot think of them all just now. There is scarcly a man to be seen in the town.

Mrs. Horace Booth was buried Monday, after a short illness of a week. Mrs. John Woodford said it was to bad you had left coming here for we were just suited for each other. Now you see what people think of your going to Washington. Mrs. Hocum told me she was down to Mrs. Parmelee.

It is a beautiful afternoon rather cool out doors. I have been wishing all day to see some one which is a shure sign of, can you tell what? I will leave you to guess.

Have had the headache or should have went down to see M. E.

Kelsey today. From what Fred Josslyn writes, Mary Josslyn (your friend) has had a nice quarrel. I have not written guess she thinks I am awful. Richard Clark has not come to Catatonk, nor have we heard from him, was very sorry to hear he was sick.

Owego has got to raise 140 more men in their town. They will be rather ashamed after their braging. Willie there has been nothing to call me out doors so I cannot think of any more news just now & as it is most time for the mail to go I must not write much more this time.

Rosa was delighted with her present. She did not know who I was writing to & was rather surprised when I told her who I had sent her message to.

Willie write often. Of course I cannot expect to see you so I must be content with a letter every now & then which are a poor substitute in comparison with the presence of the writer.

Oh, dear, when you think of five or six weeks it is a long time. All wish to be remembered to W.C.G. From one ever true, Frank

**August 30, 1862**
To: F. A. Keeler – Candor, NY
From: W.C. Gridley – Washington D.C.

Dear Frank, yours of the 22$^{nd}$ I rec'd on the 27$^{th}$ with great pleasure. However it was five days comming. Frank I wrote to you that Dick Clark had gone home sick (as I herd) but I was informed by Mr. Ketchum (of the firm) that he was in very good health & thought better than ever before.

I am glad you had the pleasure of a ride but very sorry that it made you so tired. It suits me to know that your father has a wagon to drive. Brother Ed wrote that he thought that they had raised all of the men for the WAR & no danger of draft. I hope so. I had always thought that they could.

**I have not seen anything of the Reg't the boys are with yet although Reg'ts pass every day. Frank I am in Washington but don't know how safe, the Rebels have been within 14 miles of W. & are very close now.** You ask me if I like that Sturges tribe. I answer NO but at the same time I like almost anything that I can make money out of. **Frank I have rented a store & have got a few goods.** I am in the store now.

I think Chidsey & Miss Chidsey were a very young couple. As for Ans & Sate if it is to be a match I would like to see it off &

68

let that be the end of it. Frankie, when I sit down to write a letter I am homesick to death, one part wants this thing & another that. I haven't half written this but perhaps you can read it. Indeed I would like to be thare to go to the springs with you, dear one. I am lonsome sometimes but your letters cheer me up. I think I shall stay here a while. I don't know how long. I will let you know when I come. It is time for my dinner and I must close, love to all. (ego. Amo. Tu) Yours, a dear friend Willie.

**September 2, 1862**
To: Miss Frank Keeler – Candor, Tioga Co. NY
From: Wm. C. Gridley – Washington, D.C.
Dearest Frankie, you undoubtedly know with what interest I saw its contense. Frank it is indeed so that there is many sick here. In the house where I board there are two Cap't wounded – 3 Cap't sick from the fatigue of long marches & hard fighting & a young lad that used to clerk for me when in the Sutler Bis. all of which blong to the 76 ( NYV). I learn that the Maj. Was killed, one Lieut' & one or two others wounded mortally. The Reg't went into the fight about 700 strong & came out with 32 files being 64 men. The greatest share of them wounded & but few killed, but nearly all of the officers are hurt more or less. I have not heard anything from Harder Lieu't but one of our Cap't said that Cap't Caryl was not hurt on Friday but he may be among the missing today.

**The streets have been filled with the wounded since Friday & are coming yet. Department took every hack, Buss & carriage in the city for ambulances to carry the Wounded & I guess you would have thought there was a long string. Frank I have seen hundreds of thousands pass wounded.** They were more common than citizens. Today I learn that our army has fallen back under the fortifications of Washington, some say that the Rebels hold Alexandria but I think not.

Frank I loved the army once but I can't say that I do now. Dear one I can imagine how lonesome it is there with all of the boys gone. Have they got Eugene Smith yet? There will be but little doubling for the year to come, I think in that town. If I were there I would get Lute a fellow & Ans would have to slide out (you know how), I wish I were.

I have not seen the boys yet. I guess they have not started here have they am glad that Hi Scott has gone for its all right. There are Reg'ts arriving all of the time. There is a strain upon Frank & Libies happiness & a loss to the society caused by the death of Mrs. Booth. Say to Mrs. Jno. Woodford when you see her, that you guess that's all played out.

The weather is fine rather cool. Frank I have thought that I should be home the last of this month but don't know. Our army falling back under the guns of Washington, we may be obliged to leave before that time, but I hope not. Dear one, how I long to see you. Long to meet you hand to hand, lip to lip & heart to heart. To me none but thee can sooth my raging breast. To thee do I ever look, to thee bows all my pride, hoping to find it enclosed safe within a dear ones heart. With a wish for your future happiness & comfort. You need not worry one particle for all is wright as you understand. Yours ever & ever Willie

## September 4, 1862
To: Wm. C. Gridley – Washington City
From: Augusta Keeler – Candor, Tioga Co. NY
Dear Willie, your welcome epistle came here safe Monday afternoon. Now sir I have waited three days to answer it. I promised to write often providences permiting but it has been otherwise since Monday I have been rather lazy. I came from Aunty's in the rain & have had a sore throat since, but am quite myself today. Now don't you get off your horse for I am not sick only enough to say so, just as thousands are every day & think nothing of it. I first thought to say nothing about it but knowing the Kelseys knew by Ward that I was sick, you might hear, therefore choose to tell you myself.

**Candor is nearly desolate, the men say they are going to have prayer meetings so as to get the men together, each one is so afraid they are left alone. The truth is I say they cannot find many more if there should come another draft unless they take the ladies too as the report is about the south that our men was burying the dead when they discovered that some were of the oposite sex.**

The news here is that the Rebels are very near Baltimore. The greatest excitement prevails in Owego & Ithica. In Albany on Sunday 7 of the protestant churches was closed & the ministers went & preached to the recruiting office to get volunteers. We suppose that the 109th regt is at Washington or near, have you seen the boys.

If you see Kel remember me to him & the others if you choose, his people are very well.

The girls are getting along nicely, guess Rosa Way & Henry Smith is going out of state, so his people tells.
Rosa's Pa has gone today, does not expect to be back again before the Reg't leaves. Lou Robinson was married to Bodinthia S. of Catatonk (Abe Daniels niece). Saturday eve at Mr. Roberts there was 9 couple there. Sarah has about given up going back to school in Albany till March. They have another minister at the M.E. Church, Mr. Ellis, not married, a chance for someone. Village of Spencer has made out its quotas, a company from Danby went on the cars today. Joe Judson called at Fannie Sacketts sunday. you say you are lonesome sometimes, here is one that will be company for you then, so am I often.

It has been very cold & a few frosts this week. Today is the first day it was anyways comfortable without a fire. Charlie Barager is in Binghamton & intends to be first Lieut in Captain Roberts Company. W. Sturges wife is in Candor & Susan (so talk says) is going to spend the Winter in Washington with her (W.S. wife) Asa Sackett has gone back to W.C. as for the Reg't you was in, the report here is thet E. Harder is dead, he was in the 26th, which is very sad news.

Willie how are you doing, well, hope your health is as good or better than when you went from hear. Aunt Susan Richardson wrote last week for me to come out there this fall or winter. do not think I shall. They are in Ottawa, Ill. I rather stay where I can hear from W. C. often, now you tell him what I say if you dare.

While I would just like to see you not in five or six weeks as you said it might be but in five minutes, whether you would me I can not say. I am such a beauty now with my face swolin & tied up. I was telling Sarah we ought to have company or go out calling this afternoon. It is a week tomorrow since you wrote, hope you keep up good spirits, (not ardent spirits) all wish to be remembered to W.C.G. Frank sends a kiss, can you find it. Ever thine own Augusta

**September 10, 1862**
To: Miss Frank Keeler – Candor, Tioga Co. NY
From: W. C. Gridley – Washington, D.C.
Dear Frank, your long looked for welcome & most kind epistle came to hand on monday all safe. I did not think that it would bring

71

me news of your illness but thank full it is not worse, hope you'l be all right in a few days. I went to the office today in hopes to get another letter but no. I had a letter from Asa Sackett yesterday saying he would be here this week.

**I have been running a store in here** for the last eight or ten days but now I have sold my lease at a bonus & have nothing to do. Sold for enough to pay my board for some time at $1.00 pr. Day. I shall find something to do before long.

You say there is great excitement there about the rebels. You say (talk says) they are near Baltimore, but they are far from that. They are at **Frederick City Md.** & near **Rockville**. Our men are after them. I have not seen the 109th Regt. Yet. I think they have not arrived but still they may.

You say "Rosa Way & Henry Smith are going out of state." May I infer that they intend **on "missing" the draft?** Hope they will have a huge time. Yours &c may the lord bless them. But I'd like to be there (now mind you that)

**Some of the officers of the 76th state that some one was heard to say that E. Harder of the 26th did not go into the first fight.** He said he was afraid that he would never see his Susan any more. (This is rumor) Please not state as fact from me. There is lotts of fun about it. I have seen no officil report of his death. I think not, so say to Miss Sarah she must keep her cap set. There is such a nice minister. I hope you don't talk of cold weather soon, it is hot enough to roast one. It has not rained but once since I came here, if so cold I think I shall have to be traveling back to Candor. No hopes of such here.

Dear one, four weeks have passed of the five or six & I am here with the same feeling as ever. I hope to see you soon but I know not when. My desire is equal to yours I think but cant say no more, as others say that is impossible. O hardly I would scorn the____of looking upon that face this moment if I could, I trust my affection is equal to one I think I can call my own without intruding, so help me God & you dear one, I shall not say anything to W...C... I fear he might be jellous, not knowing him. I found the kiss you sent. From Yours Ever Willie

PS Here's a kiss for you & the BABY, too and then & there we p....... can you see it

**September 15, 1862**
To: W.C. Gridley – Washington D.C.
From: Miss Frank Keeler – Candor – Tioga Co, NY
Dear Willie   Your welcome epistle has come at last & it was a welcome messenger for I had not heard from you in over a week. You write about cold weather, we are having very warm weather just now. One day warm the next we expect to see snow it is so cold. It is well the people are not like the weather.

It is so quiet that Sarah says she hopes you will bring home a "contraband," not one raised in M.D. but one farther south & see if that will not cause some excitement & get the people out in the street. She thinks there are nicer Gents out there. Captain Roberts child was buried last Thursday. He preached his last sermon sunday morning the house was full & the hall & stoop. I never saw the house so full, your two brothers were there. Cousin Will Hunt's little boy was brought here to be buried last Tuesday.

The 109th Regt are at Anapolis Junction. There goes a contraband, black as knight. Fred Parmelee thinks of going to Washington tomorrow. He wanted to know if I had any word to send to you. **The good people of Candor have got a box of lint &c to send,** ready. Mr. E. Harder is here, has been very sick since his arrival. Grandma is very much worse & Ma has been up there two days. I am just tired out & Ma says cross. That MR. BROWN that wished the soldier boy would never come back, is back in town. He has come after his Sarah. Saw him at church last eve, he said he was going to call.

Willie have you said you was going to stay there all winter, that is the story. I do not believe it, instead of four weeks I should think it has been as many months since you left, it is so dark I can hardly see. LeGrand is waiting for this so I must not write more this time. he says give his love & he is alive yet, write a little longer letter than this, if you see Charlie Hunt write about how he is. Mr. Gleason was here with W.H. Hunt. I got quite well aquainted with him. All send love, hoping to see or hear from you soon I remain as ever your Frank
Excuse the mistakes this is written in about 3 minutes

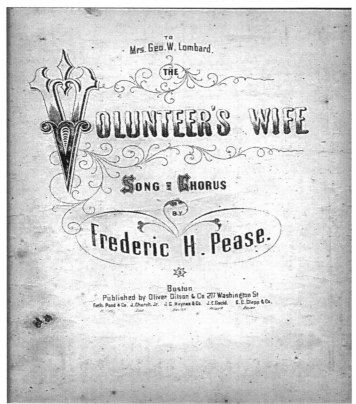

Music Courtesy of A. Sweet

### The Civil War at home – Women aid the war effort

In the letter from Francis Keeler on September 15, 1862, she mentions that: "... the people in Candor had been working on **lint** to send to the Army." This was not the annoying household fuzz we think of today. Lint was used in the medical units for dressing injuries. "Lint is prepared by raveling or scraping linen cloth" so it becomes exceptionally soft. Most surgeons preferred lint made from new linen not fabric that had been used. All over the nation on both sides of the war women produced thousands of pounds of lint, so much that the Sanitary Commission began recommending other items needed for the soldiers.

American women accepted the responsibility to manage farms, businesses and family affairs while the men fought. Their contributions sparked many feminine thoughts about more freedom for themselves when the war ended.....to obtain jobs in the business world, to vote and to manage their own lives. During the war they collected funds and goods for the troops. Women served in aiding the Underground Railroad, as spies, and continued to be active in churches and the temperance movement....and slowly the status of women in America would change forever.

## THE SANITARY COMMISSION

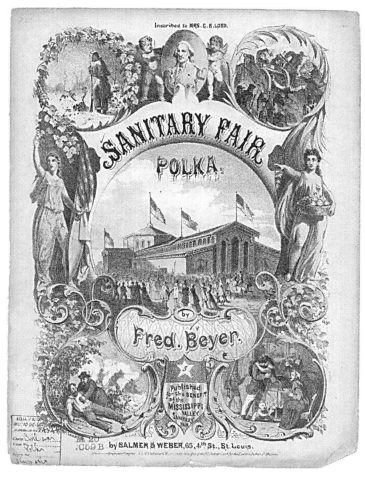

Pertinent to the story of the American Civil Rebellion and the need for clean medical facilities, appropriate food and living conditions...was the inception of the Sanitary Commission, an organization that gave succor to soldiers through charitable means. Many preferred to deal with the Sanitary Commission rather than the nefarious profiteer and storekeeper, the Sutler.

**New York Times** – July 1861
SANITARY COMMMISSION – Appeal of the Executive Finance
Committee in the City of New York
To Our Fellow Citizens

The committee addressed in the subjoined letter from Dr.
Bellows, the President of the Sanitary Commission, earnestly entreat
your immediate and hearty cooperation in the noble undertaking it
so ably advocates.

Never before, in the history of human benevolence, did a
gracious Providence vouchsafe an opportunity for doing good on
such a scale, to so great a number; in so short a time; and with
comparatively so little money. Of the immense array of three
hundred thousand men now in the arms in our defense – to be
swelled; if necessary, to five hundred thousand – the experienced
military and medical members of the Sanitary Commission declare
that one-fifth, if not one-fourth, may be saved by proper care, who
must otherwise perish. Reducing the results of individual action to
a form still more precise, they estimate that every dollar, honestly
and judiciously expended in sanitary measure, will save at least one
soldiers life.

Cannot a city like ours find forty or fifty or even sixty thousand
dollars, to save a like number of the sons, the brothers, the friends,
the fellow-countrymen now gone to battle for the very purpose of
rebuilding its own broken fortunes, of restoring, in fullest measure
its former prosperity?

Fellow citizens: We cannot afford that any one of our brave
defenders shall needlessly perish. All our interests, commercial,
fiscal, political and moral, are crying allowed for a speedy
termination of this great National conflict. In such a struggle it is
madness to waste a single hour, still more a single life. Most of all
should we avoid the ruinous delay of slowly replacing in the wasted
camp the tens of thousands which our neglect may thoughtlessly
leave to die, almost within our sight.

Men and women of New York! We beg you to awake to instant
action. Death is already in the breeze. Disease, insidious and
inevitable, is now stealing through the camps, on scorching plain,
in midnight damp, menacing our dearest treasure, the very flower
of the nation's youth. In the name of humanity and patriotism – in
the name alike of justice and manly generosity, biding us save them
who stakes in saving us – in the name of honored ancestors who

fought for the land we live in – in the name of the Blessed Being, the friend on earth of the sick and the suffering, we now commit this holy cause to your willing hearts, your helping hands; with our earnest assurance that, whatever you do will be doubly welcome, if done at once.

MEMBERS of the Executive Committee of the Central Financial Committee

**New York Times** – 1861 – Office of the Sanitary Commission Treasury Building, Washington, Sept, 26, 1861

Major-General McClellan has informed the Sanitary Commission that he has determined to immediately establish entirely new accommodations for the care and treatment of fifteen thousand sick and wounded men at Washington. Equally large hospital provision will be needed for the armies of the Ohio and Mississippi.

The experience of the Commission has so well acquainted it with the earnest wish of the women of the North to be allowed to work in the National cause, that it is deemed unnecessary to do more than offer to receive their contributions, and to indicate convenient arrangements for the end in view.

It is therefore suggested that societies be at once formed in every neighborhood where they are not already established, and that existing societies of suitable organization, as Dorcas Societies, Sewing Societies, Reading Clubs and Sociables, devote themselves for a time to this holy purpose; that energetic and respectable committees be appointed to call from house-to-house, and in towns, from stores, to obtain contributions in materials suitable to be made up, or money for the purchase of such materials, that collections be made in churches and schools and factories and shops for the same purpose; that contribution boxes be placed at the post-offices, railroad offices, public houses, and other suitable places, labeled "For our Sick and Wounded" and that all loyal women meet at such convenient time and places as may be agreed upon in each neighborhood or social circle, to work upon the materials which shall be by those means procured.

**New York Times** – December 1863
The Great Sanitary Fair at Cincinnati is in the full tide of success.
The receipts for the first two days are $20,000.

Ladies in attendance in regulation costume at the Metropolitan Fair

*The ladies in this newspaper photo are raising funds, while wearing the official Sanitary Commission Sash*

DESCRIPTION OF ARTICLES MOST WANTED:
Blankets for single beds
Quilts of cheap material about 7 feet long by 50 inches wide
Knit woolen socks
Dressing gowns or wrappers, woolen or Canton flannel
undershirts & drawers
Long loose bed gowns of Canton flannel. Small hair and feather pillows and cushions for wounded limbs. Every woman in the country can at least knit a pair of woolen stockings, or if not, can purchase them. In each town let there be concert on this subject, taking care that three or four sizes are provided.

### *United States Sanitary Association*

*A group of women in New York conceived the idea for advising and assisting the Government and Military on sanitary practices in army camp life and hospital care. They organized fund raisers and Fairs in cities across the Union to collect dollars and goods to support the troops.*

*The Sanitary Commission came into being in 1861 when the War department issued an official warrant to create the organization. Eventually the warrant was also signed by President Abraham Lincoln. When the official Executive Committee was formed it was comprised entirely of prominent men.*

*The women served ably as nurses, and provided food and*

*supplies, and clean care, staffing hospitals, camp medical units and encouraging women at home to give or make necessities for the men in arms.*

*After the war ended many women who served our country by supporting the military, under severe conditions, were not content to return meekly to the hearth. The women had aided in freeing a race of subjugated humans and helped preserve the Union. Women's experience working in the war effort added to their own quest for equality.*

*The Sanitary Commission was in force until 1865 and was the inspiration for forming the Red Cross.*

One of the well-known women who signed the original petition for the inception of the Ladies National Covenant of the Sanitary

MRS. S.A. DOUGLAS

Fair was Adele Cutts Douglas, almost always referred to only by her married name, as was the custom of the times, Mrs. Stephen A. Douglass. Her husband was the noted Senator from Illinois and a progressive thinker. Although she was considered a great beauty and an exceptional hostess, when her husband died she completely retired from public life and went into extended mourning. During the Civil War era a popular pastime among families at home was to collect photographs for their albums. Adele's picture was included in the album of a New York family, with no indication if she was friend or relative.

A Sanitary Commission
Nurse and her patients –
1864

LOC

*The Sanitary Commission was often in the news, and in many instances they were discussed in relation to the services provided*

*by sutlers. The sutler failed miserably to reach the standards of the Commission, whose wagons provided free aid to soldiers.*

**Harper's Weekly** – December 1864
TO THE SANITARY COMMISSION

The following letter suggests that the Commission shall extend their business. But we are very sure that our correspondent will see that he suggests nothing less than that the Sanitary Commission shall become the great army sutler, and that it has no authority to do so. We wish most sincerely that Private – and all other victims could be relieved of the sutler extortioners, but he must try again to devise a satisfactory method.

**"CAMP of DISMOUNTED MEN, NEAR CITY POINT, Va."**
"DEAR SIR, – None can so truly appreciate the labors of the **Sanitary Commission** as do we who are their beneficiaries in the camp and field. Their labors are gigantic, and at first sight it would appear unjust to seek to tax them with an additional burden; but when I ask only a kindness to be compensated, I hope the proposition made will be considered. "**Sutlers**, as they now exist among us, are a sort of necessary evil.' They charge us exorbitant prices for every little luxury the soldier craves, and one of their prices current would rival any yet given from rebeldom. Take a

few items : Canned fruits, $1 to $1 25: sweet potatoes, 15 cents per pound; cheese, 60 cents; onions, 15 cents; 1 ounce sweet-oil, 15 cents; butter, 85 cents – and every thing in proportion. Now what we want is that the Sanitary Commission extend their field of labor so far as to furnish the few articles we want at compensating prices. Or if the Christian Commission were to do this, they would find the Gospel of low prices an excellent adjunct to the Gospel of the Prince of Peace. This would require but an outlay of constantly returning capital, and the employment of a small army of clerks. These clerks should be discharged or pensioned soldiers, when qualified ones can be had. " Please make this suggestion, and oblige many victims, Yours, PRIVATE – – ." City Point, Virginia

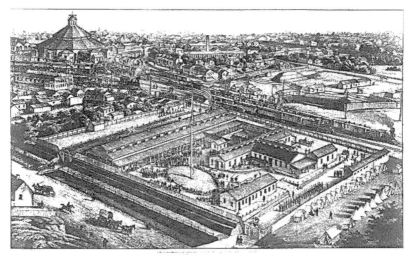

SOLDIERS REST, ALEXANDRIA, VA.

*The Sanitary Commission Lodge for Invalid Soldiers, also known as the Soldier's Rest, was located in Alexandria, Virginia near the Orange and Alexandria rail road yard.......used as a rest stop for soldiers traveling by train, and a refuge for the wounded....It was turned into a hospital in 1864 run by the Sanitary Commission. The rest hostel was originally a large warehouse and at one point housed Confederate soldiers who had taken an oath of loyalty to the Union.  Post war the facility was also a temporary shelter for United States Colored troops.*
Photo – Library of Congress

**Reminiscences of the Sanitary Commission with the Army of the Cumberland**

By – Mrs. Dr. Sophia McClelland – "Tales of the Civil War"
"To those who sit at a distance and read of the marching and maneuvering of a great army, the gay colors, the ringing of trumpets, the splendid charge, the dramatic heroism – all these have grand and pulse thrilling effect. War is glorious in the abstract; in its details it is sickening and harrowing. The brilliant uniforms soon become faded and stained, and fall into rags or show great patches. The "splendid charge" is a mad rush of maddened men, mounted on strong horses urged to their utmost speed, riding down a mass of fellow beings on foot. The reader is content with the information that "the enemy's line was broken and gave way." But when the "splendid charge" has done its work and passed by, there remains a spectacle of death and desolation in which the grandeur and glory are forgotten and horror reigns supreme. The surgeon's note book, rather than the flowery pages of the historian, tells the realities of the glories of warfare."

*SOUTHERN WOMEN IN THE WAR EFFORT*
*The women of the North were largely insulated from the battlefields. However, women of the South suffered both deprivation and bullets arriving on their door steps. Northern blockades kept manufactured goods, wool and other vital substances for life from reaching rebel shores. Items the women produced themselves; knit goods, blankets, quilts, and medical supplies, etc. went to aid their soldiers. And as on the other side of the battle where women nurses were grudgingly accepted, it took much longer for the south to allow female assistance in hospitals. Women did not always accept the government "wisdom" and took to the streets in Bread riots and demonstrations.*

**The New York Times** – Wednesday, July 17, 1861
Patriotic Work for Women – AID for the SICK and WOUNDED
The Secretary of the **Army Sanitary Commission at Washington**, has forwarded to us a circular stating that certain articles such as cotton bed shirts, loose drawers, light flannel dressing-gowns, towels, handkerchiefs and abdominal bandages, are immediately needed for volunteers in hospitals. It is to be hoped

that the noble women of the city will see to the supplying of these imperative wants of the army without a day's delay.

There are thousands of true women in the places of wealth and luxury of this City literally dying of idleness and ennui, for the want of womanly work and an impelling motive to work, who should take hold of this matter at once. It would diffuse among them a life, an energy and happiness of which they now know nothing......Let no woman who can aid hold back.......and the work needed is not spasmodic efforts of the hour but will be required till Freedom and the Union are permanently and universally re-established. "What thou doest, however, do quickly."

**New York Times** – November 1862
As you recommended the employment of "nimble patriotic fingers" in making mittens or gloves for the army I would suggest that the mittens be made with first finger as well as a thumb. It is quite difficult to pull a trigger with a mitten of the usual shape and the finger could be used or not as required. Mittens are much warmer than gloves for the same reason that four children would be warmer in one bed than sleeping alone.

**The New York Times** – 1862
Women are advised to use all moments of leisure....."with a needle making comforts for the wounded soldiers.....The Sanitary Commission is in constant need of renewals of labor, supplies and money. Let no woman waste any time while this war lasts. The sex cannot fight in regiments but they can serve their country equally effectively otherwise"...........

**The New York Times** – October 1862 – The women of the United States have done nobly since the war opened in working for the soldiers. They began by making haversacks, scraping lint, putting up delicacies and comforts for the sick and the well.......

**The Tribute Book** – 1865 – by F. B. Goodrich
1861 – NY – The Ladies Military Blue Stocking Association formed in October for the purpose of procuring 1,000 pair of stockings for soldiers reported 1,292 pair obtained by January.

**Moore's Rural New–Yorker** – June 14, 1862
Many of the husbands in Aroostook Co. Me., having gone to war,
their wives are clearing lands and doing all sorts of hard work.

*It is also reported that women are making large quantities of
blackberry cordial to be shipped to the Sanitary Commission. The
drink is believed to aid the injured by acting as a stimulant.

**Richmond Daily Dispatch** – March 1862
Ladies Defense Association
Ladies organized into an association to raise funds for a gunboat,
to protect the ancient and beautiful Richmond Capital of the Old
Dominion against the common enemy.

**"The Tribute Book, 1865" by Frank B. Goodrich** "To the
WOMEN of America this volume is respectfully dedicated by their
Countrymen."
The women of the Country – especially those of the north west
portion – have rendered other services than those we have
chronicled; the battlefield is not the only field in which they have
wrought, bearing the heat and burden of the day. The wife who in
the summer of 1861, wrote the following lines, doubtless kept her
promise, or, if not, thousands kept it for her.

"Do not stop a moment to think, John,
    Your country calls, then go;
Don't think of me or the children John,
    I'll care for them you know.
Leave the corn upon the stalks, John
    Potatoes in the hill;
And the pumpkins on the vines, John.
    I'll gather them with a will.
So take your gun and go,
    Take your gun and go,
For Ruth can drive the oxen John,
    And I can use the hoe."

*It has been estimated that more than 20,000 women of all colors and
ages and from all areas of society served as nurses and care givers
during the American Civil War.*

**Chicago Times** – August 14, 1862

One day last week the Washington Provost Marshal had before him two soldiers in uniform, of a light form, who excited his suspicions. After being questioned they admitted that they were females, and had been serving as privates in a regiment now in Pope's army for many months. They were furnished with proper apparel and sent northward.

**Chicago Times** – 1862

The Woman Major – A Row in the Family.

We have appropriately chronicled the fact that Gov. Yates has commissioned as Major in one of the Illinois regiments with Gen. Halleck the wife of a Lieutenant, who had shown both courage and devotion to the cause of humanity among the sick and wounded on the field in and after the battle of Pittsburg Landing. The correspondent of the Cincinnati Times tells us something further of her and the consequence of her appointment: "I am sorry to inform you that there is at present some apprehension of a domestic difficulty, originating out of the late commission of a female to the rank of Major in the United States army. "This worthy lady, whose bravery and Samaritan kindness to our wounded soldiers on the battle-field of Shiloh has won her the love and esteem of an appreciating public, and who has been promoted to rank by a grateful government is, I fear, about to fall victim to that most dreaded of delusions – jealousy. This lady is at present holding her headquarters on board on of the hospital steamers now lying at Pittsburg Landing, anxiously awaiting for the expected battle, to again render that comfort and aid known only to exist in the presence of angels and the attentions of lovely woman. "But what is most unhappy in the case of this lady Major is, that her once adoring and loving husband, who now holds the rank of Lieutenant, insists on being made a Colonel, and gives as a reason that his wife now commands him, from the virtue of her rank – being a Major – and that this is directly contrary to the original understanding existing between them at the day of their nuptials. From this protest of the Lieutenant I fear that all law abiding wives will hold up their hands and exclaim, "Oh! the brute.""

*And so the debate would continue for decades on the worth and rights of women.*

**New York Times** – Women and their Employers – December 6, 1863
We fear that one of the fatal errors that will be made by the working women, in their effort to obtain better remuneration for their labor, will be that of trusting their cause into the hands of professional agitators and demagogues, who will start with the idea of creating an antagonism between the employer and the employed. No more fatal start than this can be made. There is no antagonism; and, with solitary exceptions, the employer has always sufficient tact to know when he has profitable labor upon his premises, and wishes to keep it, though, of course, at as remunerative prices to himself as possible. Labor is to be looked on in the same light as we look upon a piece of goods offered for sale. It is bought at the lowest buyable rate, and sold, by its products, at the highest obtainable. The laborer who can carry his labor direct to the consumer, should always obtain for it the highest price, but the rule does not hold always. We will cite, for instance, that of the shoemaker, who, being limited in capital, is obliged to buy his leather in small quantities, paying therefor a higher price, and after the manufacture of the shoes is obliged to consume time in finding a customer, will find that he is no better off by taking his own labor directly to market than if he had sold it in gross to a capitalist, who was able to buy that of a hundred men, and an adequate stock to work them. It is to the interest of the employer to so grade his compensation to his hands as to make them feel that their positions are worth retaining, by which he can have reliance on them in emergency, and yet at the same time not to pay them at such rates as to prevent his competing with those in the same line of business. There is a point at which the indulgence of the employer becomes a positive injustice to the employee. Should a maker of shoes determine to give each of his employees twenty-five cents per pair more than his competitors, knowing that this twenty-five cents was more than his own profits, he would be doing his workmen harm, because it would eventually lead to his own failure, and consequently a deprivation of work for his men. This rule holds especially good with women, who in their strikes will have more effect upon the sympathies of their employers than men. If by these sympathies, unsupported by an actual enhancement in the value

87

of their labor, their employers increase their wages, it cannot be a permanent increase, but must end in one of two things: either in the ruin of the employer, or in his being obliged to charge so high a price for the article produced as to drive buyers to other makers. It makes no difference in this case whether the working of the rule is limited to a few shops, to a city, or to an entire country. In these days of commerce and rapid carriage, nations can enter into competition in the production and sale of goods as easy as individuals. The workers cannot always judge of the value of their labor by the price obtained for the article manufactured. The rule is oftentimes arbitrary where the risk, of the manufacturer is great. It will not do to take it for granted that because the profit on a pair of shoes, counting them by a fair cost and a fair sale, is twenty-five cents, that the profit on a hundred pair is twenty-five dollars. The object of capital should be to act as an agency for labor; to make the labor of one salesman relieve a hundred workmen from that task, and to supply labor with increased facilities, by machinery, commodious workshops, and proper avenues of sale, without charging the laborer too high a price for the use of the capital, and the services of those who have it in charge. When it fails in doing this, it is false to its trust, and must be rebuked by labor ceasing to employ it. This is the theory of strikes and combinations, and their success on either side is simply a question as to whether there is most labor or capital in the market. It the labor is unremunerated to the capital at the price demanded, it will not be purchased, but if, on the contrary, it will pay a profit it will be purchased. These are the simple relations between the employer and the employed, and no combination or strike can alter them. It will be useless for demagogues and agitators to teach these working women, who are just now struggling against a great evil, to make it still greater by leading them to believe that they are laboring under heartless taskmasters. It can do no harm to agitate the subject; indeed it may do much good, if the agitation is conducted with common sense, and does not lead to a strike that will throw them out of employment, and deprive them of five times more than they will eventually gain, even should they be successful in obtaining a trifling advance – for it can be but very trifling.

No. 22.

The United States,

To Harriet C. Twigg                    Dr.

| 1862 | | DOLLARS. | CENTS. |
|---|---|---|---|
| Nov 1 | To Services in Hospital as Cook & Nurse from 1st of Octr to 31st inclusive at $1.50 per week, 4 weeks & 3 days | 6 | 64 |
| Dec 1 | To Services in Hospital as Cook & Nurse from 1st of Novr to 30th Inclusive at $1.50 per week | 6 | 43 |
| Jany 1 | To Services in Hospital as Cook & Nurse from 1st of Decr to 31st Inclusive at $1.50 per week | 6 | 64 |
| Feby 1 | To Services in Hospital as Cook & Nurse from 1st Jany to 31st Inclusive at $1.50 per week | 6 | 64 |
| March 1 | To Services in Hospital as Cook & Nurse from 1st Feby to 28th Inclusive at $1.50 per week | 6 | .. |
| April 1 | To Services in Hospital as Cook & Nurse from 1st March to 31st Inclusive at $1.50 per week | 6 | 64 |
| | | | |

I certify that the above account is correct and just; that the services were rendered as stated; and that they were necessary for the public service.

Saml Schmitt Surgeon

RECEIVED at ___ Washington ___ the 15 of ___ March ___ 1866

___ Paymaster Quartermaster United States Army, the sum of ___ Sixty Six ___ dollars and ___ cents, in full of the above account.

1st National Bank of Washington

(DUPLICATE.)

Harriet C. Twigg

*In 1862 Harriet C. Twigg began working as a cook & nurse for the Virginia volunteers 2nd Regiment Hospital. For her services she earned $1.50 per week. When she claimed her pay in March of 1866 she received a grand total of sixty-six dollars, by check from the National Bank of Washington.*

**Moore's Rural New-Yorker** – May 24, 1862
*Free negro nurses are called for by the rebels. They are informed that "if they go willingly, good wages will be paid; if they do not volunteer they will be "impressed."

89

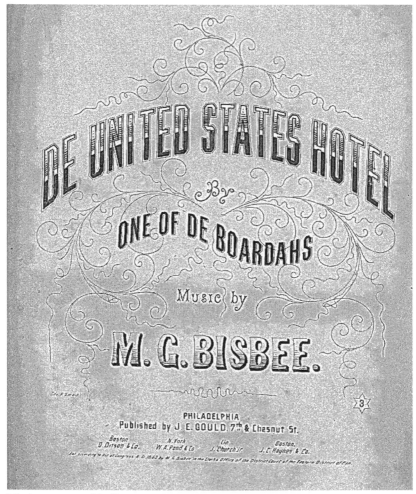

Music courtesy of A. Sweet

Lyrics: And don't you know de boardahs of de complish'd Dinah Crow, Ise took rooms for de season…Ise cutin' quite a swell, where de contrabands boards, in Uncle Sam's Hotel……….

LOC

*In several letters between Keeler and Gridley "contrabands" were mentioned, referring to escaped slaves. Often these people were put to work by the Union as cooks, teamsters, and in their own fighting units.*

**Moore's Rural New-Yorker** – June 1862
The cost to the government of deporting negroes to Liberia, Hayti, and Chiriqui, from New York will be $35 each to the former and $25 to the other places.
LOC

**The New York Times** – December 4, 1863
The Secretary of War has authorized Gov. Andrew to recruit a regiment of colored cavalry in Massachusetts.

**The New York Times** – December 9, 1863 – THE COLORED REGIMENT.
The Provost-Marshal having received authority to raise five colored regiments, has given permission to Mr. R.D. KENNEY, whose headquarters are at No. 178 Prince-street, to recruit a regiment. Mr. KENNY is acting under the auspices of the Committee for Colored Volunteers, appointed at the late mass meeting at Clinton Hall, called for the purpose of taking the matter into consideration. This corps will be known as the New-York. Colored regiment of National Volunteers, and those desirous of aiding it, by contributions or influentially, can do so by applying or sending to the treasurer, Mr. JAMES RODGERS, NO. 421 Broadway, who will furnish them with the requisite instructions.

**Southern Propaganda** – If the Confederacy prevails slaves will be so cheap every poor white can purchase their own "darky." The slave breeding business was particularly busy in Virginia.

**The New York Times** – December 7, 1863
The Fighting in Georgia the Rebels still are Running Negroes and Women in their Ranks. – Correspondence of **the Cincinnati Times.**

**The New York Times** – Published: December 9, 1863
GEN. BUTLER'S DEPARTMENT; Capture of a Noted Guerrilla Chief by Negro Troops
Correspondence of **New-York Times** – NORFOLK, Fri., Dec. 4.
The negro troops in this Department, under command of the energetic and indomitable Gen. WILD, are manifesting very creditable proficiency in their new profession, and displaying a capacity for practical usefulness which has, at length, silenced here every objection to their presence in the army. They are now in active service at several points, and but one opinion is expressed respecting their efficiency. Those especially that have been raised in this neighborhood, being familiar with every by-road, path, and hiding-place in the swamps and forests, are so many human ferrets,

from whom rebel vermin has little chance to escape. It will be safe to predict a speedy end to partisan warfare in districts where they are extensively employed. From the experiment which has proved so successful here, important results must eventually follow.

**The New York Times** – Near Chattanooga, Monday, November 30, 1863.
At the fight yesterday, at Ringgold, several of the "fair sex" were in the ranks of the enemy. They conducted themselves with a great deal of courage, and out of respect to the ladies, we make no reflections on their taste in entering the ranks with negroes and greasy graybacks. But the narrowing lines of Rebeldom need every aid on the earth above, or in the caverns under it.

**The New York Times** – September 1861 – General McClellan's position on slaves:
"There is much feeling here among leading men caused by the action of General McClellan in ordering the return of fugitive slaves, or rather, their arrest in camps and imprisonment in jail to await the claim of their masters. This in contravention of the spirit of the letter addressed by the Secretary of War.............."

**New York Times** – January 1864
.............the sale of confiscated lands for the payment of direct taxes had commenced at Port Royal, and the bidding was spirited, the contrabands were foremost in the purchases.

**New York Times** – February 1864 – Pensions To Black Troops
Senator CLARE, of New-Hampshire, will soon introduce a joint resolution declaring negro soldiers entitled to pensions the same as white troops.

**New York Times** – February 24, 1864
News From Washington – The Recruiting of Colored Soldiers at Alexandria – Governor Pierepont, of Virginia, has addressed a letter to President Lincoln, stating that he has no objection to the recruiting of colored men at Alexandria. This may lead to a removal of the embargo here on their going North.

**The New York Times** – December 9, 1863
REBEL "LOOKOUT" UPON SLAVERY
– The Charleston Mercury "improves the occasion," real or
fictitious, of the killing of a "poor negro woman" by one of the
shells from Gen. GILLMORE's batteries, to deliver a discourse
upon the beauty and value of negro Slavery. The deductions have
about as close a bearing upon the text as the ordinary deductions
of slaveholding preachers from Scripture texts. As a clincher of
the moral and discursive part of the discourse, which is not worth
quoting, the Mercury puts this: "What if the Yankees take and
occupy Lookout Mountain? The sacred code which guarantees and
recognizes the rights of the South in the interests and institutions
which now excite against her the hungry, howling horde of Yankee
miscreants, was uttered, not from Lookout, but from Mount Sinai,
Will the Yankees scale that?"
To clear up at once all rebel doubts as to the latter point, we frankly
and promptly answer by saying, No, sir. But suppose your assertion
as to the origin of the Southern Slave code should be as false as your
late boasts of the impregnability of "Lookout," what follows? While
our troops were in the act of scaling the rebel stronghold, the rebel
newspapers were proving it could never be scaled; and when the last
slave has forever disappeared from our country, we shall doubtless
have rebel preachers demonstrating from Scripture that the "divine
institution" is unassailable as the divine throne.

**Harper's Weekly** – June 1861
Major-General Butler's refusal to surrender fugitive slaves to their
masters, on the ground that they are "contraband of war" appears to
be equally sound in law and sensible in practice. He has established
a precedent which will probably be faithfully followed throughout
the war.

It cannot be complained of by the South for it rests upon the
cardinal principle of the Breckinridge party at the last election,
that slaves are property under United States Law. If they are
property, the fact that they can be of service to the enemy – like
horses or carts – places them at once in the list of articles which
are contraband of war. The practical effect of this decision will
verify the prediction uttered in this journal when war first broke out,
namely, that in one way or another, actual hostilities would prove
fatal to the slave institution......

**New York Times** – January 1864

……..Letters received in this city from Port Hudson under the date of January 12 and 13, pronounces false all reports to the effect that captured officers from General Ulman's division of colored troops had been shot. The fate of one only is unknown. The rest are either at Liberty Prison, or at a rebel rendezvous in Texas.

**New York Times** – 1864 – COLORED TROOPS IN MARYLAND. Col. BOWMAN was relieved to-day from duty on Gen. CASEY's Examining Board, and ordered to take the place of Gen. WILLIAM BIRNEY, mustering-in-officer of negro troops in Maryland.
The latter will go into the field with two colored regiments. Col. BOWMAN, one of the most energetic, yet conciliatory and discreet men in the army, will soon leave nothing of Slavery in Maryland but a tradition.

## RATIONS FOR CONTRABANDS
By order of the War Department the following is established as the ration for issue by the Subsistence Department to adult refugees and to adult colored persons, commonly called "contrabands," when they are not employed at labor by the Government, and who may have no means of subsisting themselves, viz.; ten ounces of pork or bacon, or one pound of fresh beef; one pound of corn meal five times a week; and one pound of flour or soft bread, or twelve ounces of hard bread, twice a week; and to every one hundred rations ten pounds of beans, peas, or hominy; eight pounds of sugar; two quarts of vinegar; eight ounces of adamantine or star candles; two pounds of soap; two pounds of salt; and fifteen pounds of potatoes, when practicable. To children under fourteen years of age, half rations will be issued; and to women and children, roasted rye coffee at the rate of ten pounds, or tea at the rate of fifteen ounces, to every one hundred rations.

**New York Times** – March 6, 1864 – Ovation to Black Troops
Reception of the 20th US Colored Regiment, Flag Presented
The scene yesterday was one which marks an era of progress in the
political and social history of New York. A thousand men, with
black skins, and clad and equipped with the uniform and arms of the
United States Government, marched from their camp through the
most aristocratic and busy streets, received a grand ovation at the
hands of the wealthiest and most respected ladies and gentlemen of
New York, then moved down Broadway to the steamer which bears
them to their destinations.

**Southern Confederacy** – Atlanta, Ga. – October 20, 1861
Mayors Court – Lucy, a slave girl arraigned for impertinent
language to white persons. Sentenced to 39 lashes laid on her back
by the Marshall.

**New York Times** – March 16, 1864
In the Senate yesterday Mr. Sumner presented a strong endorsed
petition of one thousand citizens of Louisiana of African descent,
praying for the rights of suffrage in that state.

President Lincoln / Emancipation Proclamation
"Lincoln and the Contrabands" By Jean Leon Gerome Ferris – printed on a
1908 calendar

*Note: General McClellan spread discontent with his public statement; "....The Emancipation Proclamation is an outrage!"*

**Southern Confederacy** – February 1862
High prices for Negros. The negros belong to the estate of James W. Reeve, late of Decalb County, were sold Tuesday last at Decator on 12 month credit at the following prices:
Dan – 25 years old – $1,400.
Henry – 25 years old – $1,412.
Jerry – 16 years old – one finger off – $1,601.
Caroline – 22 years old, one eye, not very stout, and with a child two years old – $1,377.

**September 16, 1862**
Willie, I wrote to you yesterday, tonight LeGrand received your letter saying you had not received a letter in a week. I have answered, if you have not received one last week, it is lost, you will get the one I wrote yesterday before you get this I am well, saw your father today, your mother was down to Kelsey's friday. Guess they are all well. write when you are coming, if not when you are going to stay. LeGrand says I must not write more so good by for this time, write soon, yours as ever Frank

**September 19, 1862**
To: Miss Frank Keeler – Candor, Tioga County, NY
From: W.C Gridley Washington City
Dear Frank, yours of the 15th came to hand yesternoon as safe, just in time to save this child from a backward track towards NY & Candor. I did not know but I would have to attend the funeral of one I could not part with, for I had not rec'd any intelligence from you since the one stating that you were sick & tried to laugh it off By saying that you ought to receive company or go out calling. But O, did not my soul bound with joy when I rec'd your Epistle & with what Eagerness did I investigate its contense.

Dear one yours & LeGrands arrived both in the same mail of yesterday. I will not try to reply to your note until tomorrow or Monday. I want to see if I can't get two letters from you a week as before. I think there was some little change in the Department about that time, but yet the letters may not be lost. Frankie if you felt as bad & cross as I did during the time I called at the P.O. every day for some 10 or 12 days I pity you to the bottom of my heart. They all said I was cross or something was the matter with me. I said nothing, but they would not believe me.

Fred Parmalee arrived here on wednesday, I saw him that night. I asked how all the folks were in Candor & he said all well he gues't. ("I saw gust last, she was well from what I could see") I said nothing of course. That did me some good as I had not heard from you yet.

Do you think I should bring home a **"contraband,"** that it would warm up the climate any, if so I would bring one, but I guess there are plenty there now, as you say there go's one now & it is dark, how can you see him, I cant. Firstly, that Mr. Brown had not better meet me or I may show him that SOLDIER Boy has come back, secondly: I want to know who his Sarah is & where & what she is: perhaps you think jellous, but no.

Time has run along with me very fast, until the last week & I cant say that it has. Dear one I see that you have asked the same question in your letter & note, if I intended to stay here all winter. if I had I should go back to you often, so it may be. I recon on it might suit you. I have not said I intended to stay all winter & neither do I expect to. There are some men in the city that owe me some money & I intend to stay until I get that. Please keep this to your self if you will & oblige me. I have the impression that you will see me there in about two weeks but perhaps not. I will not say positive for I don't know & so long as I can hear from you twice a week I feel contented. Mark what I say.

Asa Sackett arrived here one day last week & C. R. Sackett is here. I saw them both this Eve. Asa is doing nothing as yet but expects to soon. The army is on the move so much that Sutlers can't do much in their line of Bz.

Frank I have one of the nicest places to board & very fine room, it being the back Parlor & how I wish you could share it with me, but never mind thats all folly to talk about now.

You say that Lieu't Harder is home, sick, has he resigned or not, or what, or did he go home to see his Susan as reported here? I think the later but I hope not, for I don't think it shows much spirit of a soldier. Chs. Hunt I learn from Fred, is in Baltimore sick, he did not go home as reported. I can not tell how sick he is but not very dangerous I reckon.

As the hours of midnight are fast rolling by (Those most dear to me) & I must be up & doing in the morning shell be under the necesity of bringing this Epistle to a close, hoping to hear from you soon, a reply is eagerly looked for until arrived. Dear one, do I ever remain yours as ever till death may part us &c......From a Dear One, Willie        To Frank:

**PS   The news tonight is that the rebels have been driven out of Maryland with great slaughter, in uter confusion.** You ask to excuse mistakes, those I never look at, never think of it when I wish, if any one so make mine out its all well. I intend to have gotten a sheet of fools cap to have written this on. Yours ever, Willie

### BATTLE OF ANTITAM

*September 1862 the Antietam campaign was waged between the Union Army of the Potomac led by Major-General George B. McClellan and Confederate General Robert E. Lee leading the Army of Northern Virginia. Lee hoped to wreak havoc on Northern States that had not seen the devastation of the battles in Virginia. Although Lee eventually crossed the Potomac his troops sustained heavy casualties and were thwarted in their invasion attempt. The cost of lives lost was one of the heaviest of the war. The Union forces had approximately 12,000 men killed wounded or captured. More than 11,000 Confederate soldiers were also among the casualties.*

*Two of the authors' ancestors fought in this battle and each lost a limb in the horror of war.*

### September 21, 1862

From: Augusta Keeler – Candor, Tioga County, NY
To: Mr. William C. Gridley – Washington, D.C.   In care of Box 13
My own dear friend, my letter was not more welcome to you than yours was to me. It came safe this afternoon. The last I heard from you except your letter to LeGrand was a week ago last Friday. I did try to laugh off being sick and rather guess I have done it, for this evening I have been to a Concert at the Methodist house, must not forget to say that I saw your brother, next younger than you, there, did not speak, do not think he knew me.

Now you just wait unless you write me two letters a week you will not hear from me. I have answered every letter I have received

& one over. I did not feel cross but feared you was sick or was coming home, which I could not know till your letter came this afternoon & it was neither.

Now Mr. Willie I am here at Eleven o'clock at night safe & sound, only rather sad when I will give myself time to reflect for Grandma is much worse. She may not live the night, if so she cannot stay many days more unless better, which is almost impossible. Mother is up to Aunt Rachels, stays there most of the time. **Aunt Betsy is nearly sick for they have not heard from Charly in a week & they fear that Lucius living in the west is dead, he is where the Indians are fighting.**

I was down in Catatonk last week. It rained and I had to stay there two days. Mrs. Woodbridge & her daughter Laura was down to Aunt Sacketts. Mary Kelsey has gone up to your house, she thought she should stay two weeks perhaps more, saw Lute Hart this evening. Told her you wished to be remembered to her. She said to "give my love to Cad for he is one of my best cousins," said she did not know but you had forgotten her, as for Brown you keep still. He asked LeGrand if I realy had a gent in the Army, he said I said so. Then Brown goes right down to Hiram Wards & tells Sate somthing I can not tell just what but she has so much to do she can hardly get time to go anywhere. Poor Brown.

I am very glad you are contented, so am I. I am pleased that you have a nice boarding place, that is half. **As for Harder I cannot think he is trying to evade the fight,** he need not speak for us to know, any one that can see him would know that it had but been a step to deaths door, he was the worst looking person, so poor & weak he could not walk from here to the door without stoping to rest. He is, or expects, to go back to the Reg't this week although he better be at home, with a mothers care, if I can see. Kelsey & all the boys are at **Anapolis Junction** & were all well last we heard.

Charly Barager was home over Sunday, he said their Regt expected to leave Binghamton this week, it is the 137th regt. Kelsey is in company C 109th Regt. There is not much news in Candor, nearly everyone says they have most died since the boys left, it is so lonesome. Guess they will not make it out. I must not forget to tell you that Mrs. Joe Lyttle (Eluise Bacon) has a little daughter, so much for marrying a doctor, they were married last January, I believe, or about that time, can you go ahead of that? It is so late I must not write any more. you are as ever to me, do not fear, perhaps more so if that can be for tis daily & nightly I think of thee. Yours ever, Frank

Willie, PS, Tuesday noon, if you hear anything more about Charly Hunt being sick I wish you would tell the particulars as they have not written & aunty is very anxious. I wish you was here so I could tell you of a little thing that has happened a few days ago, but never mind, wait till you come. Ward Kesley called me Cousin Augusta last night. I told him to wait a while. Ans told Lute I was a fool if I gave you the mitten, for I never would get a better one. I thank Ans for his advice but perhaps he has forgotten that I always do as I think best, he thinks I am going with you thinking no more of you than the rest. Who knows best, I DO, do you once doubt me, Willie? But no you cannot. You asked a queer question similar to the above, I answered it on the 4 page at the close so I will not give another thought to it. I am unchangeable & let us hope for the future. So good by, yours as ever FRANK

**September 23, 1862**
To: Miss Frank Keeler – Candor, Tioga County, NY
From W. C. Gridley – Washington City – Corner of 6th & H S E
Dearest Frank, As I told you, I so must fulfil & here it comes hoping that you may thankfully occasion it & glad indeed that there is one way of addressing you (this) while others are deprived of it, & would to god that I could the way which best suits both you & me which hope it may be soon but being unable to state the day & hour, it makes me more uneasy than otherwise would be. The only reason (or nearly so) which prompted me to write LeGrand was to hear from you, thinking that you might be sick. I was somewhat alarmed about the matter (please say nothing to LeGrand of the fact. I will write him soon) little did I expect a line from you in his letter, but all was right & welcomely rec'd.

I am in good spirits, (not ardent as you said) hope you don't think that I am drunk all or part of the time, if so I am afraid you would be mistaken. Dear one, let no such thing trouble you, for it does not me & had not ought you but enough of such. How are you to-day (it will be day when you receive this) although it is night with me & going for ten o'clock.

Today is the 23rd, let me see, Friday 26 is my birthday, if the lord spared my life until that time I shall be twenty three years of age. Can you see it?? Indeed I can't.

I believe I wrote you that I rec'd your & LeGrands at the same time. I send you a paper which has the PROCLOMATION of Uncle Abe which just suits me, perhaps you will see it ere you get this, but it may suit you. Frank if you have a Co. Paper please send me one, it would pleas me much. My eyes are getting tired & I must close my scribble to one that owns my love for ever & Ever. Write soon, Yours as ever   Willie

PS I have thought of going up to see the Boys Sunday next,  CAD

## September 25, 1862

From:  W. C. Gridley – Washington City D.C.

To:  Miss Frank Keeler – Candor, Tioga County, NY

Dear Frank,  Yours of the 21st was duly rec'd & glad was I indeed to read your Epistle & to find you so well. You say you laughed off your sickness. It is better to laugh than to cry. I am very sory to learn your grandmother is so low. hope she may revive but I am afraid not. This may be an hour of deep grief to you, I cannot tell, if so May God remember you in an hour of trouble.

Dear One you say you saw my Brother Ed, think he don't know you only by reputation. Now Frank you say you have written to me one letter more than I have to you. I can't see how that can be if so I am so much indebted to you that I hardly know how to pay you but may some future day. I have written you two letters a week since I came here. If you have not rec'd them Except that week that I could not hear from you, I sent you one yesternight. Dear One, you cannot feel cross at me for I have tride my best to please you & ever shall to the best of my ability so help me God. Who, or What have I to live for Except thee, Nothing. Welcome to me indeed to know that you are there safe & sound, much more than many can say.

I rather guess you will find this letter highly perfumed for it has been covered with cigar ashes about half a dozen times, think it will not be offensive. it is to me like the one I love, for a cheerful cigar like a shield will bear the blows of cares & sorrow, feeling fine

You say you went down to Sacketts a day or two, all well I suppose. Saw Charles & Asa a day or two ago. Asa has gone to camp. Also that Mary Kelsey has gone up to our house to stay some weeks, don't know how she can stand that. What will poor Norman do, to Lute I can do no more than rendered. I think a great deal of her.

Poor Brown...I hope he will service, say to him you don't know but your Gent in the army is dead ear this. I know nothing of Harder only what rumor says. You well know that camp life & long marches will make the strongest weak, both the brave & daring & the most Timid. Nothing but the true test will tell. There are very many of our best men become sick. **Little did I think that Chs Barager would get in to the army again, but hope he will keep sober the while.**

Well, Well! They say that Drs have the best luck in raising children of any one, fair commencement I say that. I cannot beat that unless I should adopt Chs. Peters, still I have told you that. But I can't see it, you very well know what I have told you. I am quite a friend to those little ones but not upon so immediate production. I know your feelings as to the subject.

Chas. Hunt, I have heard nothing about him for some days, guess he is getting along or I should hear. I see Fred every day.

If you have anything to say spit it out. I would like to hear it, so let it come. They may call you cousin if they chuse. But say to them you guess they have got hold of the rong child. Dear one I must close this hoping the time will soon come when we shall meet again so I never part with you, dear as ever, what can I say more. Yours to death, Willie

(Small note on side of paper) **Say to LeGrand that I am very much obliged to him for Backing your letters. I am hoping at some future time to return it in some way. Cad**

## September 27, 1862

To: Mr. Wm. C. Gridley, 76 Regt NYSV – Washington, D.C.
From: Augusta Keeler – Candor, Tioga County, NY
Dear Willie, Yours of the 23rd came safe yesterday which was your birthday. I had not forgotten it. shell I tell you how it was passed by me, you say yes, well here it comes. Cousin Henry Clark is at our house & visiting round all the Cousins. in the fornoon we visited with ourselves, in the afternoon were at Uncle Walters & missed a call from Miss L Bacon & Miss Ella Benedict, in the eve Frannie had a party for Miss Annie Jameson, a very pretty lady visiting there from near Philadelphia, she is a very pretty girl & very sociable, there was nearly 30 there. We or I should say Sarah Henry & myself enjoyed it very much. By the way, Miss Susan Sturges came up to me while standing near the center of the room & says, "Where

is Cadwell, have you got him in that little locket." I said look & see, she did look & says why such a pretty locket without a picture, I will have mine taken for it. I told her she could not please me better. Then she says where is he, I stood to it that I did not know & she says I have heard bad news about you, I asked her to repeat it, she sayed she must not tell.

Henry says he should like to see you & you know he is a perfect flirt. He says if I was not his cousin he would cut you out. He calls me his wife & says you can not have me. I say yes to everything & he begins to think I am fooling him. He is trying every minute. today he sat down & talked sense for once & I have found out that he has some depth after all. he is going next Tuesday or Wednesday to visit round to other places & before he returns is going to Baltimore to see Richard Clark his brother.

The 137th Regt left Binghamton today. Fannie came to me last night & said she was very sorry you could not be there, so you see I shall get used to such talk. Pa was home, left this morning. There is not any change that I see in Candor, no excitement.

Willie you need not trouble about me for I am as ever, for we cannot tell of the future, everything is for our good although we cannot see it. You know I say that the best way is not to borrow trouble but take everything cheerful & as it comes. You are well, that is good for it is a blessing never appreciated till lost. I am writing this over to Aunt Rachels where I am visiting this afternoon. I hope you are coming soon for I long to see you. Write. From one ever the same, Frank

**September 29, 1862**
To: Mr. Wm. C. Gridley – Washington, D.C. Box 13
From: F.A. Keeler – Candor, Tioga County, NY
Dear Willie, This has been the most unhappy hour I have had in a long time & what about it would take a wiser head than mine to tell, in fact the day has not been very bright, at first I feared to hear bad news from you but the cars came & a letter, all right.

Wish you were here, dear one or some one beside my lonly pillow tonight. Grandma is still with us but her life is not long in this world. Mother stays there night & most days. This is a pen worth nothing but better than no pen. Fannie, Annie Jameson, Miss Hubbard (the last lady from Owego) & Cousin Henry called here this evening, a very pleasant call. I do think Annie is a lovely girl

& rather pretty. I tell Henry he never will see anyone else, he is so taken with her & I cannot blame him. Henry tryes to tease me by saying that he is going to write to you & tell you you cannot have me, he cannot coment for I know he never would, he thinks to much of me. He says when your letter came this afternoon that when I wrote next remember Henry to you & tell you his name is Henry not Willie as I call him about half the time. **I gave LeGrand a Co. paper to send to you this afternoon.**

Willie time seems long since I saw you. Lute received a letter from Kelsey, all the boys was well. What is Fred doing, also Asa & Chas Sackett

Sunday. Sarah, Henry, & myself went up to the Presbyterian Church. There was but few there. Thursday eve there is to be a concert by the young ladies at the Center – would like to attend. Miss Haywood has my white dress to wear.

It is about 12 o clock near another day. I will just say that it is not blue Monday with me as with Mary Eliza Wood. C.....carried her home saturday & last eve Norman went down with the horse & carriage if I am not mistaken. Did not go up very early.

Willie I must not write more although I could, but I must be up in the morning & you just hurry up that Chap for I want to see YOU but better late than never. **I have a Cousin David Keeler who is very badly wounded of the 27th Regt but we do not know where he is, whether dead or not.** good night pleasant dreams &c may God protect & keep you. from one ever the same   Frank

TUESDAY afternoon, Annie has gone, what will we all do for she took with us all very much. I am rather more cheerful today, all right again. Sarah says she is enjoying herself now Henry is here very much. all most takes her back to Albany again. This morning Sarah & myself were walking out & Lute called to us, we went over by the gate & during our conversation we spoke of Photographs & we asked to see Kelseys. she started to go in after them then stoped & looked as mischievous as ever she could but went & got a Photograph album. It was a beauty, we asked who gave it, she told us to look & the first picture was Ans...how she blushed. We had quite a laugh, also we found his sisters there. it is going to rain & I must close this or not get it to the office so just let me know when you are coming. You are partial to surprises I believe. Yours as ever, F.A.K

106

**September 30, 1862**
From: Wm C. Gridley – Washington City, D.C.
To: Miss Frank Keeler – Candor, Tioga County, NY
Dearest Frank, yours of the 27ᵗʰ came to hand today all safe but
looked for it yesterday. I am overjoyed to learn that there was one
that took some pleasure in that day, which I have sometimes cussed,
but of late. I am writing this just at Tea time & the bell has rung,
but think I shall finish it. all I can say of my birth day is that it was
spent as any other. I think Susan Sturges is minding that which is
none of her Bis. She is always up to such & her position shows it at
the present day, & as to her knowing anything but what you do, "as
in her eye." I know of but that I have called at your house, she may
call that bad news "I cant." You know HER I hope. You say Mr.
Clark would like to see me, indeed I would like to see him for Dicks
sake to know what kind of a brother Dick had. He says he would
cut me ought, I never saw that did yet there might be a first time.

You say the 137ᵗʰ has left. I saw them pass by our store
yesterday, saw Capt. Roberts & Chas B…got by before I thought
of him, had no time to follow him & speak to him, although Geo
Sturges did. The Regt come down the ave, in splendid stride &
a very fine one indeed it was. I think some of the boys said they
were going to **Arlington Hights**, but dont know certain. As to the
109ᵗʰ I learn nothing of them of late only the Co. C was in the City
today, so Chas. Sackett said & talked with him. He said some of
the boys of his Regt were in the City Gard house & he was going to
take them out. hope none of them Candor boys. Think they wanted
to **see the Elephant**, guess they have seen it. I learn that Lieut
Harders Co was very badly cut to pieces.

Nothing personal Dear One, let them talk. They may have
something to talk about e'er they are aware of it. I was taken rather
ill on saturday night & sunday did feel bad but today I am myself
again all right. Dear, I will let you know time enough to meet me at
the Depot if you like when I come home. I think this covers more
paper than yours and so I must close. say to LeGrand not to put so
many flourishes on the back of the letters, it would suit me quite as
well, say to write it plain. dont tell him that I said so, use your own
caution if you please. How is your Grand Ma is she beter. Please
write soon. I am as ever to you, that dear one away    Yours to death
Willie P.S. I think you will have a fine time to read this, do not fret if

you can't.  the same as before Willie
*(See the elephant = engage in battle)*

**October 3, 1862**
To:  W. C. Gridley – Washington, D.C.
From:  Frances A. Keeler – Candor, NY
My own dear Willie, Yesterday evening yours of the 30th came safe
& very glad I was to get it.  You say you have been sick which
made me very sad.  I hope you are better & if you do not get well
you must not stay there.  I say so for I could not be contented not to
have you where I could hear from you & know how you are oftener
than now if you are sick.  You do not speak of your birthday very
cheerfully, perhaps you was not well, you must not be discouraged,
that will never do.  Courage & perseverance is what we must all
strive for.

Henry would not rest last night till I told what made me look
sober for I at first could not look very cheerful.  he says if you are
in Washington when he gets there he shall come & see you, it will
be three or four weeks.  Miss L. Bacon & a cousin Mr. Bacon from
Binghamton was here last eve, very nice visit.  since Henry has been
here I have been going somewhere nearly every day.  Most tired of
going.  Uncle Henry is in Candor.  George Baragar & Mary Smith
(his niece) has gone to Syracuse visiting.

Willie I do not know what to write for there is no news in
Candor, except about some of the Center men.  We expect to hear
of their conduct often.  If I were some of these mens wife I never
would have another word to say to them again, such men are not fit
to live.  There is some in this place about the same.  If you and I are
not talked up in fine style I would like to know it.

The Concert at **the Presbyterian Church** last evening they say
was very nice, it was so rainy that I did not go.  It has rained, I think
every day this week.  This is fall in some respects the most beautiful
season of the year.  The leaves are turning, if you do not hurry they
will be all faded & gone.  That is the most lonesome part of the year
but they are like people ever changing.  I have not seen Mary E.
have not been down there, shall go as soon as I can.
The boys are still at the junction, some write as if they were
homesick.  They will be homesick often before they see home I am
afraid.  Tell about writing longer letters than I do, "I cannot see it"
for the writing is closer than yours so I guess we are even.  Are you

still with Sturges? How is business? Do you be very careful. I
have expected you would be sick. It has been the longest six weeks
I ever knew. It must be because it is War times for I never heard of
the like before & then to you are so far south. When you get back to
Candor you will find weeks are shorter, at least they all say so,

Fred Josslys Uncle William Josslyn & lady from Mich. is here
to Candor visiting. Grandma is very feeble cannot help herself at
all. Willie I must not write any more this time for it is late, most
time for the cars. Hurry up that bis, if I knew you intended to stay
one month two or three I should be contented & know that I need
not expect to see you, but when it is so uncertain I keep looking for
you every day or so, now I have made up my mind not to look till I
see you coming, so good by for a short time, yours ever Frank
Keeler has just come & showed part of your letter, he says you
told him not to let me see all of it or anyone else, you better not be
writing what is not to be read, so write soon. Augusta

**October 5, 1862**
From: W. C. Gridley – Washington City
To: To a Friend, Frances A. Keeler – Candor, NY
My dearest Frank, Today is Sunday & I have nothing to do but write
letters & feeling quite well would like to spend a few moments for
your sake, so here it comes an extra sheet. I have met with a lucky
hit today, & shall I say what? O yes you will say, it is this, while
fumbling over my trunk I chance to take hold of an old pare of
gloves & threw them down on the floor & when I took them up **my
large gold pen** dropted out. Which I supposed was at home, & have
scribled with an old rusty steel pen, which would make me shudder
every time I drew it across the paper.

Frank, dear one, knowing that you can keep my secrets I will
unfold one to you which may do you good to know. It is this, I have
been trying for some time to get a post as Assistant Paymaster in the
Army & think I may succede. But don't know. "as auld as Saying"
not shure of the bird until in the hand. But if I do succeede it will
be a nice thing for you & for we can be together here all of the time.
That will suit me & I trust it will you dear one.

Fred Parmelle & myself have been running around the city
this morning. Saw one or two from our County. Had some talk
of old matters which you know are very pleasant, something Fred
says sometimes when he has nothing to do. how he wishes he was

in Candor Poor fellow. I know how to sympathize with him. But guess will survive. (if not I think I have friends enough here to have my body Embomed & sent home in a box about five feet 8 inch) while I am writing this, **strains of sacred music are being utered in the adjoining room.** But O not Equal to those of one. You may guess who. It is a chaplains wife that is boarding here, a very nice lady indeed & a fair voice.

The 137th Reg't have gone up on the other side of the river, near the battle of Antietam, but don't know the exact place. **Charlie B was in the city a short time. It will be a good thing for him here, for there is no strong drink alowed to be sold here. Nor has there been since the twentieth of September.** The 109th Regt are still at the Junction I think. Why Frank P. thought the boys from Candor were going to get Non commissions in the Company, but in looking over the list I find that there are but two or three & they're all Corporals. I think such a man as Kell, ought to have a Non-Com, if any man ever should, so you see what a thing the Military is.

I have promised to write to your father but have not done so as yet, did not know where to direct a letter to him if I had written. I have two papers, one I will send to you and one to LeGrand Keeler (I suppose you have heard of him) And if you would like to read it you can undoubtedly borrow it of him. As my extra sheet is nearly full I must close, hoping to receive a letter on Tuesday the regular day for one. So I must bid you Good after Noon, remaining yours as ever, W.C. Gridley

*Charles F. Barager*

Despite the doubts Will and Augusta had about Charles Barager staying in the Army and staying sober, he became a Captain in the 137th NY volunteers, and was wounded in at least two battles. After the war he attended Albany Law University, became a successful attorney and businessmen, an active Republican, and was elected to the office of Supervisor in his town. Later he won an election for a seat as a member of the assembly in Tioga County.

**WRITING implements:** During the Civil War the government agreed to provide soldiers with quills for writing...although this was often not the case, so the writing tools would have to be obtained from home or a sutler. Wood or metal pens with metal nibs were available by the mid 1800's but were more expensive. (QUILL – obtained from goose, swan or turkey – primary flight feathers from a large bird)

**Harper's Weekly** – January 4, 1862
IMPORTANT FACTS
Constant writing for six months is done cheaper with Gold Pens than with Steel Pens; therefore, it is economy to use Gold Pens.

The Gold Pen remains unchanged by years of continued use, while the steel pen is ever changing by corrosion and wear;

therefore, perfect uniformity of writing is obtained only by the use of the Gold Pen. Gold is capable of receiving any degree of elasticity, so that the Gold Pen is exactly adapted to the hand of the writer; therefore the nerves of the hand and arm are not injured, as is known to be the case by the use of steel pens...

"THE PEN IS MIGHTIER THAN THE SWORD"

On receipt of any of the following sums in cash or post-stamps the subscriber will send by return mail, or otherwise as directed, a Gold Pen. For 25 cents, the Magic Pen; for 38 cents, the Lucky Pen; for 50 cents, the Always Ready Pen; for 75 cents the Elegant pen; and for $1.00 the Excelsior Pen. Morton – No. 25 Maiden Lane, NY

**October 6, 1862**
To: Miss Fran. Keeler – Candor, Tioga County, NY
From:  W. C. Gridley – Washington City
My own dear Frank, Today your letter of the 3rd came to my view & hastily did min o'er its contence. You say mine letter made you very sad.  I was afraid it would after I had time to think over what I had written you.  But It was to late for it had gone.  I then thought that I had did wrong in saying anything to you about it. (being sick) for I new you would worry about me, but e'er you get this you will be informed as to my health.  No I can't speak of my birthday as being any more pleasant than any other day, & if did not.  You can guess how I feel if someone else did.  And tonight I am sitting by this table & talking with you as freely as though I was at your house.  There, my **pipe** has gone out & I must light it again.  There it is lit again so here we go in the language of the poet:

> "Then smoke away till the golden sky
> Lights up the dawn of the morrow
> For the cheerful cigar like a shield will buy
> The blows of care and sorrow"

Dear one, My courage is still good I think, if not I think I should have been under the sod before this. You say Henry would not rest until told him of the cause.  Also that If I am here when he comes to the City of Washington that he will call & see me, but I think before the time rolls round I shall be in Candor, at least I hope so. I would like to see him very much.  I see you have not forgotten to be on the go all of the time.  all I have to say is to go & enjoy yourself, but do not cary it to far for you know the consequences.

You speak of the Center Men. You may also say the same of the Corner ones. I can't talk to you on that subject now, but wait till I come back, it is no doubt that there are many who seem short for subjects to talk upon & so they must have something. Thank the LORD we are not the only ones.

It seems to me that Candor is blessed with concerts this fall is it not? You say that it rains nearly every day. I wish I could say so, for it has not rained any to amount to shucks for a month here. It has been so warm the most of the time that it is very uncomfortable at night without the windows up & nothing but a sheet for bed covering so you may judge the weather.

I wish that I could hear from Mary E. I have written to her some time ago & have rec'd no reply perhaps she docs not care to answer it. But she can do as she likes as to it, all I care to know is that she has rec'd a line from me. If you see her please ask her if she has heard from me? You say the Boys write as though they were homesick & I don't doubt it & think they will be more e'er they go back to old Candor. They do not know what it is to be from home, but guess they will learn. *Although amid the sound of cannon roar & that everlasting tap of the drum, with now and then a squeal from the fife, they forget home and its pleasures.*

I am still with Sturges & Bro. Biz is rather quiet just now as the Army are up the river & the greater part of the supplies are taken from Baltimore instead of Washington as before. City travel is good. Dear one, you may think it is a long six weeks for you commenced looking for me the next day after I left home. That is what makes time so long. If you had not commenced looking for me untill now you would not have had to look so long. I am happy to say that I am in as good health as ever. I must close this, so good night. (my love to all) hoping to hear from you soon, I remain as ever Yours till death, From your own Willie.

*During the Civil War images of cannon and patriotic symbols such as the flags, shields and freedom caps, were found on many items. The above is a gutta-percha tin type case.*

A field piece loaded with "canisters," (tin cans packed with small iron balls) could cause multiple casualties with the effect of a giant shot gun.   The 13 inch mortar "Dictator," could send a 200 pound shell nearly two miles. Quaker guns, were often used as a ploy to fool the enemy, what looked like cannons in defense lines were found to be logs painted black. At a distance they were convincing. The log in the following photo was mounted by the rebels at Port Hudson, Louisiana.

Dictator

Quaker Gun

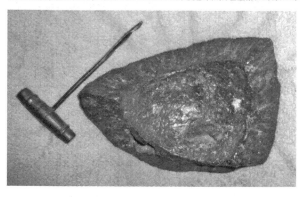

Fragment of mortar shell weighs 40 pounds and, at 6 inches long the GIMLET was one of the most important tools for the artillery. It was used to clean debris from the vent of artillery pieces.

**Richmond Daily Dispatch** – March 1862 – Cannon Metal
Iron is valuable just now for making cannon, why does not the
Governor or some other man in authority order those at the different
street corners to be taken up and recast? The corners of Mobile
are full of cannon stuck upright in the ground as posts, to keep off
the drays, and Richmond can boast of a number used for the same
purpose. There is one on the corner in front of this office.

*All kinds of metals were necessary to the war effort. This Civil
War receipt dated June 1864, indicates that about 100,000, (one
hundred thousand pounds) of Quincy Ingot Copper would arrive
from Detroit to the purchaser at .45 (forty-five) cents a pound, cash.
Winterhoff & Company were the Brokers, with offices at No. 66
Beaver Street, NY*

**Harper's Weekly** – June 8, 1861 – An Immense Gun for
FORTRESS MONROE
An enormous rifle cannon is just being finished at Pittsburg for
Fortress Monroe. The length of the gun is 16 feet, length of the
bore 14 feet, diameter of bore 12 inches, diameter of the gun at the
breech 48 inches, diameter at the muzzle 25 inches. The ball will be
12 inches in diameter and the wright about 600 pounds; The rough
casting of the gun weighs 78,000 pounds; finished, it will weigh
50,000 pounds. The chamber has 21 groves.

**The Gateway Guardian – Atlanta** – February 25, 1861
Siege of Sumter
Every gun fired from Fort Sumter costs on average $13. Every gun
fired by the state will be an average expenditure of $9. A prominent
officer of Fort Moultrie informs us that by a calculation
It has been ascertained that when its batteries open the cost per diem
to the State at that fort alone will exceed $15,000. Pretty heavy
that. But it is the surest way of mastering the fort, and we had better
spend money than lives in its acquisition.

*A well known Confederate siege weapon was known as **"Whistling
Dick."** It was an 18 pound gun and part of the defenses at
Vicksburg in 1863. It made a loud whistling sound when shot. This
cannon helped sink the Union gunboat Cincinnati. By the time the
war was over the gun had disappeared and has never been located.*

**Moore's Rural New-Yorker** – January 18, 1862
The News Condenser
*The government is sending large quantities of gun cartridges &
army wagons west
*The government expended 22 millions for fire arms since the
Rebellion began
*The Federal fleet near New Orleans & Lake Ponchartrain has
captured several rebel steamers

*Telegraph wires at this time consisted of seven twisted, rubber
coated wires strung along everything from trees to fence posts.*
**THE TELEGRAPH**
**The Philadelphia Inquirer** – August 1861
HURRAH FOR THE TELEGRAPH
On Tuesday afternoon the work of setting the posts to which the
telegraphic wires are to be attached, was commenced in this city
under the superintendence of James Street, Esq., the enterprising
agent of the company. The first post was set a little south of our
office, and we are pleased to notice that the work has been continued
four blocks down Main Street, then one block east where it strikes
the State road and is being rapidly pushed forward in the direction
of Fort Crittenden.  Success to the lightning rods!!
**– The Salt Lake City Mountaineer** – July 13, 1861

## THE TELEGRAPH

Communication was a significant factor for the Union in winning the Civil War. Of the many methods of sending messages; drums, pony express, flags, birds, & balloons, the railroads and telegraph were all important. In the 1840's the United States government spent approximately $30,000 to build telegraph lines between Baltimore and Washington. It was one of the greatest technological advances of the era. By 1861 many small corporations, as well as Western Union and railroads had constructed telegraph lines connecting the continent.

President Abraham Lincoln granted unprecedented war time powers to Secretary of War Stanton. During the war Stanton had every telegram routed through his office.....total information control. All data could be censored and disseminated by this agency.

REBEL TELEGRAPHIC News – **Richmond Daily Dispatch** – From Charleston – Our batteries have kept up a brisk fire upon the Yankees, who appeared in much larger force than usual at Gregg and Wagner.............

The first US military telegraph Corps was established during the Civil War. The original four military telegraph operators were, Brown, Strous, Bates and O'Brien  LOC

MAGNETIC WIRE NEWS

**New York Times** – September 9, 1862
THE REBEL INVASION OF THE LOYAL STATES
It seems to be settled that a force of at least 40,000 rebels has
crossed the Potomac and taken position at **Frederick, in Maryland**,
about sixty miles west of Baltimore and about forty north from
Washington. They have been permitted by the Government to cross
without resistance. **Telegraphic** reports from the Capital would
almost lead us to believe that they had been invited there….for we
are assured that the Government is perfectly satisfied with their
position and that none of them will ever return. We hope this may
prove to be true….but we would rather see it proven than give full
credence to it in advance. As we remarked yesterday, we have too
many of these official assurances already on hand unredeemed to be
especially eager for more.

**Telegraphic News** from Louisiana as reported in **the Richmond
Daily Dispatch** – August 9, 1863
Col. Logan is again at work. A few days since, he attacked the
enemy, 700 strong, near Jackson, East Louisiana. He routed them
completely, killing a large number and capturing 200 prisoners and
two pieces of artillery. This is official.

**New York Times** – March 3, 1862 – The Independent Telegraph Co.
At the meeting of the Board of Aldermen last evening Alderman
Dayton moved that the Board take immediate action on the
application of the Independent Telegraph Company for the privilege
of raising poles for their wires in the City of New York

**By Jesse H. Bunnell – Served the Union Army in a band of "wire
tappers" for four years, beginning when he was 18 years of age.**
"Under Both Flags" – 1896
"Priests, physicians and telegraph operators are, by reason of their
peculiar professional position, in possession of more secrets than
any classes of men……The telegraph operators of the grapevine
wire during the Civil War were, of necessity, the depositories of
many and important secrets, plans of campaigns, orders of march,
objects and intentions of commanding officers, the cooperation and
assistance sought and expected when and where. All came into the
keeping of, possibly, a mere lad or by whose humble position only
entitled him to moderate compensation, while the betrayal of the

secrets which, of necessity, were placed in his keeping, would have offered temptation to older, wiser, and far wealthier men. To the credit of these lads who served the Union in those days of trouble in flashing orders and commands, which have made the grandest chapter of our nation's history, to be recorded, that no Benedict Arnold was found in their ranks."

**New York Times** – October 1863 – News of the Rebellion
The military telegraph between Chattanooga & Nashville has been closed to the Press!

*Note: Andrew Carnegie, 1835-1919. He was appointed Superintendent of the military railway, and the Union Government telegraph lines in the east in 1861. Carnegie rendered significant service toward winning the war.*

**ERIE RAILWAY TELEGRAPH.**
OFFICE, Erie Railway Depot.

TO THE PUBLIC.

The Nature of the Telegraph business is such that errors and delays are occasionally unavoidable. The payment of once and a half the amount of the usual tolls on any Message will insure correct delivery by a repetition of such Message from the place of destination to the party sending it. On Messages not so repeated and insured, no responsibility for errors or delays in transmission will be assumed beyond the amount of tolls, and in no case for errors or delays occurring on other lines. All Messages will hereafter be received subject to the above conditions.
C. TILLOTSON, Supt.

April 11th 186 3

Received at ........... M. by Telegraph from Owego

To .......... Union

Come on first train
Your son has lost
an arm
J. Bishop

*Telegram sent in 1864 notifying parents to meet their son at the train station due to his war injuries*

**October 7, 1862**
To: W C Gridley – Washington, D.C.
From:  F. A. Keeler – Candor, Tioga County, NY
Dear Willie Your welcome epistle came this afternoon or rather there was two, one was dated 2nd and the other the 5th which was better than none.  I am very well, although not quite as strong as one year ago at this time, & was very glad to hear you was up all right. Yes, I am very glad that you found your pen for a good pen is half in writing.  As to your prospects in business I am very glad they are so fair & there is one that ever wishes for your success, & hope to have the privilege of ever sharing your joys & sorrows, fortune or adversity whatever it may be for what is your interests is mine also. I long to see you it would be great pleasure to be with you where ever you are, that you know.

I do not wonder that Fred is lonsom, he was very attentive to Miss Way before he left perhaps he thinks of her, he said he would write to me perhaps he is afraid to.  I do hope that **Charles Barager will have to keep straight & sober.**  Kelsey & the other boys said they rather be a private.  Pa *(Ira Keeler)* has all letters directed here, sometimes at Owego Care **of Ahwaga House.**  Peter Brink & Lady are going to housekeeping in a few weeks.  Your papers did not come tonight, will be here soon.

Willie this evening is splendid out doors, the moon shines light enough to read by.  Lute came up here just dark & wanted me to go down to the Church & play on the Melodian, did I tell you that I was playing for ME.… for three or four Sundays while Miss Bacon is in Montrose.  Henry & Fannie came here & found I was there, came down & we came near to going out & locking them in for it being dark we did not see them.

I went over to Fannie's & there saw a Mr. Turner, brother of Mary.  Robert has gone to War so he said, & Mary is in NY City at school.  Henry says he is going to Binghamton about the 25th & he is going to Washington also, says he shall find you if you are there, he is going tomorrow for the Great Bend where his Father lives. Grandma is living but not able to help herself.  Uncle Walter Hunt fell from the scaff'd in the barn down to the floor head first, came near to breaking his neck, cannot turn or move his head & was very much bruised, do not know if he will get well yet. The roosters are crowing, can it be 12 – no, only eleven, they better wait an hour. Mother is over staying with Grandma, everything is so dull it is just like Sunday. I must not write any more tonight so from one ever the same, F.A. Keeler

Write soon, yes I rather think I can keep a secret, so you need have no fears about writing your business or anything you wish for I love to hear any thing from you or about you. Augusta

Wednesday Your paper came this after noon. It has been as warm today as in July. Willie I am happy to hear that you (like myself) think of coming to Candor soon. I look for time when you will be here. You will tell me when you know if you are to stay & how long you will stay here. If not stay there you will stay here this winter or not. Time flys & a few short weeks will tell all.

It is most car time so I must close, I love to read your letters. They speak of my own thoughts although I do not write them, you know I never write though, I cannot, your letters make me wish more earnestly to see you. How little I ever thought one short year ago that a simple sheet of paper would be so welcome to me. Time makes great changes. I have not seen Mary Eliza, have heard that Norman did not go there for a long time after she returned from Candor. Guess that is not true, good night, write soon & think I am ever the same, Augusta

The Ahwaga House in Owego, NY

*Many years after the Civil War, the Ahwaga Hotel and Owego streets remained much the same as when the Keeler and Gridley families visited relatives and businesses in the village.*

**October 10, 1862**
To: W. C. Gridley – Washington, D.C. Care of Box 13
From: F. A. Keeler – Candor, Tioga County, NY
Dearest Willie, before me is your last kind letter which came last evening. I did not receive it till about ten. Sarah & myself visited Jennie Hart yesterday & had a nice time the first time since she moved up to Mr. Harts. In the evening Norman made his

appearance, after his work was done, we had a sing, I played for them. Norman made a fine remark during some of the jokes that was flying, something was said about The Blessing I would get if I did not stop. I told him (pretending to take it the other way from what he said it) that it would take a minister to give one that was worth anything. Then he said that I would get one before long, he expected. I told him not till he got his first. he was waiting to see me get one. I told him not to wait, for him & Mary was the oldest & I would wait for their example, & Mrs. Hart told him I was right. he did not say more about you. here I am all out somewhere so I took this oportunity to write, the first I had today. I intended to have written so it would have gone tonight, it is to late. Uncle Walter is getting better & we think he will be over his hurt all right in a few weeks. There was a dance at the Phoenix last night. Hubert did not keep very straight, sorry to say.

**The report was that Captain Roberts was ded & that he was sent home which caused some excitement. Word came that his body was at the depot at Owego although no word was sent to Mrs. Roberts. People in Owego supposing it was so, some men came up to the funeral yesterday. Mr. Williams went to Owego to see about it & after inquiring found that no telegraph had been sent to Owego, neither was there any corps there. I think it was to bad for Mrs. Roberts, still we rejoiced that it was not true for her sake.**

It has been very warm this week till today which is cold enough to have a fire. Willie dear I cannot help looking & thinking of your coming if the time does seem long to me sometimes, but the longest time is short when we think how the years fly. I have put bars to the door & it is raining which makes everything look lonsome. I will be thankful if the time comes when I shall be as strong as I once was for I get tired sometimes. Mother says do nothing, more truth than poetry.

I had a call from Mr. Dunbar the other day. Willie did I ever write to you that Mary Josslyn was married, I pity her. Fannie has been over to Newark, visiting. She speaks of you every time I see her. I must tell you what she said when you come home. I was much amused. **There has been several hirers arrived in town & prospects of two or three more, raising soldiers for the War.** The girls have come & I cannot write as they are talking so fast, so I must bid you goodnight & hope to hear soon. All send love so does

little Sis. While I remain yours ever the same, Frank
SATURDAY

As I did not get your letter written in time I will ad a few words, it has been raining all day. Uncle Walter is getting quite smart although we feared at first he would not. Since Henry has left it is very lonsome. he made his home at our house while here. It is very cold, you may just keep still for I am not going to look for you till I see you coming, expect you will surprise me as you often did last winter.

The boys at the junction are well. Mr. J. North has got home. have not seen Mary yet but shall try to see her next week. Guess she is very buisy. Write soon for I love to hear from you since I cannot see you. do not see any of your people, Willie dear you must not get discouraged that will never do, for where there is a will, there is a way. yours now & ever Augusta

## October 10, 1862

To: Miss Frank Keeler – Candor, Tioga County, NY
From: W.C. Gridley – Washington City D.C.

Dear Frank, Your triple sheet came to hand all safe today & welcome to was it. Making short its journey, only two days. I also rec'd one from home. But had to write two letters to get it, & a third one had Started but guess hadn't rec'd it.

As to your letters I cannot describe to you with what feeling I read them. You know, I'll leave business any time to read one if rec'd so perhaps you can guess. You hope to have the privelage of sharing with me joys, sorrows, &c. Yes dear one, that has ever been my wish & so it shall be so long we both live, & I know of no reason why that we are not as likely to live some time as others. You know what I have so often told you that no one except you dear one can claim that privelage, & how I long to be with you this night, this hour, this moment. I know fulwell your thoughts & at some future day shall be granted, & as we have talked before, it shall be soon after I return to the Town of C....but cannot say how soon, but may it be soon for your sake dearest.

You can if you wish with perfect safty, prepare for the journey, hoping it will be a source of perfect joy to you, & so far as I can, by any excertions on my part it shall ever be. You know dear one, the wishbone that we broke I think I never told anyone my wish as yet, but I think from all prospects that I can see it is coming to pass in due time. When its past I will notify you of the event. Might but you would like to know it now.

Saw Fred tonight he is feeling very well, think he has had a letter from Miss or he would not feel so well. He has never said anything to me about you since he first came down. I think he's somewhat suprised at my not saying any thing about you nor any sign.

Did you attend **the fair at Owego** Frank? When you see Peter Brink wish him much joy for me, please. I did not know that you sat up until the Roosters began to crow now-adays. I began to think you had forgotten some of your old tricks, but I see not. There you have been making music for the lonely people of Candor. Then Rob Turner has gone to War? I wonder if he has a Comm. Your uncle Walter had quite a fall I should think. I shall spend a part if not all of the winter in Candor, which will suit you I know. Frank time Changes everything, may it change for the best. You speak of wrighting thoughts, I write what suits me best. Frank I do not feel just right for writing tonight, so you must excuse the scribble.

Dear one, I enclose you a piece of Sesch music given to me by a Lieut of my old Reg't. The music is very good but the words you will not like of corse. This music is an exact copy of the original gotten up at New Orleans on steel plate. There is another called **My Maryland** but I have not succeded in getting it yet. The music is better than the others.

Frank, I am rather tired after working all the day & must close this by saying "firstly & lastly" that my health is good now & hoping that this may find you enjoying a better one still. Wishing to hear from you soon I send love to all, but the greater share reserved for yourself.

As the impression on my finger by the ring, (it is nearly the size of the ring) so is the impression of its owner on my heart. (I know it for I can feel it) But I must bid you good night, pleasant dreams &c. Write soon, I remain as ever yours   Willie

## "MARYLAND MY MARYLAND"

The despot's heel is on thy shore appeal,
Maryland! Maryland!
His touch is at thy temple door,
My Mother State! To Thee I knell,
Maryland! Maryland!
Avenge the patriotic gore
For life and death, for woe and weal
That flecked the streets of Baltimore,
Thy peerless chivalry reveal
And be the battle queen of yore,
And grid thy beauteous limbs with steel
Maryland, my Maryland, Maryland! My Maryland!

*The song goes on for nine verses, and was written in 1861, sung to the tune of "O Tannenbaum"*
*It became immediately popular in Maryland even though it was supposed to inspire the state to join the Confederacy. This is the song Will Gridley was trying to obtain copies of at the time of writing his October 10, letter.*

Included with this letter: Electors for President of the US

For Electors of President and Vice President of the United States,

| | |
|---|---|
| HORACE GREELEY, | PRESTON KING, |
| OBADIAH BOWNE, | ALONZO W. MORGAN, |
| JAMES S. T. STRANAHAN, | HIRAM HORTON, |
| GEORGE RICARD, | ALLEN C. CHURCHILL, |
| ABRAM J. DITTENHOEFER, | EBENEZER BLAKELEY, |
| WILLIAM H. McKINNEY, | JOHN CLARKE, |
| THOMAS B. ASTEN, | JOHN J. KNOX, |
| ISAAC T. SMITH, | THOMAS KINGSFORD, |
| GEORGE OPDYKE, | GEORGE W. BRADFORD, |
| GUY R. PELTON, | JOHN E. SEELEY, |
| ALEXANDER DAVIDSON, | JEDEDIAH DEWEY, |
| JAMES W. TAYLOR, | MYRON H. WEAVER, |
| CHARLES L. BEALE, | JAMES ALLEY, |
| THADDEUS HAIT, | JOHN W. STEBBINS, |
| JOHN TWEDDLE, | WILLIAM BRISTOL, |
| CORNELIUS L. ALLEN, | JOSEPH CANDEE, |

JOHN P. DARLING.

# THE ITHACA JOURNAL.

## PARAGRAPH CORNER.

### Ithaca, Wednesday, December 11, 1861.

From the Philadelphia Press.

### The Countersign.

Alas! the weary hours pass slow,
The night is very dark and still,
And in the marshes far below,
I hear the bearded whip-poor-will;
I scarce can see a yard ahead,
My ears are strained to catch each sound—
I hear the leaves about me shed,
And the springs bubbling through the ground.

Along the beaten path I pace,
Where white rags mark my sentry's track;
In formless shrubs I seem to trace
The foemen's form, with bending back;
I think I see him crouching low—
I stop and listen—I stoop and peer,
Until the neighborhood hillocks grow
To groups of soldiers far and near.

With ready piece I wait and watch,
Until my eyes, familiar grown,
Detect each harmless earthen notch,
And turn guerillas into stone;
And then amid the lonely gloom,
Beneath the tall old chestnut trees,
My silent marches I resume,
And think of other times than these.

"Halt! who goes there?" My challenge cry,
It rings along the watchful line;
"Relief!" I hear a voice reply—
"Advance, and give the countersign;"
With bayonet at the charge I wait—
The corporal gives the mystic word;
With arms aport I charge my mate,
Then onward pass and all is well.

But in the tent that night, awoke,
I ask, if in the fray I fall,
Can I the mystic answer make
When the angelic sentries call!
And pray that heaven may so ordain,
Where'er I go, what fate be mine,
Whether in pleasure or in pain,
I still may have the Countersign.

A BAD LOOK OUT.—Through the loop holes of Fort Lafayette,

A CON. FOR THE CAMP.—Q.—Why is a lover who composes a pretty sonnet to the features of his "object" like a soldier? A.—Because he knows how to write about Face.

☞ Captain Nathaniel Gordon, of the slaver Erie, was convicted of piracy Nov. 9th, in the United States Circuit Court, before Judges Nelson and Shipman. He was sentenced this morning to be hung Friday, Febuary 7, 1862.

**October 13, 1862**

To: W.C.Gridley – Washington, D.C.   Box 13

From: F. Keeler – Candor, Tioga County, NY

Dearest Willie,  Your kind epistle came this eve on the cars & very glad was I to get it & better pleased still to hear that you was well. I will remember what you have so often told me.  Willie I so often see those that we cannot trust that I often am surprised that I ever could love or have confidence in men, you know what I have said on that subject when a certain Gent convinced me that I was wrong. I cannot therefore cary out the plans laid out one year ago but am doing quite the other thing, now do I fear that we will not be as happy as others, yes.  Willie I have a confidence in one that will not be easily shaken.

Willie you write you should spend a part or all of (I suppose the winter in Candor, although the word winter or whatever it was was left out so I cannot think what it was but winter.) When you write let me know your calculations if it would be right.  I do not know just what you mean by my preparing unless you are coming home soon which I hope is so for which I hope is so for I long to see you, not that I wish to hasten the hour that I may be all yours (for that will come in its own time) but I want to look at you & know that you are here.  Now I have been talking rather free for me.

Tuesday.  Mother stays up with Grandma most of the time so this letter is not finished yet for my time is not all my own. Grandma is more feeble.  Uncle Walter is not any better, sometimes they think he will never be better, as it is over a week & he does not get better.  The little house on the sidehill Mr. Humestons house, was set on fire & burned Saterday night.  They do not know who done it.  Prof. Towner's Musical Convention is next week at the Babtist house.  I am very anxious to go for I think there is a small chance for improvement in my voice.  I told LeGrand yesterday perhaps you would be home before long, he said then he expected to have a sister in the army before long.  He got his ears boxed right smart.

Now Willie this is one of the worst letters ever written so you may just please burn it as soon as you read it, if you can read it at all.  It is most time for the cars so good night.  Write soon, I am with much love, yours, Frank

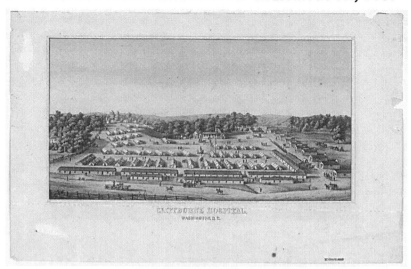

Cliffburne Hospital, Washington, D.C.

*The American poet Walt Whitman, 1819-1892, volunteered as a nurse in Civil War hospitals.*

**Moore's Rural New-Yorker** – October 18, 1862
Mrs. Lincoln distributed one thousand pounds of grapes to the inmates of the various hospitals about Washington City during the past week.

**Many of W. Gridley's excursions around Washington, D.C. were near hospitals and the Washington Arsenal.**

**Harper's Weekly**
March 1861 – ARSENAL AT WASHINGTON – In connection with the military movements now proceeding at Washington we publish herewith a view of the Arsenal at that city.  It stands on the junction of the eastern branch with the Potomac, and is surrounded on three sides by water.  Here are foundries, work-shops, magazines, laboratories, and every thing necessary for the manufacture of implements and materials of war.  At the present time the Arsenal is a scene of great activity.  In front of the Arsenal stand a collection of foreign brass cannon, some of which are trophies taken in the battle at Saratoga, Yorktown, Niagara and Vera Cruz.

Washington Arsenal

**The Philadelphia Inquirer** – August 1861 – Affairs at the Arsenal
The activity noticeable in every department of the ARSENAL
shows that "no step is to be taken backward" by Government in the
prosecution of the war. The entrance and carriageways are blocked
up with army wagons, carts and other vehicles, heavily loaded
with arms for the regiments, provisions for the army, huge shells
on their way to be filled, and all the requisites of war. Splendid
parks of rifled cannon, from ten to thirty-two pounders, ornament
the lawns, huge guns lie about on the wharf and in the shops ready
to be mounted, while the tattoo of hammers and buzz of saws bear
evidence to the life within. Rifled and round shells, grape, canister
and shrapnel, mine and pistol balls, in immense quantities, roll out
ready for their mission of death, under the manipulation of many
hands, bright guns go up upon their wheels and turn their dark
mouths towards the blue hills of Virginia, while a constant tide
of muskets, rifles and bayonets pours in and out of the spacious
armories. The regulars, who formerly guarded the entrances, have
been assigned other duties and the responsible position is now filled
by Company A, Captain Moffitt, of the Twenty-sixth regiment.

**INTERESTING FROM WASHINGTON ARSENAL**
The Sanitary Commission says the EVENING STAR, visited the
new building just erected by Mr. Job Angus, (under direction of
Commissioner Wood), near the railroad depot, for a temporary
resting place for the soldiers as they arrive here. The commission
examined the building minutely and expressed themselves satisfied
with the arrangements made for the comfort of the men, and

approved in all respects. The building will be completed by night.
It is 300 feet long, with sleeping and eating accommodations for
2,000 men. Great pains have been taken to have the structure well
ventilated and ample provision has also been made for proper
drainage. Bathing apparatus has been introduced, and other
necessary provisions made conductive to the health of those who
may be temporarily quartered therein.

## October 14, 1862
To: Miss Frances Keeler
From: W.C. Gridley – Washington City D.C.
Dear Frank, Though shades of darkness often fall upon me, yet
I still survive. The recolections of home & dear ones left behind
when in a land which nature made beautiful in all respects, is now
made the home of those suffering ones known in times of war.
Often do I think as I pass to & from my boarding place, **of those
now in hospitals (being only three of them on my way) which
may number its inmates not only by the hundreds but by the
thousands & thousands of brave ones, who have left the fireside
of a friendly home where loved ones are mourning their absence
day by day**, but to him who leaves Father & Mother has a strong
courage. Although not equal to him who leaves behind object
of his affections none can comprehend, only those who have the
opertunity of being made acquainted with its feeling, especialy those
who never expect to return.

Let not the above excite you dear one, tis nothing but one of my
Theological strains. Perhaps you have seen or heard of them before.
Glad to know that you had so fine a chitchat with Coz Norman. I
think its time he had the Prefix, don't you? You tell about Herbert
thinks that Charlie has gone & died must have some one of the
family to fill his place.

Well Frank, I have been down Town since I began this & as
you see back again. What an idea that was, to report the death of
Capt. Roberts. Tis strange what some will do. Yesterday it was cold
enough I can tell you here. I did not freeze but came near. It rained
last night, today quite mudy. You say that you get tired soon, all
that has been caused by over-exerting yourself when you had been
sick & yet very weak. I hope you will be careful with your health.
I want to see you alive when I get home again (please try will you)

No, dear you never told me that Mary Josslyn was married, but LeGrand did & that was what he had in his letter that you sent apart. Lets hear (in your next) what Fannie has to say, spit it out. I think it will wound no one.

It is a strange thing to say that while some are passing out of this world, there are some escaping in. Then the prospects is fair to raise another company there soon of infantry. I thought there were some when I was there that began to look quite interesting. "I did not see it." You say I may just keep still. I can do so if that would suit you best. But the question now comes would it suit I? I will thus far venture to say that I can keep still. Both hands and mouth, if in accordance with my lovely Queen. I trust you will see I have not forgotten how to tease yet.

Dearest one I have a paper which I got while down Town, I will send you. I shall also enclose a few envelopes Backed so that you need not trouble LeGrand when he is busy. O, Frank I forgot to say that I rec'd yours of the 10th today all right. Dear, you can't receive my letters with any more pleasant feeling than I yours. Mark what I say. O, In the paper you will find a story marked thus (a grid of 3 x 6 lines) which I have seen to perfection long ago. Tell me what you think about it when you have read it. I think it very true.

Well I must close this. Love to all of the friends & a bundle to little Sis. Hoping to receive my commision soon together with its prize. And as we met, so ever we part, from your Willie.
*(There is no evidence that W. Gridley ever received this commission)*

## October 17, 1862
To: W.C. Gridley – Washington, D.C.  Care of Box 13
From: Augusta Keeler – Candor, Tioga County, NY
Dear William, Your most welcome epistle came safe last eve, do not be sad, for if we give up to such thoughts we would always be so. The sky is not always clowded, as for those poor soldiers you know I pity them. I would love to spend my time if I had the strength, to help take care of them. We mis those that have gone but I must not talk about them more, it is a very exciting subject to me, ever, you say tis only one of your Theological strains, I often have such thoughts of those poor sufferers who is suffering for my comfort.

From what I have heard they had quite a dance. **We hear that Cap. Roberts is Chaplain, not dead, do not know how true.** As for me I do not doubt but you will see me alive. Do you ever get tired when you are busy all day. Grandma does not get any better & Mother is there most of the time which keeps me very busy, by the way that makes me think that I wish you would tell me about what time you intend to come & with Ma's being gone most of the time I would rather know a little beforehand, it would be more convenient that if we had no sick friends. I do not expect that you can tell exactly.

I will not write what Fannie said. I rather tell you. Mr. Cross has gone to war. Mrs Cross has a by two days old. Sarah thinks she bares the Cross. You must not tell it for Sarah's sake. Mrs. Jacob Wilbey has a little daughter last night. Hurrah! for Jacob. Mrs. Dodge (Alice Merrill) has lost her little one. This is enough news of this kind, it will spoil you I am afraid.

If you are so willing to obey your Queen I shall not have much trouble in being obeyed, or do you obey but one who you tease. I like that Old maid, she was not convinced as I am by what others say, you send such a piece just to see what I will say, you just find out if you can, of course I would not tell what I think.

I hope you receive your commision soon. What & what is the prise if it is what you wrote about two weeks ago & you succed do you intend to go back there?

I was up to Prestons & Frank asked me if I would like to buy a pair of white kids. I had a notion to inquire if they were quadrapeds. Sarah says "she can't see it," I forgot to tell you it had rained all the week. perhaps you knew it, but no snow. O dear, Ans took Ella Trusdal up to the dance, not Lute. **The boys here have moved from the Junction toward Washington.** Much obliged for the paper, so good by, As we part so may we meet, Frank as ever

**Moore's Rural New-Yorker** – October 18, 1862 – The News Condenser
*The departure of the Central American free negro expedition has been postponed
*One hundred and thirty eight members of the New Bedford, Mass. Fire department are in the army
*Prince Salms-Salman excellent Prussian officer, is raising a Prussian brigade in New York for the Union

*It is said that 350,000 heavy English navy blankets have been imported into the South within the last six weeks

*A Key West letter, dated Sept. 29th says Col. Morgan issued an order freeing all the slaves within his department

*A man named Louis Napoleon was hung in Richmond, Va. A few days ago for counterfeiting Confederate Treasury Notes

*The mouth-pieces of the Southern Rebels in England are beginning to abuse Garibaldi for expressing sympathy with the North

*The Herald's dispatch from Washington says Gen. Lockwood is liberating slaves of disloyalists on the eastern shore of Virginia

*Speculators following the Rebel army in Kentucky, buy up confederate script which the troops scatter, at 60 cents on the dollar

*Gen. Pope has refused to employ Chippewa Indians in the war against the Sioux. He does so from motives of public policy

*Among the imports of the past week we notice $520,000 worth of guns. At $20 per gun, this would make an importation of 26,000 guns

*Gen. W. T. Sherman in command at Memphis has ordered that for every boat fired upon, ten secessionist families shall be expelled from the city

*The drafted men in Cleveland are paying all the way from fifty to sixty dollars to three or four hundred for substitutes for the nine months service

*A private circular has been issued by the rebel Government to proprietors of newspapers forbidding the publication of the emancipation proclamation

*S. W. Smith, merchant at Palmer, NY, recently had his pantaloons stolen from his bedroom, the thief fishing them with pole and hook through the window

*Among 1,200 wounded rebel prisoners now at Sharpsburg, no less than 86 regiments and six batteries, all of which took part in the battle of Antietam, are represented

*Gen. Lee is still conscripting with remorseless energy, seizing all under 45 within his reach, taking citizens walking the streets accompanied by wives and children

**October 19, 1862**
To: Miss Keeler – Candor, Tioga County, NY
From: W. C. Gridley – Washington City

Dear Sis, Your kind letter of the 18th came safe on friday but could not answer it until today which you will be apt to get tuesday next.

I saw Kelsey Hart, Jud Allen & Geo DeBoyce in the city the other day. I asked Kel how he liked soldiering & he said you know if a man was out would not be apt to go again & while we were talking Geo spoke to Kel & said ask him when he hurd from Gust last. Kel said that he would not as that would be a leading question & so when they were all done I said I hurd of her by the way of Mary Eliz & that closed the subject.

As to your plans of one year ago I now nothing but would like to very much. If you are satisfied I am glad of that & as for me I have nothing to say.

Frank, I know your dealings fullwell & hope you never will have the opertunity to change them. I did write you that I expected to spend all or part of the winter in Candor & although you had to substitute the word winter it is not strange & think it very likely you may have had to substitute many others, for I never look over a letter to see, I think that I am not the only one.

Dear Frank, as I have said before that I should come home as soon as I can get matters straitened with the Gov. US which I hope now to be soon but cannot tell the day or week. The Reg't have two pay Rolls made out & expect to be paid soon. There are certain posts offered that of your own tast, if any.

I did not mean every thing for time may as well as season require different. I do not wish to have you think that I am dictating about your affairs for I am not. I only wrote that you might have the time for all things.

Dear Frank, the weather here is very pleasant although somewhat chilly. I have been troubled for some days with a severe headache & some thing of a cold, but nothing more than in any other climate. feeling quite well today, & hope this may find you in good health.

Mr. Geo. Sturges went to Candor last week perhaps you heard so, he is going up to pack apples & send them here &c & no one but W.R.S. & myself in the store, which lessens the help for the bis. which makes it harder you know.

I think that I'll go up to see Mr. Sturges this afternoon, he has a very pretty woman I think. I have not had a chance at Washington to party yet but think I shall soon, as have had an invite. how do you like the music? There is a much perter one if I could get hold of it, but have not been able yet. Write me about Mary & Norman I want to hear, she has not answered my letter as yet so guess she dont intend to. Well Frank I must close this as is most diner time, love to all, some to Sis   Yours Ever & Ever Willie

## October 21, 1862
To: Miss Augusta Keeler – Candor, Tioga County, NY
From: W. C. Gridley – Washington City
Dear Augusta, Your kind letter of the 17th came safe yesterday but I was tired last night & could not reply. Sorry to hear that your Grand Ma is not any better. You say Mrs Cross has a "by." What kind of a thing is that I'd like to know. That cross is born by a good many, yet tis not a nessary thing.

Jacob is having good luck. That Miss Alice has just come around. I have been looking for it some time, acording to reports. As to obeying, I will let you know soon enough. Then the old maid story suits you. I will know what to send you here after commission. Yes I will show it to you when I get it & it's value. I would have told Frank P. unless they were quadrupeds, I did not want them.

That makes me think of a story I have read. Perhaps it will not suit you. There has been a woman stolen away from her native home, she being in a rather interesting way. Time elapsed & the offspring at hand, of some little time after the ship was sacked the child lost & the woman thrown upon a desolate isle where she found nothing but an old goat, after looking around some time discovered the old goat had a pair of kids & she being in some pain in the cause of her lost child said she would nurs them & did so & in short time was taken from the isle but her two kids had to go with her & ever after went by the name of the Goatess. Thus ends the first section. I suppose Lute don't dance so Ans must have some one. Dear Frank, the boys, some of them were down here & also the quarter Master, Mr. Thurston perhaps you know him. I see Fred every day, he is well. Things go off very well, Dear One, I may be home in a few days & may not in several weeks, I can't say, but wished I could. Charles Hunt was in the City today so Fred said but did not see him. I am so tired I cannot write any more so you will have to put up with this. My love to all &c & as we met so shall we meet again, from yours ever so, Willie

**Moore's Rural New-Yorker** – October 18, 1862
THE WAR'S PROGRESS – Facts, Scenes, Incidents, Etc. – A NEW
CONFEDERATE FLAG
By a late act of the Confederate Congress a new flag has been
adopted. The imitation of the glorious old Stars and Stripes has
been done away with….the stars and bars of the Rebel rag are a
disgrace.

**Harper's Weekly** – June 1861 – FRANCE – Secessionist Flags Not
Recognized
Secessionist flags do not find favor in French Ports. The ship
Matilda, from Charleston, flying the Palmetto, attempted to enter the
harbor of Harve on the 29th of April, but was not allowed to do so,
until she hauled down the rebel abortion, and hoisted in its place the
"Stars and Stripes."

**The BONNIE BLUE FLAG** was a marching song, written in 1861
to celebrate the new secessionist flag. White stars on a dark blue
rectangle, it was the first flag of the Confederacy.

*The Confederate flag controversy would continue for the next
hundred years, and more. Two well known incidents follow:*

*Wayne Ripley was a Florida state Senator from 1951 to 1953, and
1959 to 1961. At some point during his public service the following
newspaper article was written:*
**FLORIDA SEEKS LAW TO PROTECT REBELS' FLAG**
*Tallahassee, Florida, (UPI)*
The flag of the Confederate States of America should not be used
for wiping an auto windshield, State Senator Wayne Ripley said
yesterday. Ripley won committee support for a bill prohibiting the
mutilation, defiling, or casting of contempt on the flag.
He said he was shocked into action by the sight of a man wiping
his windshield with such a flag."That flag stands for states' rights
and is a symbol of what Southerners fought and lost their fortunes
for, and it should be shown respect," he told the Senate's General
Legislation Committee.

*And, in 2015 the State of South Carolina became the center of a passionate debate on the presence of the Rebel Flag flying on state land. A similar flag had been seen in the hands of a mass murderer. Eventually the banner was removed. But, hopefully this did not remove the respect due the people of the South who fought and died for the Confederacy.*

## October 22, 1862

To: W. C. Gridley – Washington City D.C.  Care of Box 13
From: Augusta Keeler – Candor, Tioga County, NY
Dear Friend Willie, After waiting your welcome epistle came safe today. I did not know but you was sick & was very glad to hear you were not. Mother is still up with Grandma. Grandma is much worse so that Ma is there all the time. I just came from there & Grandma was not any more comfortable. Uncle Walter walked up here yesterday.

Candor is very quiet most of the time rather more lively this week. Prof. Towner Musical Convention at the B church did call out some excitement. I do not attend for you know I cannot sing. Therefore I do not think I would make much headway getting up there alone before so many. Rosa Way & H. Smith are going to be married Lute says, within three weeks, hope they will. That reminds me of a request that Lute made, she wants me to write for her & tell you she would like your Photograph, she had a present of a photograph album & has some for it. Ans gave it with his & his sisters in it. Fred does write to Rowena Way, she said so. George King from Chenango Forks has been visiting here, came Monday & went last eve on the car, rather a short visit & I heard from all of my friends. received a letter from Henry some time ago, have not answered it, when I received yours today I thought I would not write in three days just let you wait a week as I did.

It is very cold today the weather is very unpleasant most all think it will snow. last night we had a thundershower about midnight which I enjoyed very much. I love in the night to lay awak & hear it rain, it is company for me when I am wakful. now did you ever hear of anyone not sleeping just when they ought

I saw Geo, Sturges saturday go up the street. It must have been very pleasant for you to meet the boys from Candor one time, most people like to see familiar faces. I would like to see their faces once, they are missed very much. They do not know how often we speak of them. sunday there was 4 young men at church & all the girls was there which made Lute feel very bad. I believe she thought Kel was perfect.

I did not expect you wished to dictate me, that was not what I ment. Willie I cannot write you about Mary & Norman for I have not spoken to Mary in a long time, do not know when I shall ever get down there the weather is so bad, she was here last. it rains very nice, has all day, shall be so glad when the fall rains are over.

Dearest Willie I must not weary you by writing more this time for Sarah is teasing me so that I can hardly think what I am writing, beside what is most annoying of all is this poor paper & pen, hoping you are enjoying yourself & good health also. I shall have to bid you goodby for this time, all wish to be remembered to Willie; so do I. Pa has just come home. I am waiting to see you, Ever your own Frank

I hope you may be successful in getting your pay & that soon. it has been most six weeks & I am getting anxious to see Willie.

**October 24, 1862**
To: William C. Gridley – Washington, D.C.   Box 13
From: Frank Keeler – Candor, NY
Dear William, Here I am in the front room by the table & the room in beautiful confusion, Sarah is singing & every idea I have (if ever I had any) gone, guess the wind has carried them for it is blowing very hard, have just come home, have been to see Grandma, she is failing very fast. It is cold & snowed just enough to say so. People are going by to the convention, expect there is to be a concert this evening.

There has been some talk that there is to be drafting in this county. I doubt it. Mr, Barber's son from Pa came home on a visit & they came & told him that he must go. I do not now Mr. Thurston. Rowena Way said last night that she had a letter from Fred & that you was well, which I was very glad to hear, do not think she will make much asking so many questions. Lena Williams received a letter from E. Hans of Spencer yesterday. He said there was 9 sunstroke in their company. Rather warm weather they are having. I must say that it looks lonsome out doors. The leaves falling & rain & mud to think of winter for I am not partial to that season.

Do you have warm weather, if so it will spoil you to come north as Charly Hunt wrote when his people wanted him to come home this winter. have you received those two papers, now Willie what do you think.

2 P.M. Mr. Dunbar has called & your little ........Sarah says that you will be jealous & she would like to know if you are one of that kind. I say never. Now Willie you know that is never to be. I am not, but Sarah will not be convinced, she tries to torment me all the time, she gets her pay, for I ask her if he still calls her the idle of his sole. There now I must not write any more for I have to go out in the other room.

**The deceased Capt. Roberts has written a letter home to the Editor of the Gazette flatly denying the charge of his departure from this world,** says he is still in camp & closes with an appeal to the friends at home to write often to the soldier boys. Write often & come soon, from one ever the same, Frank

## October 26, 1862

To: Frances Keeler – Candor, Tioga County, NY
From: W. C. Gridley – Washington City D.C.
Dear Frank, Your welcome note is before me and happy indeed was I on receipt of it & ever shall be. I am afraid your grandma cannot stay long with you according to report. But may she go to that home where pain & trouble are no more. I am glad to hear that your Uncle Walter is getting smart again. I suppose he has got over talking to you about me has he not?

You say you do not attend the Musical Convention. I wished you could and would sing. You know nature never favored me with that tallunt, although I have a fine tast for music & love it dearly, but that is no good.

I saw Lieut. Oakly & Truman North the other day. Lieut went back to camp & Trum staid over night. Fred, Trum & myself went to **the Theater & had a fine time,** did not get out until 12 o'clock & then went home. I think it was the first that Trum had ever been too. I expected nothing else than he would get into the Guardhouse although he had a pass, but by the by a pass is good for nothing, after 91/2 o'clock, but the Guard let him pass being with us. don't you say a word, now mind or they will all know where it came from.

Dear one, I hope your heart not so weaked as in case I could

142

not write the self same-day of receipt of your letter that you would rejouce in giving me the pain of a detaintion of that nature, when accompanied by full reasons. No dear one, I trust not. I think I have a friend too true for any thing of the kind. May God bless you the only object of my affections, it depends upon you of my happiness or misery. Dear one I long to see those before in days gone by.

It has not stormed here in some time until today, the streets have been covered with dust two inches deep & the air quite chilly, today it has been raining all the time.

Saw Capt. Krom the other day. (chanced to meet him) he had been stoping in the City some three weeks he said, has left for his company now quite well, he was tickled to see me, you may guess. As for Rosa Way & H. Smith I hope they will get married soon if they like. I have no objections in the least, all is well. Trum asked me when I was going home, I told him I thought in the course of 4 or 5 weeks & he said I expected about Christmas or before, you can understand.

And as to Lute, I will send her a photograph but I think her proper way was to have applied in person, if she wanted a favor. Say to her I will send it, talk not of the above.

I don't get any line from Mary, I dont know what is the matter, if she dont answer it soon I shall strike her from my list so mark me unless explained. I am not to be trifled with. Fred I think there is no doubt corresponds with Miss Way. She may & of corse would deny it.

Fred & I think of going up **to see the boys at Beltsville** next sunday if it is pleasant, Frank I must close this, I forgot to say I recd your paper, your own true ever Willie

**October 28, 1862**
To:  Miss F. Keeler – Candor, Tioga County, NY
From:  W. C. Gridley – Washington City D.C.
Dear Frank, Your welcome epistle is open before me dated 24ᵗʰ recd today, very glad to hear you well & hope so may be it. It has been quite chilly all day although we have not had a stove in the store yet. Think we'll put one up tomorrow if it dont get so cold we cant. We havn't thought of seeing any snow yet. I would like to see 2 feet of snow just to see how the people would act.

You speak of the concert, I wish I could have been there, we would have had a fine time. but no, I am here at my room hoping to be there some time not far distant. As the draft goes so I go if they expect of such a poor miserable thing as I am.

Why Frank, you & I will be of the same waight in a few days I guess, for I have lost 18 pounds since I came here. That ring so often looked at & thoughts of another never flee, is quite loos upon my finger now.

I do sometimes dread that cold weather up there but after all it is the best. I know that Fred & Rosa Way were corresponding by Fred being so contented. I think he did not get a letter from her the first two weeks he was here, he was so homesick but tis now he dont care, the things is all right. Talk about sunstruck now that is not so, it might have been in the month of August but not now tis not a frequent thing for 100ds are often sunstruck every day on long marches without rest or water.

You say the winter is a part of the seasons which you are not partial to. I can say I am but not to that mudy & rainy weather connected with its (come & go) if I may so use the phrase. I have rec'd 2 or three papers from Candor I don't know which.

Now Frank how may I understand you, have you a regular appointed Post Master in the village besides the one at the other place C.C.? You say Mr. Dunbar has called on my little WHAT? I cant understand such kind of a word if word it may be or what? O wall, if I loose the first, I'll be sharp enough for the next, to go on. All is well that ends well. I know how it will end if I know myself & I think I do. You tell Sarah that your Soldier boy is far away in the southern clime may never come home again & think she that you would like to be alone. If so shes much mistaken guess, but enough of such. Tell the Idle there is but one to worship & that he who worships woman forgets his God.

Saw Fred today as I passed the store, think he is well. Dear, you know how I long to be with thee. I am looking & waiting. My best love to all the friends. While I remain yours till death that ever true & unchangeable, Mortal Willie – to a dear one, Frank

**October 29, 1862**
To: W.C. Gridley – Washington City D.C. Care of Box 13
From: Frances Keeler – Candor, Tioga County, NY
Dear Willie, I received your last letter yesterday which I was very glad to get being rather lonsome. (Sarah & LeGrand are singing & I doubt if you can read this) Grandma has gone to that long rest.

She died Saturday morn at 2 o'clock, was buried on Sunday. I can hardly realize that I shall not see her every time I go over to Aunt Rachels.

Mary Kelsey called here yesterday, she has been sick, she was sick up to your Mothers & she says she has not been well since. I spoke to her about receiving a letter from Washington, she said she received one & had tried several times & she thought she should this week write & asked when I heard last. I told her not very lately as I had not had one since Thursday. Mr & Mrs Whiton from Conn. Has been at Mr. Kelseys & to their other friends, they were some relatives of yours. Have not seen Lute since Friday, do not play at M. Church. Miss Bacon has returned, a good thing off my hands. Dalton Dootlittle is not expected to live. The Presbyterian bell is just ringing perhaps for him, there has been several sick.

Uncle Walter is quite smart & inquires nearly every week if I have heard from W.C. I always tell him, he says you are about right.

You spoke about Truman, I have his photograph, wish Kel would get his for me, he promised to send all the girls one but he is a soldier, They tell anything. it is just like Sunday every day scarcely a person to be seen from morning till night. I Wish the War would close so the boys could come home.

How does Charly Barager or do you never see him? Will, now you just keep dark while I tell you that Mary Eliza said that Leon Chidseys wife had to be married, although I do not believe it.

In about four weeks is Thanksgiving. Monday morning the ground was covered with snow, today is very pleasent for the first day in some time, the sun shining on the trees makes every thing look beautiful. You say you are coming in 4 or five weeks, see that you do. I have got to close this for Sate is talking so fast I can hardly think what I write, now Willie what would I not give to see you & know how you look. Write often, so good by     Every thine own Frances

**October 31, 1862**
To: Frank Keeler – Candor, Tioga County, NY
From: W.C. Gridley – Washington City D.C.
Dear Frank, Your kind letter of the 29th came today & glad was I to receive it. Your lonesomeness I believe I know how to share with you & bear my own too. But the time will come when that shall be forgotten & hope to be known no more. You dear Frank that I long

to be by your side. But could I tell you of Southern Ladies here. (they are like choice butter in the market, none of it.) But O! for the Girls of York there are none to equal, perhaps you may think me jelous but no I judge from observation

Perhaps Sarah & LeGrand take pleasure in trying to bother you, that's all right

And your grandmother has gone to that long rest & I hope she is at rest where nothing troubles. This of corse has a tendency to increase your loneliness but soon it will wear away. You can guess how I feel to go home and find GrandPas room vacant. It troubles me to speak of him, I should not have felt so if I could have been there & seen him once.

Then Miss M.E.K. has called upon you at last & I am sory to learn of her illness. Our folks did not writ so Mr. Whiton & Lady from conn have been out, I would like to have seen them. I am not aquainted with Doolittles.

You speak of soldier boys as though there word was nothing. You must'nt class me as such for if so I might prove so.

According to your theory you say it is just like Sunday every day, tis not so here, there is no sunday so all the same, tis all sunday with you & no sunday with me. Yet there is one day out of 7 that I don't work but tis not Sunday. You may look for the boys in vain, there is three years ahead of them & I fear you will not see them or many of them e'er that time.

I have herd the boys say that they had a good deal of fun with Sam Chidsey. I did not know what it ment, but hardly think it that. I do not know how Mary Eliz could know anything about it, if so all I can say about it, they are green, not well ripened. (I think this will do.)

I have not seen any snow. You must be very cold hearted up there I guess. it has been very warm today like Sept.

I went to the P.O. today, no letters for the firm but mine. I let him see the back (W.R.S.) & he says that looks like his hand writing & asked who wrote such a hand & I told him a fellow in Candor, he said no more.

You say what would I give to see you. I can answer it: your old shoes & perhaps hat. You now I could not wear them but my paper is nigh scribbled o'er & I must close, Love to Frank & the rest, so good night, Ever yours Willie

(Fred is all right I think, see him every day, & as to Chas B....I

146

have never seen him since he came to Washington. Think they are up on the uper Potomac, think will get to fight before long. Will is here all right with the exception of a hard cold....Willie)

## November 2, 1862
To: W. C. Gridley – Washington, D.C. Care of Box 13
From: Frances Keeler – Candor, Tioga County, NY
Dear William, Today is sunday & a beautiful day just like summer no need of a fire today. I did not attend church today, not quite energetic enough. Sarah says lazy although I plead sick, as yet she is not convinced. Peter Brink & Lady are to Aunt Rachel Josslyns. Jerome Richardson came on the car last night. a notice was read in church today that on thursday eve at half past 7 there was to be a wedding service performed at the M E church. Then good by to Rosa & Henry. Where are you today, how are you sick or well. I truly hope you are well & enjoying yourself for I am lonsome enough for two or three it is so dull. Candor looks like a deserted village. Why do you not write about the army, you have said nothing in a long time.

Tuesday. Your letter came duly at hand last eve on the cars & was very welcome, for I looked anxiously, you better take good care of yourself, I rather think that climate does not agree with you. Mr. Oakley wrote home (so I heard) today that their Regt. Was going to Texas, we hope it is not so, their friends are not pleased to have them go so far south, but such is life & we must all part in some way either sooner or later.

Today is election, **one span of horses** ran away broke a wagon standing side the wood, then ran into Mr. Marshalls wagon doing some damage. They were frightened by the rail cars.

Frank Josslyn has gone to Mich. with his Uncle Wm. Josslyn to live. Mary Eliza said that she heard that report from their neighbors down there. I guess I shall see her this week, when I did see her I tried to joke but she took it cool. I told her something & asked her if Norman did not tell her of it & she said he never told anything, now you & I know better. On the first page I wrote that I was trying to be sick, I am all right just as you say you are, only no cold.

Then you think Mr. W.R.S. was inquisitive, so do I. Susan Sturges is at Catatonk, if not I should have been down there this week. Pa is home today & usually well. LeGrand is all ok, he likes to tell me he has not got any letters, then after I really think

147

he has had none he gives it to me. Mr. & Mrs. Joel Robinson were both thrown from a wagon last week, it is doubtful if he gets well. Cousin Chas Sackett & Lady live in Baltimore this winter. Today it has been very cold, the weather is no two days the same. Willie why do you not write what you are doing. Kel writes that they are getting fat, why don't you?

Mother is hurrying me for to help her so I must not write much more nonsense, guess you will get tired before you get through reading.

I went down to Church sunday with George Barager & Sed..... dear me how people did look, I do not think they had had their eye open before that day. Most of the young people from above was there, George Woodford, Freman Booth & nearly ever one betwen here & there. It was rather amusing to me, I would like to know what they would say but enough of this.

I long to see another one dear to me, one that stays so long, but patience is the best virtue & I must practice, write often & accept love from one true friend   Frances  to dear friend Willie
PS  do not forget to write if you think best when you are coming, do not think me impatient, you know I can not dictate the ways of a higher being who rules all things.

**Moore's Rural New-Yorker** – November 29, 1862
The News Condenser
*The Health of Florence Nightingale is improving
*A Rebel paper published in Louisiana is printed on the inside of ordinary wallpaper
*The country through which Gen. Grant's army has recently moved is said to be filled with cotton
*A mass of copper weighing 47,923 pounds has been unearthed at the Meanard mines, Lake Superior
*The Supreme Court of Georgia has decided the conscript law of the Confederate States to be constitutional
*On Saturday week there were 9,375 men in various camps in Massachusetts awaiting marching orders
*The number of hogs shipped over the Erie Railway last week was ten thousand two hundred and nineteen hogs
*The Postmaster General has given orders for the redemption of postage stamps that have been used for currency
*Gen Burnside's forces on the Potomac consist of three grand

armies, nine corps, 30 divisions, and 70 brigades

*At the last dates from Vicksburg, fresh meat was from forty to fifty cents per pound and everything else in proportion

**The handsome sum of $14,520 per annum will be realized by the income Tax on Members of congress.**

*The St. Louis correspondent of the New York Tribune says there are now four hundred of General Pillow's negroes in that city

*Up to the first of the present month 210,000 men for long and short terms of service have taken the field from New York State

*The City of Cambridge Mass. Has reduced the salary of the mayor for the next year from $1,500 to $1,000 on account of the times

*The Troy Times says that $500 dollars worth of shinplasters have found their way to Newbern, N.C. and circulate freely

*The Tribune says the Navy department has secret agents in Europe and is advised beforehand of all movement of Rebel vessels

*American silver coin is very plentiful in Canada, but it is hinted that samples are not such as have been made at United States Mints

**November 4, 1862**
To: Frances Keeler – Candor, Tioga County, NY
From: W. C. Gridley – Washington City
To my dearest and only loving Frank,

Your indeed very kind letter came yesterday **while I was in Baltimore** buying some goods & did not in consequence of it receive your letter until today which I regret. But its here at last.

Dear Frank I fret not about anything. What I said in that letter I only said to tease you, if I could. I said nothing that need come in contact with our matters. You know dear one that when you wanted to go anywhere & I was away & had a chance to go notwithstanding that I loved you dearly & far above all, as it would shut so many prying eyes & knowing that I could trust you to last with the same feeling as though I did it myself, and now dear Frank I need not go back to any date to find the proof of your sincereity for I have it every week & also have it before me on the table & as to mine you can find it over there, dear one none but thee would I love, none but thee could I love. Now that pasture must be sweet for sheep to like. Twas so with me. I think that I have found the one for me & never yet once doubted her true love, tis <u>My own dear Frank.</u> It seems that I loved her ages before she knew it. But now she knows it & may she be ever blessed.

Dear Frank you speak as though I doubted you. Never never did I once doubt you. How could I doubt you when I love you to the bottom of my heart, tis ever my own dear Frank from morn till night & night till morn, and how sorry I am that you should think of such a thing. I can not for Dunbar or any other Boy.

Dear one I must say that your letter came very much sooner than common it being marked the 1$^{st}$ (Sunday) & arrived on Monday. I saw Mr. Wm. Hunt, Charlie & Dick Clark & all well, had but few moments to talk. I was in a hurry. I saw Chas. Sackett the other day, he stoping in Baltimore. **Heard from Asa Sackett last night, I think he is at Harpers Ferry, all well.** Saw Alb Robinson of candor 109$^{th}$ he is fine shape as fat as mud. I should have stoped & seen the boys yesterday, but had no time to spend. I suppose that I shall hear of Rosa & Henry's marriage soon. I am very glad that Rev. Haywood has preached his farewell sermon for I never liked him for only one thing & that is the shortness of his sermons. Lute has always been a dear friend to me and I love her much. Hear nought of Mary Eliza yet how is it, does Norman go that road as much as ever? How are all the folks? I must close this pity thing or scribble. Hoping it may find you well, to one I love, Frank. From your ever true Willy

Well good night & pleasant dreams, long to see thee

*On a separate piece of paper Augusta included a patriotic poem her sister wrote:*
Throughout the wide world
Our moto shall be
"Vive le America"
Home of the free.


**November 7, 1862**
To: Miss A. Keeler – Candor, Tioga County, NY
From: W. C. Gridley – Washington City D.C.
Dear Frank, I recd your letter yesterday. But Frank I did not have time to answer it last night as your Coz Asa Sackett was here & I had to **go with him to the Theater** & also he staid with me the night. I was very glad to receive your kind letter O, very much so indeed.

You say it has been a beautiful day. I am glad to hear that. But, Frank I cannot say so of today for it was snowing when I got up this

150

morn, & has continued to snow all day & is snowing yet (9 o'clock) I saw the snow on our back stoop where it had not melted about 5 inches deep & O how cold. No dear Frank I hope you are not sick, I can't think of such a thing.

Who did Peter Brink marry? I have never heard as yet. Please write in your next. Well I see you have some fun in C.....after all, they are not all dead yet. Mr. Smith & Lady are now numbered with the Matrimonial corps & joy go with them as they travel.

You ask where are you today, I answer at my room & went to the store once, how are you! Quite well thank you. I cant say that I am enjoying myself as well as though I could see Frank, my dear Frank.

I am sory you are so lonesome, I wished I could help you. But think I am in a short time. You ask why I do not write about the army. I do not know positively any more about the army than you do as we can learn nothing only from the papers the same as you get.

Some of the boys of 109th said that they were going to Texas but I dont think so, the Col. Only has thrown in an application. I think the boys will feel cold tonight, I have no fears of they're going so far south yet. There will be a chance by & by for them all to go I think, which I hope. **We have NO election in washington so all was quiet**. By the way I had a letter from Mary Eliza the other day. I dont see how she came to write.

Dear Frank I have'nt time to state every little thing that those soldiers do, so lazy as they all get after they've been in camp a short time I think. I do write a good bunch of nonsense & so often that it ought to cover all. You ask what I am doing, the same as I have told you yet. I think I shall change my bis in a very short time now. It will be to go north & soon.

Dear Frank I can read as long a letter as you can write, I guess. Well I guess your walk to church will shut the eyes of some of that race & I am glad am I. You know e'er this by my last letter what I think of such. tis all right with me. Wall I must bid you good night for I have but a moment to get this into the office. Love to all & to dear Frank, Yours ever the same   Willie
PS I have changed my boarding place tonight. Fred is well he says I wish I was in C.....& so do I, all is well. Your Cad

*A popular photo to add to albums in the Civil War era was that of "General" Tom Thumb (Charles S. Stratton) and his wife. He was a performer in the Barnum's American Museum. Billed as one of the smallest men alive, he and his co-star "Commodore" Nutt (George Washington Nutt) traveled throughout the world on exhibit. The show was often at theaters in the Washington, D.C. area.....adult admission, 25 cents, and a child under 10 could attend for 15 cents, a show attended by W. Gridley*

## November 10, 1862

To: Miss Frank A. Keeler – Candor, Tioga County, NY
From: W. C. Gridley – Washington City

Dearest Frank, Your kind favor of the 7th came this morning all safe. It is so dark that I hardly can see to write but I must write or scrible some hoping you will be able to read. Yes dear Frank if I could have been in place of that letter you know I would. I am Glad to hear that you are contented But would not for it to be any other way dear one. I am feeling very well today, say nothing of business, I talk not of that.

Well what did Truman have to say about me as of corse something. What is the matter of Rhoda? I think myself that Truman would like to be back to Candor & I doubt not many others. I did not know of Mr Norths sickness. Tis not so much the hard living as it is other things that you may guess that they would like to be home for. I heard Kel say that you know if one was out of it (war) he would like it & I think he is as true a man as any of them.

152

Well, dear Frank of your description of the weding I think you must have had a very large time considering the number. You speak of the style. I think I never would be married in that position. I would rather be married in a barroom for it would be smaller, understand me.

is any thing said about Ufant & Eliza & then Norman is as constant as ever, you can poke Mary any? I have rec'd Marys letter & answered it. think I said so in my last. Rec'd a letter from Wood today, all well from what he says. And so you say cold weather & so it seams it has Roda and Henry together. hope that the warm weather will not loosen the icy bands O wall, enough of such.

Fred & myself went out on the Ave to take a walk yester night found all quiet along the lines, but with one exception & that here & there along the way were groups of men discusing the removal **of Geo. B. McClelan** from his command which in the morn was the first it was heard of & it is for disobeying orders of which we have satisfactory proof & has allowed the Rebs to escape unmolested to their fortifications at **Richmond** to which they are fast hasting.

Great excitement is prevailing every where but all will be hushed in a few days, after they read Sec. Stantons letter on the subject. I have some confidence in G.B. Mc.....but lost the greater part of it while he was on the paninsula, as I thought that an unjust move & do to this day, & I think that it was all his plan. Dear Frank I will ask Kel the next time I see him.

Dear Frank the little ring of which I obtained from you in a manner of which you was hardly conscious at the time has given me more actual pleasure than any thing I know, because I could look at it at any time & know that it was true (as the giver) as a token of deep love for me, of which my sole & Body are the only served & that I never forfeit. I die first.

O, dear Frank I long to see you & hope to at a time not far distant, dear one if I do say it many have tried to gain the affections of your Willie but never have succeeded, only my own Dear Frank & can I say she tried in that manner, no, & had she, she never would have been entitled to this small piece of paper but Frank, dear Frank you know there is one upon whom you can trust & lean for support in times of all afflictions, so good Night, Your constant friend Willie PS I learn today that Mrs Dodges (Miss Merrell), Eldest daughter lies buried in the soil which Bill Gridley owns upon the hill near the house, fine place, all at present

**November 12, 1862**

To: W. C. Gridley – Washington, D.C.

From: Augusta Keeler – Candor, Tioga County, NY

Dearest Willie, It is with pleasure only known to those that look long for a letter from one dear to them does. I received your last two letters this eve, both came to me at the same time. I had feared you was sick knowing that you had not been very well & you may know I am ever thinking of you & as Sed says I count the days between the letters although she little knows what I think, I am lonesome indeed. I am & I always feel a lonliness when the object of my every thought is out of sight.

You did not gain that ring I will not say fair (although they say all is fair in love & war), but I cannot help what is past, I am glad that you find pleasure in looking at it. Indeed I was not conscious of your object at the time & not till you brought the one I wear but when I found out I thought I had sold myself as the saying is when one gets the start of the other I did not expect anything of that kind from you, the last of all persons, therfore you will understand how you obtained it so easy.

yes Willie I can trust you & ever did & I often think how much for you know it is something I seldom do, I learned young that the world was full of deception & I never had but one friend but you that I fully trusted & that was my dearest Cousin Maggie Richardson & since she died I have had none till I learned I <u>had found a friend ever trusting in you.</u>

Yes I was sick with an ugly cold & sore throat but the throat is well but the cold is not so easy to get rid of, I have been staying in the house for a week & trying to get rid of it. Otherwise I am well for me, I have not gained back the color in those cheeks but that will come in time. I have been sick some of the time since you left but have not been so as to stay in the house when I wanted to go out anywhere, but I am getting quite fleshy, I first thought I would not tell you that, I had not been as well as when you was home in the summer, but I am well now although look as pale as ever so you will not have anything to worry about, now I am very well. I just as live tell you, not have you hear it after you get home as you did before, enough.

Peter Brink married Hattie Hull (or Hall) of Oxford. Henry Smith & Lady returned today. I am sorry for Rowena, they have broke up housekeeping & she has to board.

In every letter you write you hope to come back soon. Please tell me how long soon is. Rosa, Ans, Mant, & Eliza are not going to be married till spring. when I try to joke Mary E. says that is no use, she talks about him freely. We had snow on the ground saturday, sunday & monday, now it is gone & quite comfortable weather today.

**I am sorry to hear about McClellan for I am his friend you know.** Lute & Lau said yesterday that they were going to Elmira today & stay a week or so. Did you not know that Rhoda is not a favorite with the young people of Candor nor never will be. I had some sweet apples that Keeler bought of your Pa today, you know I do not eat any other. Potter is going to New York soon. Albert has got the other store filled. I am glad to hear Fred is well, guess Rowena would like to see him. Mrs Dodge will feel the loss of her eldest, I have no doubt. I saw Lau Ward today, Mary E. says Mr. Ward told Norman he need not go by every time, he told me he did not see how he could keep it.

You cannot tell how much better I feel since the cars came for it is a week since I received a letter & I told Ma if one did not come tonight I should know something was up, it is all right now, you will not get this as soon as usual but do not worry for all is well. I did not direct your paper to your box perhaps that is the reason. **It told about the quota for the town of Candor, we have 8 over the quota.**

Frank sends a bundle of love to Willie & hope it will not be many months before she will see him safe & well in Candor. What if I had tried as many did to get Willie, would I have been happy without his love also, no never – what is life to a woman without love, we should die. Life would be a blank. I never thought of trying to gain your slight thought of affection for I had heard you was anothers, enough I was mistaken, happily for me I hope. Not much of consequence anyway. Truman said that "he was down to Washington & saw my friend Mr. G…& he had not been very well but was all right now. Mary E. spoke about you & I told her what Truman said which I was very sorry for afterwards for she told your people of it. I will be careful after this, you know experience is the best teacher. Willie I guess this will answer for both of your letters, it is so long. Yes dearest Willie I was so glad to get your letter & know that you are well. I guess I will not repeat it again, give my love to Kel. Here I sit in the front room by the table alone, poor **melodeon** is sadly neglected. Henry Clark expected to go to Baltimore last week. I have not answered Mary Josslyns letter. I ought to forgive & forget (but that is the Sackett of me) it is hard work after the past.

Ever the same unchangeable Frank

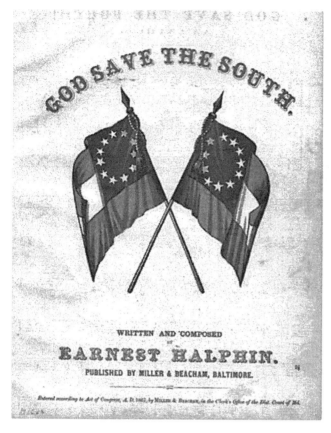

Throughout the War Southern Soldiers also sang in prayer and patriotism.

# 9 OF PRESIDENTS AND GENERALS, of Cabbages and Kings

1865

Confederate President J. Davis

General Robert E. Lee

## PRESIDENT ABRAHAM LINCOLN

"He heeded the call and for four long years he led – though many bled and tears did fall – 'till the reign of unity and freedom for all"

*The photograph of President Lincoln was taken by the great Civil War photographer Mathew BRADY. In 1842 Edward & Henry T. Anthony opened a daguerreotype gallery in New York City featuring Brady photographs. In 1902 Anthony merged with Scoville and Adams Company founding the ANSCO Corporation, located in Broome County, New York*

LINCOLN AND LIBERTY – by **Jesse Hutchinson, Jr.**
Sung to the tune of the "Old Rosin the Bow"
Hurrah for the choice of the nation,
Our chieftain so brave and so true,
We'll go for the great reformation,
For Lincoln and Liberty too!
We'll go for the son of Kentucky,
The hero of Hoosierdom through
The pride of the "Suckers" so lucky,
For Lincoln and Liberty too!

**The Illustrated London News** – February 22, 1862
General McClellan has forbidden the Hutchinsons to sing their anti-slavery songs in camp and has ordered them back to Washington. The legislature of Michigan has sent a petition to Congress stating that as slavery is a cause of the war it should be swept from the land.

*(The **Hutchinsons** were a popular American singing group specializing in four part harmony. They did sing controversial songs regarding abolition, women's rights and temperance. General McClellan's views of slavery were not in line with government policy and when President Lincoln received notice of the banishment of the Hutchininsons he immediately countermanded McClellan's order.)*

*Both Augusta Francis Keeler and Will C. Gridley used stationery honoring General McClellan, whose image was embossed on envelopes and stationery. "Commander of the Federal Forces on the Potomac."*

**General George B. McClellan** – 1826-1885
George McClellan, born in 1826, became interested in the military at an early age. By 16 he was accepted into West Point Military Academy and studied classic military tactics. He also wrote a manual for cavalry and designed a saddle for the mounted troops. In 1881 he was appointed by President Lincoln as both Commander of the Army and General in Chief. He had no doubts about being able to handle both positions, claiming "I can do it all."

General McClellan and his Peninsula Campaign were avid topics among the population in 1862 and the thoughts expressed in letters from Augusta and Will on the subject reflected those of many Union Citizens. They supported McClellan but were horrified by his ignoring Presidential orders.

McClellan's Army of the Potomac was the greatest military expedition ever produced by America. Over 190,000 men composed his forces but this huge force of might did not produce the expected military victories.

His very public opinions opposing the federal governments' interference with slavery, and an open preference for those of his own race, gave many people grave doubts about his character. However he vehemently opposed secession, and was extremely popular among the soldiers. "Little Mac" was not exactly a team player with politicians, the war department or President Lincoln so he was eventually fired from his position as General-in-Chief.

A very widely published removal from head of the armies did not make him retire from public life. In 1864 he became the Democrat nominee for President opposing Lincoln on a different front. Once again his entirely independent opinions lost him support when he did not agree with the Democrat platform. After his loss in the presidential race he eventually ran for governor of New Jersey where he served from 1878 to 1881.

**The Philadelphia Inquirer** – August 1861
General McClellan – a correspondent of the Tribune says that our brave Philadelphia General is regarded by the Sturges Rifles, his body guard, as invincible. "They say he never makes a mistake, and I verily believe these eighty three men would cheerfully march forth to-night alone, to attack the Rebel army at Manassas, if General McClellan should give the order and lead the attack.

"General McClellan is one of the least pretentious of men; he generally wears the simple blouse of the riflemen, with not even the starred shoulder straps to denote his rank; a man who never wastes time; who is indefatigable in his pursuit and attack of the enemy, and equally untiring in his efforts to secure the utmost comfort of his men, compatible with the circumstances of a soldier's life.

When his line is on the march, he is ever among the men, with a kind and cheering word for every company; a pleasant look, or a kind salute, or hearty grasp of the hand for every officer or private with whom he is brought on speaking terms by business; and in a fight he is always at the front of the column, in the thickest of the danger, encouraging his soldiers by cheering word and fearless deed. He takes soldier's fare with the rest. Asking no better food, and no more luxurious bed than the newest recruited private under his command. If he sees a man without proper shoes or clothing, he has that man with his captain sent to his own quarters, where the man is served with the garments he needs, and the captain receives a reprimand that leads him to look more closely after the comfort of his men in future."

**The New York Times** – June 30, 1862 – IMPORTANT Rumor Gentlemen connected with the Army who came over yesterday afternoon by the Richmond Train, report that McClellan is falling back and burning his fortifications as he leaves them. This is a strange proceeding, if true, after the repeated war bulletins which the General has issued to the North that he would press the enemy to the wall, and be in Richmond in a few days. Our telegraphic intelligence from Richmond makes no reference to such a move on the part of McClellan as given above.

**Harper's Weekly** – September 1862 – McClellan
Once more we hail thee, Chief! The nation's heart,
Faint and desponding, stricken to the dust,
Turns back to thee with the old hopeful trust,
And childlike confidence, and love. Thou art
Our Chosen Leader. We have watched thee well,
And marked how thou hath borne the taunts and sneers of those
whose envious falsehoods harmless fell
About thine head; how, unmoved by their jeers, Thou hast toiled on
with patient fortitude,
Winning from all the Legions under thee
A love which is almost idolatry;
Thy one sole aim thy Country's greatest good.
Press on, young Chieftain, foremost in the van!
The hour of need has come-be thou the Man!

346

---

### THE PRESIDENTIAL ELECTION IN AMERICA.
##### GREAT M'CLELLAN MEETING IN UNION-SQUARE, NEW YORK.

MR. C. D. SHANLY, of New York, whose sketch of an open-air political meeting in that city we have this week engraved, writes, under date of Sept. 9, as follows:—"The nomination of General M'Clellan by the Chicago Convention for the office of President of the United States was ratified last evening in this city by an immense Democatic 'mass meeting' in Union-square. This meeting was called in the name of 'the friends of M'Clellan, in favour of free speech, a free press, and the rights of the people, and all who hope in peace and re-union.' Five large stands were erected on the south side of the square, and from these, which were brilliantly lighted with Chinese lanterns, the orators of the night, surrounded by their friends, held forth for some hours to the assembled multitude. The German stand was placed close by the statue of Washington, and at this point the scene was very striking. A powerful calcium light had been placed in a distant part of the square in such a position as to concentrate its rays upon the bronze statue, illuminating it almost to whiteness, and projecting its shadow, sharp and black as a *silhouette*, upon the buildings behind. Sometimes a skyrocket would curve high up against the dark sky, and, bursting directly over the statue, descend upon it in a shower of sparks; at which the honest Germans, who are great M'Clellan men just now—would grasp each other by the hands, accepting the omen as one favourable to their nominee. The meeting was of a most enthusiastic character, indicating a considerable degree of popular faith in the new candidate for the presidency. I send with this a Sketch of the scene described above. The boys that figure in it are trading in M'Clellan badges, which they dispose of at fifteen cents apiece. A terrible accident occurred in the course of the evening, by the bursting of one of the calcium lights, which caused the death of at least two persons, fearfully scorching and maiming several others."

---

*(Sutler Gridley seemed to admire McClellan, but the general was often imprudent in his positions and many of his opinions went against government policy)*

Excerpt from the pamphlet: **The War for the Union – From Fort Sumter to Atlanta**

THE FIRST YEAR OF THE WAR   By William Swinton

As the chief force of the rebellion – the head and front of the offending – was collected in Virginia, it became a necessity to place here an army of proportions fitting it to foil the purpose of the enemy touching the capture of our Capitol, at the same time to drive the opposing force out of Virginia.

With this view a grand army of over 200,000 men was collected at Washington, and placed under the command of **Maj. General G.B. McClellan**, whose name, from a series of successful minor operations in Western Virginia, which another than he had planned and executed, had acquired a halo that did not properly belong to it. It was not until sometime afterward that the *constitutional inactivity*, which seems to be a part of General McClellan's nature, and that secret sympathy with treason that has always made him tender of hurting traitors, began to be appreciated, and hence it was for many months our armies were kept at a dead-lock, thus giving the rebels the opportunity to prepare their plans, and the rebellion its best ally, time, and we were put in a position of humiliation before the world.

*(General McClellan was not the only officer embroiled in controversy, interesting or heroic situations....on both sides of the war there were many differing opinions on the conduct of hostilities. There are numerous tales of those whose bravery is remembered.)*

**Moore's Rural New-Yorker** – September 27, 1862
McDowell vs. Brodhead
No one officer in our army has been placed in a more unpleasant position before the country than Maj. Gen McDowell. The following was written by Col. Brodhead, of Michigan, on the battlefield a few moments before his death, two balls having passed through his body. The original letter was covered with his blood.
Dear Brother and Sister:
   I am passing now from earth, but send you love from my dying couch. For all your love and kindnesses may you be rewarded. I have fought manfully, and now die fearlessly. I am one of the victims of Pope's imbecility and McDowell's treason. Tell the President, would he save the country he must not give our hallowed flag into such hands.
   But the Old Glory will triumph yet. The soldiers will re-gild its folds now polluted by imbecility and treason.
   John, you owe a duty to your country; write, show up Pope's incompetency and McDowell's infamy, and force them from places where they can send brave men to assured destruction. I have hoped to live longer, but I die amidst the clamor of battle, as I could wish. Farewell! To you and the noble officers of my regiment I confide my wife and children.

*(The above missive was forwarded to President Lincoln with a lengthy response from Maj. Gen. McDowell)*

**Richmond Daily Dispatch** – March 3, 1864 – Major-General
Pope's Fiction
Major-General John Pope, the prince of Yankee Tiara, is going to
write a history of his campaign, it's likely to be a good fiction.

**New York Times** – March 1864
News from Washington – General Meade's Conduct at Gettysburg
    The Committee on the Conduct of the War has been for several
days past investigating the conduct of General Meade at the battle of
Gettysburg. Generals Sickles & Doubleday have testified that after
the first days of fighting, General Meade wrote an order to fall back
17 miles, and but for chance a retreat would have been ordered.

**General Joshua Chamberlain** – Honored by US Medal of Honor
At the battle of Petersburg he was wounded, mortally....
promoted by pity for his death to Brigadier General, but fooled
everyone and lived to command under his new rank. On his horse
named Charlemagne, he accepted the Confederate surrender at
Appomattox.

**DEATH DID NOT STOP HIS PROMOTION** – Interesting News
from the Confederate States
Major General Daniel Smith Donelson, born in 1801, was a nephew
of President Andrew Jackson, graduated from West Point and
became a successful planter and the Speaker of the Tennessee State
Legislature. He served in the Civil War with the rank of Brigadier
General. The Confederate War Department promoted him to the
rank of Major General in 1863. However, after gallantly serving a
cause he believed in, he died of chronic diarrhea.....at least a week
before his rank was elevated.

**General Robert E. Lee**
The plantation home and land owned by Robert E. Lee was
confiscated by the Union armies. The property was transformed into
Arlington National Cemetery in 1864.

**Confederate News Article**

STEALING REDUCED TO SCIENCE

It is said that Sherman's thieving crowd surpass London pickpockets in their profession. They have thoroughly mastered their trade, that it is a thing next to impossible to conceal articles so that they cannot find them. It is useless to bury articles, especially metal as it is said that it is not an uncommon thing to see a rogue going about a man's premises trying every hole and corner with his ramrods in search of silver plate.

We are not informed by what means they find other articles, but presume their success is generally the result of long habit in their avocation. Sherman's "army with banners" is not such a terrible thing, but from Sherman's robbing corps the people may well pray "Lord deliver us."

General A. E. Burnside, best known for his unique facial hair, was not a particularly gifted soldier or businessman. So, postwar he became a politician.

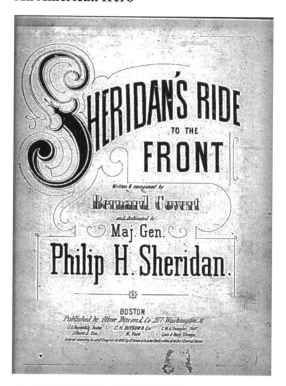

General Philip H. Sheridan

The personal headquarters flag of Philip H. Sheridan, spring through summer of 1862, when he led the 2nd Michigan Cavalry and rose from Capt. to Major General.
Photo of Flag Courtesy of Ron Katchuk

**General Philip H. Sheridan in the Shenandoah Campaign.**
"Generations of schoolboys in the Northern States have learned the lines beginning, "Up from the south at the break of day." This picture represents Sheridan in 1864, wearing the same hat he waved to rally his soldiers on that famous ride from "Winchester, twenty miles away." As he reigned up his panting horse on the turnpike at Cedar Creek, he received salutes from two future Presidents of the United States. The position on the left of the road was held by Colonel Rutherford B. Hayes, who had succeeded, after the rout of the Eighth Corps in the darkness of the early morning, in rallying some fighting groups of his own brigade; while on the right stood Major William McKinley, gallantly commanding the remnant of his fighting regiment – the Twenty-third Ohio."

**Richmond Daily Dispatch** – March 21, 1864
Lt. General Hood in the Saddle
"The Atlanta papers published the following extract from a private
letter from Lt. General Hood to a friend in that city:
"I am told some of the old women in trousers in our country fear
I am not in good health, and that I have to be tied or fastened on
my horse, etc. Since I came here I have been riding all over this
country with General Johnson and have been in the saddle every
day enough to have fought two or three battles without feeling any
inconvenience from it whatever. I ride with perfect comfort to
myself, and expect to walk with a cane before long. I tell you I am
in good health and as young as ever, and am ready and in as good
condition to fight a battle as I ever was; so do not trouble yourself
about me." *(Hood was the advanced age of 33 years in 1864)*

**New York Times** – March 1864
News From Washington – The Battle of Gettysburg
General Humphrey was again before the Committee on the Conduct
of the War to day. The committee are still collecting evidence
in regard to the Gettysburg battle. General Hancock has been
summoned to appear.

**Confederate Press** – Lynchburg, Virginia – March 1864
General Robert E. Lee
A friend who traveled with the General on his way down from
Gordonsville to Richmond says he has a very hale and vigorous
appearance and looks as though there were a dozen or more
good campaigns in him yet. He is a man of fine commanding
presence, six feet or upwards in height, and weighs probably the
rise of one hundred and eighty. But for his white beard, which he
wears entire but trimmed short, and his slivery hair, he would be a
comparatively young looking man, barely more than in the prime
of life. The General is affable, polite, and unassuming and shares
the discomforts of a crowded railway coach with ordinary travelers.
He travels without staff or other attendant. He is first to rise and
offer his seat to ladies, if any difficulty occurs in seating them. He
talks freely about affairs generally but had little to say at the time
we write concerning the army and the country. At one station
where an eager crowd were gazing at him he suddenly remarked, "I
suppose these people are speculating as to what is a foot now!" He

speaks quickly, sometimes briskly, and with the tone of one who is accustomed to command. His countenance is one indicative of more than his habitual tolerance and amiability would lead one to expect. He looks the stern soldier. The General is as unostentatious and unassuming in dress as he is in manners. He wore a Colonels coat (three stars without the wreath) a good deal faded, blue pantaloons, high top boots, blue cloth talma (cape) and high felt hat, without ornament save a small cord around the crown. Thus appeared our great chieftan, our hero patriot, our Christian soldier, our beloved Robert E. Lee as a rail road traveler.

*This song was so often sung that Maj. General Sherman grew weary of listening to the tune.*

## MARCHING THROUGH GEORGIA

Campaign of Maj. Gen. W. T. Sherman 1864 – Work's publisher, song writer, soldier, George Frederick Root

> Hurrah! Hurrah! we bring the Jubilee!
> Hurrah! Hurrah! the flag that makes you free.
> So we sang the chorus from Atlanta to the sea,
> While we were marching through Georgia.
> How the darkeys shouted when they heard the joyful sound!
> How the turkeys gobbled which our commissary found!
> How the sweet potatoes even started from the ground,
> While we were marching through Georgia.

"Sherman's dashing Yankee boys will never reach the coast!"
So the saucy rebels said, and 'twas a handsome boast,
Had they not forgot, alas! to reckon with the host,
While we were marching through Georgia.

There will forever be debate about the personality of General George Armstrong Custer. Although a West Point graduate, he finished very last in his class. During the Civil War his courage was tempered by his frequent distain for official orders. He was a fierce fighter, and a dashing young General, usually wearing a vibrant red scarf.....but the Battle of Bull Run in his history was overshadowed by "Custer's Last Stand" at the battle of the Little Big Horn where he and his men lost their lives.

Music dedicated to U.S. Grant – LOC

The popularity of General U.S. Grant was shown in the election of 1868 when he became president of the United States of America.

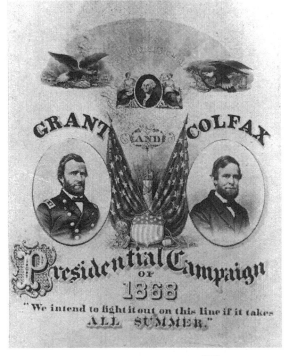

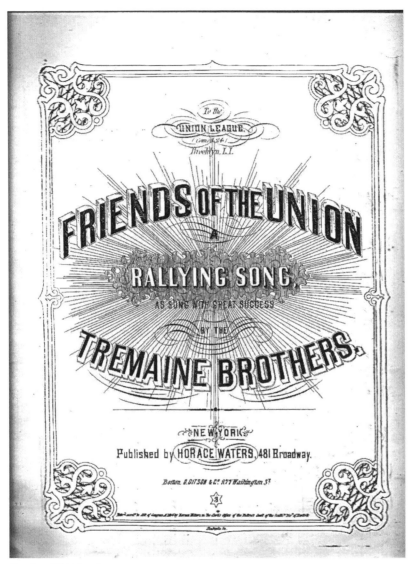

Courtesy Allen Sweet

Photo Courtesy of R. Katchuk

**December 6, 1861** – Albany, NY
From: Sarah W. Keeler – State Normal School, Albany
To: Francis A. Keeler
Dear Frank, I received your letters this week and one from Mary. I was so glad to hear from you that I shall answer them immediately. I am glad LeGrand has gone to Binghamton: I hope he will write to me. I sent him a paper yesterday. Yesterday there was public exercises at school; and my desk mate read a composition. I received a letter from Frederica and there were only about half dozen hard cuts in it. That is very few, considering. The school closes eight weeks from today. I wish you could come out examination week and bring LeGrand? You would be well paid for coming. Hattie would be pleased to have you. She spoke of it first. Miss Butler (teacher) says we ought to have our clothes ready as soon as possible; because during the last month we shall have to study all our spare time. Do you think our folks would be willing to get me a summer silk to wear the last day? I thought perhaps you

175

would get one cheap by buying it in the winter. If you think not, do not say anything about it but all the young ladies are going to wear light silks in the closing exercises that are to be in **Tweddle Hall** for the first time.

Write soon and tell me what you think about it! Do not show my letters to you to the connection for they will only gossip about them. I will do what you asked me to in your last letter. I think the Adelphic Union values their Bacon too high at 20 cents. I wrote to Sarah Kelsey last week. The Senate met in the Capitol Monday. I am going up some Friday evening to hear the speeches. I suppose it is very intertaining. I have a slight cold in my head but it only makes me sneeze a little.

I am going to write Grandma soon but, dear me, I owe five letters and guess they will not be paid in some time. A great many of the students went home the night before Thanksgiving and stayed till the next Monday; but I thought it would only make me discontented. I heard a regiment came last evening but do not know from what place. I have not been to school today as I sneeze too much so I have some time to write. Do not worry about the news you are to receive in a week; it was merly whether I passed out of my studies as I hope to do. I interrupted my letter to receive a call from Miss Johnson, a very pleasant lady. She attends the same Sunday School that I do. I guess all the young ladies in Candor will soon be married if they continue. I do not approve of it, however. There will be only six weeks vacation this winter, and begins in February. I am not going to get another bonnet this winter. Velvet ones are quite fashionable, trimmed on the top and flowers inside. I guess your cloak is in the exact style: at least, it is in Albany. Shawls are chiefly worn to school. The skating park is opened for the season and the ladies anticipate a splendid time. It is illuminated in the evening by colored lights. I do not have any time to go. Give my love to Father, Mother and all. Write soon for I like to hear from you often! Your affectionate sister    Sarah W. Keeler

The ALBANY STATE NORMAL SCHOOL opened in 1844 in an old rail road depot and in 1849 moved to a larger building in downtown Albany. Men and women each had their own private entrance to the school. During the Civil War patriotism was high and a Normal School company was formed from most of the men enrolled at the institution and their friends and family.

TWEEDLE HALL – Albany NY Normal School campus In 1861, Albany's Tweedle Hall hosted a meeting for conciliation, concession and a compromise on slavery. The wealthy families in the area generally owned three or four slaves, who, according to written reports, were usually treated kindly and lived and worked amongst the family. Graduation exercises for the Normal School were also held in Tweedle Hall.

ADELPHIC UNION – This was a student run literary society, probably founded in 1790's. It believed in expanding education by including many topics not included in school studies. The organization hosted debates, and discussions on religion, politics slavery, music, poetry and essays. Sixteen year old Sarah believed the 20 cent dues were too high.

**September 17, 1861** – Albany Normal School
My Dear Father,

I arrived here safe on Friday evening at eight o'clock and am at Uncle Henry Sacketts house    I have been down to the school and tried to get a good boarding place but I could not find many.  Uncle Henry does not want me to board down in the lower part of the city because he thinks the people are not very good and he wishes me to board at his house for two dollars per week and they will do my washing. I can find but one good boarding place and there I should be obliged to pay three dollars per week besides my washing. Do you think I had better board at uncle Henrys? It is only a pleasant exercise to walk from here to the school and I shall not have to go alone for there is a young lady in the next house who is going to The Normal School and she says she will call for me every morning. Please write soon and tell me which to do.

I wrote to mother Sunday but I have not had time to write any since till now. The school began yesterday morning and everyone says I have got to study very hard. Uncle Henry went to New York last night and will come back to night. Professor Cochran presented me with three pamphlets this afternoon; he is a very good teacher. Harriet is very kind to me she has taken me out walking every day. I like the city very much but sometimes I am lonesome when I think that I am two hundred and forty miles from you all. I took the eleven dollars that LeGrand got from Mr. Ward and the ten dollars that you left for me which made twenty one and I used $6.40 to come here with and I have got 14.60 left. I shall money and take the fourteen dollars for my board. I shall not need any more money in seven weeks. I must bring my letter to a close. Give my love to all of our folks when you see them and think kindly of your absent daughter.

Sarah W Keeler, State Normal School, Albany

**February 4, 1862**
From: O.B. Preston, Fort Lyon, Alexandria, Va.
To: Miss Frances A Keeler – Candor, Tioga County, NY Highly Esteemed Friend, You will doubtless be somewhat surprised at receiving a letter from me at this time but finding that I cannot find girls enough in Virginia to suit me, I shall have to come back to Candor & see them who I have no reason to consider less than friends…Hoping you

will pardon my presumption (if you are pleased to call it so) I will proceed with my letter…

I have been calculating to write to you for several months but no favorable opportunity has presented itself to me. Presuming you will pardon my long silence I will try and be more neighborly. We soldiers consider it as sort of a prerogative of ours to address anyone who we think enough of. And as I take it a particular privilege to write to you, you can use your own judgment about answering it but you must remember that if you do not answer this you need not look for any more from me. When I take a retrospective view of the past I recall with pleasurable emotions the many happy hours I have spent in your company. Yes Augusta be assured I enjoyed myself exceedingly well when at Candor and I hope to have the pleasure of seeing my old friends again…I have that neck tie which you presented to me & I intend to keep it to remember you by. What do you girls at home think of their soldiers who have left their dear friends at home, Fathers Mothers Sisters & Brothers to fight for our once glorious country & uphold the Star Spangled Banner? I think I can imagine how our Christian friends are praying for our protection and safe return…

But I have lengthened out this uninteresting epistle to a more extended space than I intended & I will close hoping to hear from you soon…..Please write soon. Your friend O B Preston
PS Direct to Alexandria Va., Co K 26th Regmt NYV

**Monday April 28, 1862** – Roanoke Island N.C. Camp Stanton
My very dear Brother Marshall, & Sister Julia how do you & your Father & Mother do? I hope you are all well. I hope my dear Father & Mother, Eustis & Lucia, & little ones, Howard & Viola, Uncles, Aunts & Cousins & all of my dear Friends are well. And my prayer to God is that it may be well with them & you that we may all meet again soon. My dear prescious Mother sent me in a box with Cousin Thomas things. A big cheese, a lot of cookies, & dried apple, eggs (but three of them got mashed) Letter paper, News papers, &c. I made some souse of the apple & finished eating of it this day noon. I have ate them all up now. I thank my dear mother a thousand times. Oh! But it choaked me all up – I could not help but crying – because my very dear dear prescious Brother B.P was not here to help me eat all those good things! I have not heard from him since I wrote to you & Mother last, but hope I shall quite soon

dear soul. I pray for him every day he is not killed, or wounded as I can see by the list. And I hope he is not sick. Oh that I could know that he is well & enjoying himself I would feel better about it. Newbern is 120 miles from here, Have you received your letter I wrote to you latest, March 30th or 31st? Has dear Father & Mother received a letter from me dated April 12th by Henry Sherwin. Ive received Mothers last letter & those papers. Cheese dried apples, cookies, eggs &c the 22nd of April. Give my love to my dear, beloved, prescious Father & Mother. I pray for them every day that their lives may be spared & mine that I can see them before long. I hope my prayers will be answered quite soon. Tell Father I will send him 40 or 50 dollars or more by Capt. E. H. Converse when he goes home to put away safe for me or he can use some of it. I will try & get that of Mr Chamberlain for him. I shall write to mother again about that time the amount of money &c that I send. Pay day comes off again quite soon the 1st of next month. I shall get quite a pile then with that I have got, I expect. I will write how much I sent. (if Capt Converse will carry it.) And how much I keep to my self. Give my love to my dear brother Eustis & Sister Lucia & little ones kiss them for me. Tell them I pray for them every day. And, Oh I pray for you all as one, dear ones, that God will spare my life & yours so we may see each other again soon. Give my love to my Brother Howard when you write or see him also to Viola. Tell him to write to me. Tess Eustis & Livia I have not received a letter from them yet. I wrote a letter to my dearly beloved & prescious Friend Rhoda Harper day before yesterday, & one to my dearly beloved & prescious sister Martha & Caleb yesterday, but I shall not put either yours or theres in the post office till after the 1st of May without there is a mail that goes before that time. I want to pick you some May flowers & send them. Peach trees were in blossom about the 1st of March, they blossomed quite full, apple trees are in the blossom now. **The 6th Regt NHV have been in one battle since we have been out here. There were 2 killed & none wounded. One was Curtis Flanders of Co. F. the other was in Co. G. I have not learned his name yet. They were 4 Regts went out in May, Gen. A. E. Burnsides expedition from here, N.H. 6th, NY 89th, NY 9th (Hawkins Zuaves) & Penn 51st, the Zuaves were badly cut up they made a wrong move, they charged upon them a mile off & got tired out & were beaten but our Regt. stept up in there near & fired one volley into them & they fell like hail stones**

& the rebels retreated instantly. **They got complimented very high from Gen. Burnside & other big officers, I have been in no battles yet neather have discharged a gun since I have enlisted, I am helping my country in a different way. I take care of the sick & wounded. I have been in the Hospital 7 weeks or more. I had rather be in the Brigade Hospital than in the camp on one or 2 accounts. I get a little more pay & a bed to sleep in.** May 1st, my dear Mother, Sister Lucia, and Julia & Viola, I wish you merry May, all of you. Julia wish your mother Wood for me give her some of the leaves & flowers if you please. I will give you a list of the leaves & flowers I send you. There is the Fig leaf, Apple blossom, Boxwood leaf & blossom, mint & other leaves that I don't know the name of. I must close now. I shall write to my dear Father & Mother next & Eustes & Lucia next. My love to all. Good bye for the present Dear Father, Mother, Brothers & Sisters all as one. From your most affectionate & loving Son & Brother Joshua T. Hunt

Roanoke Island, 1862, where the letter was written by Joshua T. Hunt

Map – LOC

The battle on Roanoke Island occurred in February 1862 and was captured by Union forces. Camp Stanton was established in 1863, named for Secretary of War Edwin Stanton. It was used for the recruiting and training of African American Soldiers.

*The next letter was written by B.P. HUNT, brother of the previous letter writer, Joshua T. Hunt. Although the letter was written after the Civil War, a photo was included with it of B.P. in uniform, playing the fife...he survived the war but civilian life was difficult for him. Both letters and photos are courtesy of R. Katchuk*

**Burrillville**
**August 17, 1868**
My Dear Mother
I dont know but you will think I have forgotten you. But I have not. I received the postal card that Lucia wrote. I ought to have ritten to you before now but have been sick about it. have so much on my mind, and so much in debt I do not know when I ever shall get up there again. Sarah, Ella, Amy have gone to the shore for two weeks. they went yesterday and I am left alone nights. I board up to Ant Marany's we are all well. I have not got but this half sheet of paper to write on now. Mother I got the letter that Martha rote to me when you was down there but did not answer it. It seems quite a task for me to write. I am so forgetful. I have got very poor memory since I fell off of the Church. My head troubles me some. I wish Julia Joshua and Howard would write to me. they do not write any oftener that what I do. Mother I will try to write more next time. Mother Jesus is just as good to me as ever he was. I do not live so near him as I ought to, but my trust is in him, he will keep us. I feel that he is the only one that can keep us if we trust in him. I shall have to get more paper to write on next time than here is, for I have

only just begun to write on this subject. I will try to write more next time, Mother I want to see you very much and all the rest of you, hope I shall sometime, must close now. God bless you all is my prayer. So Good By your poor son, B.P. Hunt

**October 3, 1862**
To: Miss Francis A. Keeler – Candor, Tioga Co. NYS
From: Truman S. North – Beltsville, Maryland
Friend Augusta, I take the liberty of addressing a few lines to you hopeing you will not be offended at it….if you are you can let me know and I will not do so again. **We are in camp 13 miles from Washington in a wheat field on a gentle side hill faceing the Rail Road that runs between Washington and Baltimore. Lots of cars running by here and lots of soldiers** passing to War, the boys are enjoying themselves as well as could be expected under the circumstances. We are all getting fat….just as fat as matches. There is not anything to write about here at all…it is one thing over and over here…in the first place in the morning we get up to roll call and then go to the creek and wash…then we have squad drill then go to breakfast…after breakfast we rest until nine o clock then we have company drill for to hours then the next thing is dinner… at 2o clock we have battalion drill that takes till about 5 o clock and then go on Dress Parade after that is supper by that time it is dark then we lay in our tents until 9 o clock then go out to Roll Call and then go to bed. The bed is the ground with a few Brush spread on it then a blanket…it is not like being at home and getting in to a good feather Bed but it goes verry well…sleep tip top…would like to be at home a few days and call in and see you Girls and have a nice little time with them and you too…I wish you would send me your photograph to me so I can see how you look….besides I want it because I would like to hav all of my friends so I can look at them once in a while and I take you to be one of them….I know that I am to you…Please answer this soon…do not show it to any body…it looks so I'm forgetting how to write…never was any hand to write letters…any way write all the news…give my respects to all…By the by I was down to Washington the other day and saw your friend Gridley… he was not feeling first rate at that time…saw Fred Parmele…he is first rate…getting fat. I do not think of any thing more at present so I will close…give my respects to Sarah & Legrand. From your true friend…Direct to Truman S North Co. C 109th Regt, WDC NYV

CAPTAIN JAMES HOPE – soldier, teacher, ARTIST,

1818-1892, was born in Scotland, brought to Canada in 1827 by his widowed father and shortly thereafter became an orphan, apprenticed himself to a wagon maker in Vermont, attended Castleton Seminary for two years, and did not hone his natural artistic talent until an injury disabled him for several months. He painted his own portrait and thus received many commissions, but continued to earn a living teaching at Casselton Seminary. In 1841 he married Julia M. Smith. By 1852 he was established enough to open his own art studio in New York City where he spent winters for 20 years. When the American Civil War swept the land he recruited a company of soldiers and was made Captain of Company B, 2nd Regiment of the Vermont Infantry where he served for 18 months. Participating in numerous battles he sketched the war from a first-hand perspective. While seriously wounded he viewed the Battle of Antietam and recorded the bloody field in pencil. Returning home, he did paintings of his war drawings some on massive canvasses. His wife remained in Vermont raising their children even during his sojourns to NYC....until 1872 when the family moved to an area near Watkins Glen, NY.

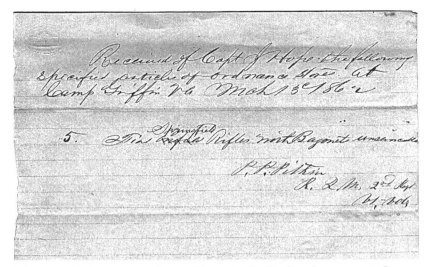

*This receipt is to Capt. James Hope in 1862 when he presented five Springfield rifles to the Quartermaster of 2nd regt. Vermont Volunteers.*
Photos of THE BATTLE OF ANTIETAM, By Hope & portrait of James Hope, LOC

**January 28, 1862**
From: C. L. Terwilliger – Camp 109th NY Vols –
**Near Petersburg, Va.**
Friend Menzo, I received your of the 22nd this morning and was glad to hear from you and learn that you all was blessed with good health. Well Menzo, it found me well and hardy but is vary cold down hear, now at present and begins to look much like winter now but thare hant any snow hear but cold enough to make that all up. you spoke of good sleighing up thare, how I wish that I was up thair this winter to have some fun and enjoy myself with you and the rest of the young folks agoing out a sleigh riding and going to your Singing Schools and other places of amusement. I think that I could pass the time off much better than I can in the army, for thare haint any place to go hear and have any fun.

only once and a while go out on the **Picket line and have some fun with the Johnies and then that don't go vary well sometimes for thay git mad at us and commence to gun us and then we let in to them with some shells and then thay haf to dig fort their whales and hide till we quit shelling them and then thay will come out again as thick as Black Birds all a long the lines and once and a** while some of them will come in our lines and give them selvs up and go north to live with the Yankies for they ar tired of fighting and so am I for it is hard business to maike a living at, don't you think so?

you say your folks has sold and what is the caus of that, have you got tired of farming, I got tired of that a long ago and went to war for a change and it hant the nicest place in the world so just as long as you can keep out of it do so for thare is nothing like freedom to a man when he goes to war it is like going to states Prison for a while, but I hant got long to stay any way and when my time is out I will stay out of it and try. Well I dont no of anything or any news to tell you this time that will be of any interest to you. I must tell you that since I last rote to you that I had bin promoted to Orderly Sergt of the Company and I dont know but I will soon be higher than that for every thing is working favorable for me now, well I will close for this time in hopes of hearing from you soon again, give my best respects to all of the folks, no more this time, very respectfully yours, C.L. Terwilliger

Challenge at the picket line

### June 2 (probably 1862)
To: Sarah Keeler…From: Eliza E. Limbold – Brooklyn, Michigan
My Dear Sarah, I have looked long & anxiously for a Letter from you but as you perhaps know have received not a word, & after due consideration have finally concluded to write again, just six months since I wrote you. What can you have been doing all this time? for six months is time enough for a great many changes. I am at home now & shall remain here during the summer, wet weather all things jurminating. I shall go back to Kassin Institute where I have been

the past winter & half of the spring terms. I liked it very much & formed many pleasant acquaintances & friends, but none whose friendship I value more highly that I do that of yours, you do not know how many times I have read & reread those kind friendly letters of yours......

Everything remains about the same with us yet, we are farming of course but Pa is not able to work but very little, has the Rueumatism so he is obliged to walk with a cane. Ma is well but very lonely as we all are. Pa feels as though he had lost his staff & support & has little courage to do anything. We have an Irishman who does all the work. Charlie & george are going to school this summer. Charlie has grown to be a large boy & grows to be like John every day. He has a thousand little ways that often remind us of John but he is to sickly & poor & we sometimes tremble for fear that he too will be taken from our family circle. George says he remembers Augusta well because she used to hold him & talk to him.

THIS WAR has created great excitement around here. Ma is very much interested & if it were not for the petticoats I do not know but she might volunteer & join the army. You know she was always quite a politician but the funniest of all is James is down in Miss. & we received a letter from him a few days since by which we see he is a CESESSIONIST. I hope he will not join the Southern army. I hardly think he would unless he was forced to. Pa has just come in & I must bid you good by for this time for I suppose he has a letter for me. Hoping to hear from you very soon I remain yours with much love & esteem......Eliza T. Limbold  PS  Give my respects to all, kiss the little ones for me, my love to Augusta & yourself.  Ma sends love.

**To: Cousin Shedy** From: Your Cousin Joe
Dear Cousin Shedy, I received yours of the 18th today and was very glad to hear from you. I hardly expected you would be well enough to answer my letter when I wrote. So you see I was agreeably surprised for the last I heard of you was that you were very low. I am so glad you are not so poorly as reported. As for unworthy me I am well in as good spirits as ever. I am glad Cousin Nelly is there for she will be so much company for you. She is not one of the dull kind, she can make time pass pleasantly. I know by the tone of her letters. You wished to know if I have seen Jeff Evans, I

saw him the day before the last battle was fought. He was there at
ALEXANDRIA and was well at the time. I have but just returned
from an expedition up the Potomac river only we wernt up as far
as Edward Yessy with a military train and was gone five weeks
and came back all right, although this WAR IS DANGEROUS to
encounter. We are at our old camping ground near the **Navy yard
in D.C.** and probably I shall stay there till another battle. As there
is no news to write I will close. Your cousin Joe Write as soon as
convenient, I give my respects folks.

Unknown heroes of the Civil War

**March 12, 1863**  To: Sister, From: Charlie
Dear Sister, Mothers letter of the 9th inst. I received yesterday and
as I have a chance to answer it now I will do so. For some days we
don't yet get a chance to write. I have been lucky enough to only
be detailed twice to work two hours at a time while w......etc. but
some of the boys have had to go to work pretty near every day It is
quite likely that next Thursday we will have a full Co. and be sent
to Harrisburg thare to be assigned to some Regts. we don't know
what one yet. It does not seem as if by next 4th of July you would
be a married woman and I should rather it would not be so, you cant
find any one only James Dickinson but use your own judgment. I
did not mean to say anything about it (knowing if I did it would be
of no account) but I hope you will enjoy yourselves at any rate. If
you leave home we will have to hire someone.....at all events. Tell

mother not to work any more than is good for her health for she has yet got $100 to dispose of and then it is quite probable that we will get another hundred dollars LOCAL BOUNTY. By the way W.G. Sterling told me when I was coming away that he would be ready to pay Edwards bounty in two or three days. I forgot to tell you when I wrote. Send me all those photographs I have in that box. If there is no other way send by mail one or two at a time. My health has been very good and all the boys ditto. Give my regards to the Jones & Dickinsons (Jim included) and any one else who inquires after me. Tell Gene to write for after he gets to following the plow his fingers will get hard and stiff and he cant write as well as he can now. Write soon, I am as ever your brother Charlie

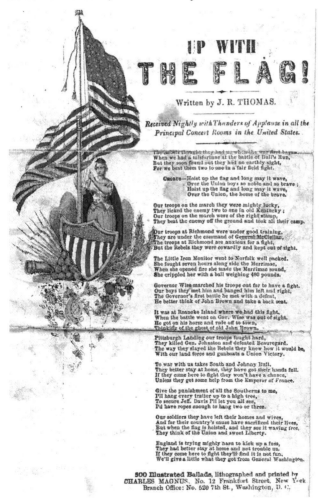

*Letter above written on the back of BALLAD by J. R. Thomas "UP WITH THE FLAG"*

**January 3, 1863** – From John V, Camp near Bellofkin……..
(Part of letter to Brother Isaac & part to Mary V.)
Dear Brother, I now seat myself to answer your most kind and
welcome letter which I received last knight on 6th. You did not say
weather you was well or not nor enny the rest of the folks. I write
you a letter new yesterday and was very much under the weather but
I am some better now and I hope that these few lines will find you
all well and in kicking order – well Isaac, you wanted to no what
to do with my money if I never come back home again from war.
Isaac if you want my money till I come home or till you find out
weather I am kilt or I am taken sick and dont get well you can keep
it. I think that it is safe as long as you have it. If you don't want
it you can give it out to some man that is good for it, as if it were
your own. Or Isaac if I never come back I want you should take
my money and divide it among my own folks, give an equal share
to Eleanor and Mary Jane and Uncle Daniels wife and kids and you
keep equal share for yourself. It won't be but a little to each one
but it may do them some good but I hope that it may be my happy
lot to live to come home to see you. **I think that this WAR will
close this winter but I am afraid that it will not. I am tired of
this campaign. I have been fiting the REBS long enough for this
time and for any other time. It is very pleasant down hear and
we dont have it very hard down hear. All we halve to be is we
halve dress perade at half past 3. All that takes about one hour.
So no more at present. So good by, John V.**

Well Mary I wish I could have been up there to visit Uncle
William with you at Christmas and visit the forestvilles. If Elecity
Rogers and Edison Parker is married I hope that someone will
cut the bed cords (rope) and let them down and give them a good
hazing. If I was up there I would do it myself and put them to bed
and tuck them up good. Ash Richards and Joseph Richard is well.
Edwin Gile is well. BS Sanders is well so no more at present, so
good by, write as soon as you get this…..this from John V. to
Mary V.

Sugar Shack

**March 25, 1863**
Dear Brother I got your letter on the 23rd and was glad to hear from you and to hear that you was well. Don't you worry about home, try and take care of your self until you come home then we will have a good time. Boys is down to the sugar camp boyling sap. They got to barels yesterday. You wanted me to make you some sugar cakes. Take care of your self till you come home and I will have them cakes ready for you. We don't hear any thing about the WAR at present, it seems as if they aint a going to do nothing rite away, only keep our men down thare and let them dye. You must rite all the news – you must be a good boy and keep your nose clean. I wish you was hear. Good by,

**May 28, 1863** (Pennsylvania)
Dear Friend, I seat myself to pen you a few lines to let you know that we are yet a live and hope you are. I begin to think that you were a sleep. Our folks has got their potatoes planted and is planting their corn today. Your folks have got every meadow and every field on the old place plowed up except the hog paster and it the hogs has rooted up that so bad buckwheat can be sowed without any plowing. We heard last night that VICKSBURD was taken. How true it is we do not know. I hope that it is the case, the word came to Titusville about a week ago that RICHMOND was taken and they bought fifty eight dollars worth of powder here and they shot and carried on all day and some of them did all night and they said that they was hardly a man in town but what was drunk. Hugh is over to daves Shearring his sheap. They took theirs and yours to Sporty yesterday.
I must close for the present so good by  F. P. Kerr

*The surrender of Vicksburg with over 30,000 Confederate troops, to General Grant in 1863 was cordial. The meeting of Rebel Pemberton and U.S. Grant to discuss terms of surrender was conducted with courtesy, salutes and handshakes.*

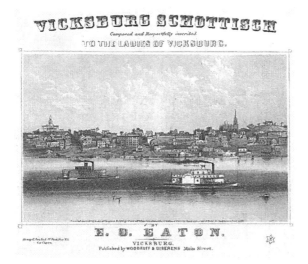

*The Vicksburg Schottich was music composed in 1865, in honor of the Ladies of Vicksburg for their perseverance during the American Civil War.*
LOC

**Moore's Rural New-Yorker** – August 9, 1862
THE WAR'S PROGRESS – Facts, scenes, incidents, etc.
IMPORTANT **FROM RICHMOND**

The following statement by a gentleman of Essex Co., Massachusetts, who has resided several years in Richmond and who has lately returned from that city, as published in the "Boston Traveler." The people of Richmond are confident of the final success of the Confederate arms. This confidence is increased by the result of the late battles and they have more confidence than heretofore in their Confederate currency. Before the battles it required 250 of their shinplasters to buy a dollar in gold, but when he left he exchanged their notes at the rate of $2 for $1 in gold. The only kind of property that does not rise is the slave property. Negroes sell nominally for about the same as before the war, but owing to the currency they are really not worth more than one third or one half their former value.

*Hay fields in Candor*

**March 25, 1863**
To:  C Kerr –
Sutler – 169th Regt.
Co. C. Glancester
Point, Va. % A.
Davile
From:  Hiram,
Dear Cam, I
received a letter
from you to day
and was glad to
hear.  The rest of the folks is all will, I wish you was hear to help us
in the sap bush this spring, it would be more pleasant to have you
hear than it would be to have you a weigh down in the land of Dixie.
You said that the rebel calvrly came up to your pickets.  Look out
for them, they are feisty sharp fellows.  You don't now when to trust
them.  I herd that the president has cald for six hundred thousin
more men.  If they take that many more men I don't now what some
of the people will do.  **You must hery and come back by the time
the draft takes place.**  Miller Belknap has got the long ferlow.  He
has gone the way that a good meny that has gon the same road that
he has gon.  His funrel sermon is a goin to be preachd two weeks
from mondy at the chapl by Scofield.  We boiled us to barals of
sap to day and sugared up.  There hant bin much of any sap yet but
it bids fare for a perty good run of shugor this spring.  The rods
is giting very bad a bout now and is broken up we cant hardly git
along the road.  Was hard times out hear this winter.  HAY is from
$25 to $30 dollars, a..?..is $200 and $250 a hundred.  Corn $5.50
doller a bushl, flour $17.50 and $18.00 a barel, pork barel $17 and
$19.00 dolars, butter 20 cents, tobace $100 a pound.
Your folks are giting a long first rate with ther work and all looks
first rate.  You must not have any trouble a bout your things for they
get through.  You need not worry for if any thing happens I shall rite
and let you now all a bout it. You must be a good boy and take care
of your self through the danger that is a round you.  Think of the
welfare of your self if you hapen never to return to your friends on
the earth.  Ther is a beter world than this if only you are prepared for
that day and then you will escape.  HIRAM

**November 1, 1864** – From: Sara Keeler – New Rochell (Mamaronack, NY postmark)

To: **Mrs. Frances A. Gridley** – West Candor, Tioga Co. NY
Dear Sister, Last evening I received a letter from Father and one from Rose each bringing the welcome intelligence that you had a son, and that you were well as possible under the circumstances. No one could be more glad that I am. I wish I could start right off and come and see you. It seems as though I was just the one to come & stay to be company for you. But my school will close Thursday the 10th and I shall be home the Monday after. Wish Cad joy for me a thousand times and kiss the young gentleman for his aunt Sara. Don't name him till I come home. Every morning I take a long walk before breakfast and one after & feel much better for it during the rest of the day. Last Friday it rained and wet me to the skin before I got to school, and had to run home in the rain. So I cought a bad cold which has ended in a cough. "MARYLAND, my Maryland," is a free state today for the first time. The cause of Liberty is advancing!  This morning just as I returned from my usual walk, saw Henry Cornell who came down to tell us that there would be a meeting at the Quaker church, and two speakers there from the west. I went and heard them and besides one of the quaker ladies. Mr. Henry Cornell escourted me home with his fast horse, and just nicely cut out our young trustee Mr. Tompkins. I was sorry for I like Mr. Tompkins best, for he is not such a prodigious flirt as they tell me Henry Cornell is.

Mrs. Richard Cornell, our trustees wife says she will not let me go home, for her children are doing well and she wants me to be here and go to the parties this winter. I saw Miss Barnes last Sunday who said she would introduce me to some very fine young ladies of her acquaintance, and that I would find the society very pleasant, but now that I have made up my mind to go they cannot tease me to stay. Ida Carlow has been in Rockland County nearly three weeks, and I have been very lonesome without her. She is now in the city, at Sarah Sullivan's and will return in a day or two. LeGrand is coming down here at the close of the term, and we will shop a day or two in the city. Is there anything you would like to have me get for you there? If so, send word & I will do my best to get it. Tell Cad not to forget to **VOTE FOR ABRAHAM**, and do all he can to defeat the **COPPERHEADS**. I was very sorry to hear that Roswell Woodbridge was dead. What an affliction to his wife and children.

I have a thousand questions to ask about the friends at home but will let them go till some other time. And now, love, and kiss my nephew for me and let me hear from you soon, Ever your own Sara, PS Ida has just returned. Excuse this writing as it is dark.

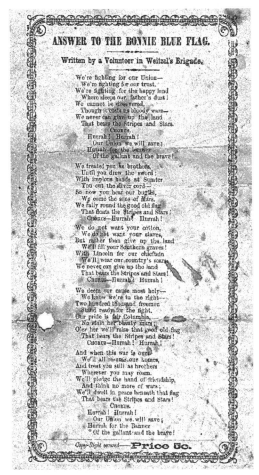

**Sunday Evening December 13, 1863**

In Camp near New Iberia, Louisiana

Dear Sister, its with pleasure that I take the present opportunity of writing you a few lines to let you know of my helth which is verry good at present and hoping this will find you all enjoying the same blessing  it has ben a long time since I have wrote you a letter a very long time and it has ben so long that I am amost ashamed to write but I will do better for the future and would like to keep up a corisspondance with you.  I have wrote a number of letters to Turing and have received a number of letters from him.  I think that I have not ansred the last one that I have receivd from him.  Well I have been in the service now about Sixteen months and I have seen some thing of the war and a little of hard ships but I have got a long very well so far.  I have enjoyed good health most of the time we are now in camped near the village of New Iberia La about 130 miles from New Orleans La we are laying here in winter quarters  how long we shall stay here I can not tell but I think for some time yet.  I receive letters from my wife most every mail she is well and our little boy he is getting to

195

be quite a boy. I received his likeness a few days ago we call him after Father Ruben B. Smith he is now tow years three months old. And is a fine looking as you can find any whare I wish you could see the little fellow your self I am in hops the time will come when I can bring the little fellow to Killewog and show him to you. I would like first rate to hear from Lib. I wish you would write to me and let me now her address so I can write to her. How does Peter and Mary get along. I have had a little coraspondance with Orson. I got one letter from him and anserd it but have hurd nothing from him since. Well I will have to tell you some thing about the money I save in the company. I sent home all of the money that I have drawn from the goverment and for the last four months I have made 7 dollars a month extra making $20 dollars a month and in the four months $80.00 dont you think that is pretty well for me. I think I shall be able to save enough while in the army to buy me a house and lot of my own if I have the luck to live till the war is ended and I mean to. I commenced this letter last evening but I did not have time to finish it there is a order for the regt to be filled by recruiting, one non commisioned officer    Is to go home for that purpose, there is need enough of it as our regt is geting small. Well Ann I hardly know what to write there is but little news a stiring in this part of the world. I do want you to answer this letter tell Almeda and Truing to write to me. I will agree to ansuer all of the letters any of you will write me. Be sure to write and let me know Elizabeths address so I can write to her. Give my respects to James and to Almede, Annett Wuring also to O. W. Smith and family and to Peter Young and family also to Alexander Philps. This from your ever loving brother. PS Direct Co E 114 regt NY Vol New Orleans La. Jos Smith
*This small paper, "Answer to the Bonnie Blue Flag," cost 5 cents, was mailed to Truing Hitt in December 1863 From J. Smith of Company E 114th Volunteers then located near New Iberia, Louisiana*

**January 3, 1864** – Greene, NY
Dear Almedia, I received your most welcome letter and were glad to hear from you I have written to your Mother once but received no answer so I thought best not to write any more. I am well as usual I have kept house all the time since Joseph went away to war, till the first of November and now I work for my board with Reuben I like it better, this winter wood cost so much I have to pay ten shillings

for stove wood by the cord. If I got a good place I think I will work for our board next summer it's the cheapest for me. Little Reuben was two years old in September. . He sends all his money home to me. He was wounded in the battle **at Port Hudson** on the 14th of June the buckshot went in his head over the left ear. It hurt his head considerable, I saw a man that come from there he said Joseph had been shot in his head, now he said it made him crazy for some time. I have not had a letter since the last battle. Joseph is in the 19th army corps under (Maj. General) Franklin Banks division under Col. Perka, Captain Dedira, he is in Louisiana they have been to Texas and returned back again, I gineraly got a letter once a week but I have not had one in over two weeks now. I will make some inquiries about a school for you the schools around here are engaged for the summer. The woman I work for now has two children and Mr Coven tends the mill, I would like to come out there but I think you might or some of your folks come and see me, I should be very glad to see you, the stage from the forks comes every day here. Direct letters to Joseph S. Smith Co. E 114 Regt. NY Vol, New Orleans Louisiana. If he is not thare they letters will follow the Regt. He would be glad to here from you I know he would. I hope you wont forget to write to me again so good by this from your Aunt Eliza
Phebe E. Smith, Chenango Co. NY
Give my love to all the folks taking you a large share for your self
Alimedia C. Hitt

*The battle of Port Hudson resulted in 5,000 Union casualties and 7,200 Confederates. Although the Union forces won this conflict the cost in life was massive.*

**Illustrated London News** – February 8, 1862 – The Confederate States
Richmond reports the arrival of the **British steamer GLADIATOR** at Savannah and the Confederate Steamer Vanderbilt at Charleston, both vessels having run the BLOCKADE. The former vessel, which had been waiting at Nassau for some time, was laden with arms, stores and clothing.
*(Steamers were used effectively by both sides of the conflict.)*

**March 11, 1864** – Franklin, Louisiana

Dear Nephew, Once more I take the pleasure of writing you a few lines to let you know of my health which is very good at present hopeing this will find you and your folks all well. We are still encamped at Franklin but we expect to leave here soon as we have all things ready for a march. Our wollen blankets and sutch things that we could not carry on a march hase been boxed up along with our large tents and sent to New Orleans. I think we shall go as soon as Monday. The 13ᵗʰ army corps that were to go with us arrived her I think it was yesterday and are encamped near here at present. **To regments of negro soldiers passed here to day they are commanded by white commission officers, they made a good appearance and are well drilled. They done some good fighting at Port Hudson and all they want is good officers to lead them** on, we expect go from here to Shreveport whare we her the rebs are pretty well forty fide. I hear that we are to have as many as 15,000 cavelry to go along with us if we drive the rebs from Shrevport. I think we will go from thare to Texas but time will tell. I am in hopes to have some good news to write in a few weeks. The weather is warm and pleasant the fields are green with the new blades of grass and the treese of the forest have put forth thar new leaves. We can here the mocking bird singing his merry song from early dawn till sun set oh what a beautiful country this is and I would like to live here among orange trees if it warnt for this wicked rebellion that is bringing poverty and starvation to the inhabitants of the land whare it rages. Tring I wish you would write and let me know whare to address a letter to your aunt Lib so I can write her a letter. I have hurd nothing from her in a long time. I received a letter the other day from Alexander Phelps and was pleased to hear from. He talks of having an un common smart boy. How is O – Tring how does the copper Jacob prosper in Killowaog and how did the Election go. Write me all the particulars what has become of Theadore Yarington is Fred Yarington married yet. John Preston girl is married to a man in my company by the name of Wm Newby. If you see any of Johns folks tell them that Newby is well give my love to Annett and all of the children and to your father and mother. I will write a gain when thare is any thing new to write about. Please excuse the mistakes and bad spelling, this from your friend and effectionat Uncle Jos S.Smith

**October 13, 1864** – Tibles Plantation

Dear mother I now set down to write you a few lines telling you that if you do not stop writing such letters I will not write at all    I have not been in a batle nor more that I do not expect to. we are in the reserve corps. I have not even seen a reble only what was a prisoner. you hear of our being in a batle long before we are knowing of it. I prefur the suny south in preference to the windy north. we have weather here that would make hay up in your county. the leaves ar on the trees like July in your county. now I want to know how you or father gets along with the tannery. tel father to fix the old mil up right so when I come home that I can run it. how is butter and factory cloth. I herd that butter was 23 c and coten cloth had folen off 30 c on a yard.  how does most like that if that is so.  tell all the boys to write and I will as soon as I can.  I have not been home sick at all but if you do not stop writing such letters I shall not be at all.  I like it here first rate. I got a letter from Uncle Pettr this morning and one from Nettie. I have writen to Arhley. now I want to know whether you have had eny rain up ther or not. I had forgotten thet mony thet I borrowed of Charles Phelps....yes I saw father when I came by Killawag.  Buter is 75 cents a pound here sugar 22.  Some of the boys have got the disentry so bad that they turn up and shit over 5 rows of tents and turn out hardtack.  **I want you to get a piece of hemlock bark and scrape the inside of it out that that has got the strength and send it in a leter fine like powder for stop the shits.  I have not got them yet.** I want you to stop worring about me. I am near the south site rail rode  but thare is more than 30 thousand men in front of me I am a coming home again that so I don't feel the least bit alermed about it our men captured a spy Sunday morning and he is to be shot to morrow he diserted from our lines and went in the rebels lines a then cam back and got a map of our bristworks and was a going with them when our men got a hold of him  when I came up the James river they was **a steamer** just ahead of us but our steamer cought up with her. she had on board a lot of sailers and I saw Sammy Brooks on her and I got up on our vesil and talked with him acrost. I little thought of seing him thare. he said thet he was a going to Getty point.  I tolt him thet I was a going to the same plase.  now don't believe every flimsy report that you hear.  I sent for the Marathon Meror my self.  paid a dolar and a quarter for a year so that you could git all the news about us.  Welle writes for the paper he is with us all the

while. all the old headlines say they they will not be eny fighting after the election. all the able soldiers cry Old Abe and he will be elected. I had a bout as leave go in a batle as not as soon as our men get the south side railrode they ar whipped. we ar in a bout 3 miles of it. now for mercys sake don't write another such a leter  as you did last. send Aunt Libbies address so thet I can wrote to her how darnt low I look in my photygraphs. I have not found nothng yet but what I can put up with very well. has the crick raised so the old mill could run eny. the 109th is with in a bout a half a mile from here. I have seen some of them they say thet Fernando Runge was killed ded on the spot. thet is all I can think of now so good by. yes I had a blanket stole up to syrecuse but I dont kned them at all.  my bunk mate is Arnold Bunnal  as good a fellow as ever breathed
Jerry Hitt
*(The above letter was written without any punctuation or capital letters, but some have been added to make it easier to read.)*

**September 5, 1864**
*From **the London Herald, reprinted in the Richmond Times*** **Dispatch**
The independence of the Confederate States is a fact accomplished……..

## 11  DRUGS – SUCH AS THEY WERE

*During the American Civil War many thousands of solders lost their lives due to battle wounds.  Illness, diseases and accidents claimed as many lives as bullets.  A man had about one in four chance of surviving the hostilities.  Typhoid fever killed both blue & gray more often than battle injuries.*

*Wounds to arms and legs almost always resulted in amputation and infection.  Poor sanitation, fevers, sunstroke, dysentery, scarlet fever, smallpox and many other diseases added to the death toll.  Medical officers did their best with the tools and medications available.  However, it was often patent medicines whose main ingredient was usually alcohol, home remedies and whiskey, that were in great demand for illness and comfort.  It was common for solders to request home remedies from family and friends, such as the October 1864 request for* **hemlock bark** *to cure diarrhea.*

*(Camp Stevenson, Ala. was established as a medical facility and refugee camp.  It was also a vital railroad link)*

Camp Stevenson, Ala.  **March 27 (1864)**
Dear Sister, As I have time to write some to day I thought that I would write to you.  I am well and hope this will find you all the same.  **Three of the boys in our company has got the mumps and some more of them begin to complain of sore jaws and I think Milt Knox is going to have them.**  Sol Darling and John Winner was here day before yesterday and staid one day and one night with us.  They expect to work near Chattanouga.  Sol agreed to write to me as soon as he could and let me know where they are.  Tom Swan is at work near where we was incamped in wanhatchie Valley and is incamped on our old Battle field, he is here this morning he said that he came up to see the boys and then he was a going back.  Tell father that I dont get more than half of my papers now and when I do get them they don't get here till some time after the other boys get theirs.  So I wish he would have it stoped entirely for it dont pay to have it come in that way.  I should like to have the paper well enough but I want it to come when it should, the other boys that take the same paper get it nearly a week before I do.  I have not received the paper that Granma sent yet.  The weather here now is very warm an pleasant the snow did not last long, and the ground is getting about dry again.  I have not got any war news to write.  You see in

the papers that Gen Grant has command of all of the U.S. forces and that Smith has command of the Potomac army. things look now as though this corps will be likely to stay where it is this summer at least we hope so. I have not much more to write this so I will close.
from your Brother Ira
Letter courtesy of R. Katchuk

**New York Times** – July 1862
The "Surgeon at Work" introduces us to the most painful scene on the battle-field. Away in the rear, under the green flag, which is always respected among civilized soldiers, the surgeon and his assistants receive the poor wounded soldiers, and swiftly minister to their needs. Arteries are tied, ligatures and tourniquets applied, flesh wounds hastily dressed, broken limbs set, and sometimes, where haste is essential, amputations performed within sight and sound of the cannon. Of all officers the surgeon is often the one who requires most nerve and most courage. The swaying tide of battle frequently makes him a prisoner, and sometimes brutal soldiers will take a flying shot at him as they pass. Upon his coolness and judgment depend the lives of a large proportion of the wounded; and if they fall into the enemy's hands, military rule requires that he should accompany them as a prisoner. An arrangement has lately been made between General Howell Cobb, of the rebel army, and Colonel Keys, of the army of the Potomac, by which surgeons are to be considered non-combatants and released from custody as soon as their wounded are in the hands of the surgeons of the enemy.

**March 1862** – New York Times – Soldiers Relief
Protect your health. No sensible man will leave the city without a supply of Holloway's Pills and ointment. For wounds, bruises, sores, fevers, and dysentery these medicines are the best in the world. Every English and French soldier uses them. Only 25 cents per box or pot.

**Union News** – 1863 – Dr. Sweet's Liniment, advertised as the "Soldier's Friend," could be used for both human and horse.

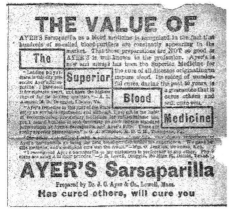

**Ayer's Sarsaparilla,** prepared by Ayer & Co., Lowell, Mass. Price $1 per bottle: six bottles in one package $5. Sold by all druggists everywhere. For strumorous, & scrofulous complaints, expelling foul humors and eruptions and ulcerous sores. It will cleanse out the vitiated blood!  1863

*This dark bottle contained a home remedy, the small corkscrew was necessary to open the container.*

*Clear glass Cupping jars were used to draw the ill humors from the body.  Heat bottle, place on skin mouth side down, create suction & blister of blood will form.*

**Richmond Virginia Whig** – January 25, 1864
A new remedy – The Surgeon General (CSA) at this city wishes to acquire a supply of the roots of the plant known as Side Saddle Flag, for use as a cure of smallpox.  It grows abundantly in South Carolina.

*Another request to folks at home, found in these vintage letters, was for a supply of SMART weed. Used as a dye for clothes it was said to repel insects, or as infusion in alcohol for coughs, or chew the roots for toothaches, or with vinegar to thwart gangrene.*

*In the letter of March 21, 1862 Francis Keeler discusses her experience having teeth pulled. The procedure was probably done with a tool similar to this.*

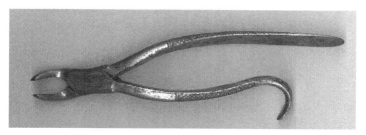

**Forged steel Dental Extractors used from the 1800's through the Civil War era and beyond.**

Often dental problems were dealt with by itinerant practitioners who learned by experience, or not. Barbers, veterinarians, blacksmiths or druggists were frequently called into service to attend teeth of human and animal alike. The instruments were rarely cleaned between uses. Many dentists were apprentice trained others self-taught. After the Civil War there were still only three dental schools in the United States. The most common method of treatment was extraction. Fillings were composed of gutta percha, lead or less savory materials. Pain control, when available, consisted of alcohol consumption or opium concoctions or perhaps cloves packed near the offending tooth. If fear of the procedures did not incapacitate the patient there was always infection and/or shock that might deal a deathly blow.

**Rebel News – October 1862** – North Carolina
There are now 86 new cases of yellow fever
**New York Times** – December 30, 1863 …there are three hundred cases of small pox among Union prisoners at Danville, Virginia.

*The need to invent modern medical treatments for injured soldiers led to some bizarre apparatuses....*
*The Wonderous Aesthetico-Neuralgicon*

*1864 – Medical discovery by homeopathic system of medicine. This device introduces medication into every tissue of the body, through the nose and will* absolutely cure all ailments. *It consisted of numerous suspended tubes & jars, pumps and sprays and filled half a room.*

*Chloroform and ether were used, when available to abate the pain of amputation. However many soldiers still died from lead poisoning, and other infections. Germs were more of a danger to life than firearms, and claimed many casualties.*
*And perhaps, at times, the most modern of medicines were dubious cures, but time often heals*

**Forestville –** September 26, 1864
Dear Cousin, I received your letter this evening I acknowledge I aought to have written sooner We are all in good health Father is as well as he was before his illness He had no Dr took no medisine I dressed his foot three times a day I had not the least hopes at the time I wrote to you of ever seeing him well again He was ninety two years old the fifth of last March Yours, ASG

**Southern Confederacy – Atlanta, Ga**. July 1, 1861
Medical Purveyors Office
BARKS WANTED! The best prices will be paid for the following barks: Stem, branches and root of dogwood (root preferred), branches and root of white willow; root, trunk and branches of American Poplar (called also white wood, canoe wood and Tulip tree), roots preferred. These barks must be carefully dried and securely packed. They may be brought to this office or sent to Mr, L. W. Waller, Botanical agent Cartersville, Georgia
George S. Blackie, Surgeon and Medical Purveyor – CSA

## 12   WAR STEEDS

During the War of the Rebellion it is estimated that more than one million horses and mules were killed.  In Gettysburg alone three to five thousand perished.  The equine sacrifice is noted in numbers, along with the count of soldiers who died in battle, on many monuments in Gettysburg National Battlefield Park. Horses and mules carried the war – soldiers – goods – arms – ambulances – "war rode on the backs of the equine population."

General Hooker at Chancellorsville, May 1862... riding a seasoned war steed

*General Robert E. Lee was almost as famous as the horse he rode throughout the Civil War.  For five years "Traveler" was a constant in the life of the Southern General........the horse lived to be 29 years old.*

**The New York Times** – July 18, 1861
1,000 DRAUGHT HORSES WANTED
Suitable for the Quartermaster's Department. They must be strong and sound, between 6 and 8 years old from 15½ to 16 hands high, and calculated to endure hard service; none others will be inspected. Apply at the Howard Stables, corner of Grand and Mercer sts. R.N. Eagle, Captain of Cavalry – Inspecting and Purchasing Officer

**Salt Horse** – The army mandated daily ration of 20 oz. of salt beef or salt pork....but was packed in strong brine so long that men could not tell what meat it was supposed to be so they called it horse.

**Moore's Rural New-Yorker** – October 18, 1862
***In St. Louis, on Tuesday Week, some Secessionist miscreant mixed poison with the horse provender in the Government stables. Between 50 & 100 horses have died

***General Robert E. Lee has sent a dispatch to the widow of General Kearney, promising the return of her husband's horse and accoutrement

*Since the beginning of hostilities, the Sanitary Commission advocated the formation of a special Ambulance Corps, when implemented the corps saved many hundreds of lives. United States Generals objected saying such vehicles would be very unmilitary. In 1862, Secretary Stanton agreed to the proposal and the Sanitary Commission efficiently provided horse drawn ambulances, proving their worth on the battlefields of Antietam by conveying wounded soldiers, both blue and gray, to medical care.*

**The New York Times** – July 1861
............Heavy draught horses exchanged hands at $125 & $150 each. Government agents have purchased 41 horses at an average of $122.50 each. Their limit for the best is but $130 each and horses must be 15 ½ hands high, sound, active, an average weight of 1,100 pounds, long tails and dark colors preferred. Those purchased were for baggage wagons and artillery. Dealers and farmers can find a ready market for this class of horse as there is a requisition for 1,000 head at the quoted prices.

**New York Times** – July 11, 1861
NEWS FROM CALIFORNIA by the **PONY EXPRESS**
Fort Kearney, Wednesday, July 10
The Pony Express, with the following summary of intelligence for the Associated Press, passed here on the 8th inst. At 11 P.M.
.....There was a fair demand for money for Monday's steamer, at easy rates. The next eastern bound steamer will be the St. Louis which goes armed with two fine brass pivot guns and a Dahlgren

gun, besides small arms, sabers, and all the necessary preparations for making a vigorous defense in case of a hostile attack....

The news since the departure of the last Pony Express is unimportant.

............The **San Barnardino Patriot** of the 22nd represents that Secessionists are recruiting all through the tier of Southern Counties. Mexicans are being enlisted and every one who can raise a horse is busy drumming up recruits............

**The Evening Post Weekly:** New York – November 1861
PURCHASE OF HORSES
The testimony shows that the horses purchased for the army, in a majority of instances are of the most inferior kind and have broken down or fell dead on the road......
**REPORT** on file:
The undersigned having been summoned as a board of Survey, to examine and inspect the condition of horses forwarded to this regiment from St. Louis and report the result to your headquarters, would respectfully report that we have examined said horses and find 76 fit for service, 5 dead, and three hundred thirty undersized, under and over aged, stifled, blind, spavined, and incurably unfit for any service, said horses being a part of the Missouri contract.
Very Respectfully, David McKee, Major, George Rockwell, Captain John Schee, Lieutenant:

The committee has testimony of over half a million dollars sunk in hay contracts. The quartermaster paid $17.50 per ton for hay in bales which on examination is found to be prairie grass and hay of a very poor quality..........Hay from stacks and in abundance along the route could be obtained at $6 to $8 per ton..

**Moore's Rural New-Yorker** – February 8, 1862
Since last June there have been purchased in Maine & carried out of it to the war about two thousand horses.

**MORE BEASTS OF BURDEN**
**Richmond, Virginia Whig** – January 1, 1864
Camel Train – A train of camels is running from the Humboldt salt mines to Virginia City, packing salt for the Humboldt Salt company.

This is found to be a cheap mode of transportation. Each camel is able to pack from 800 to 1000 pounds. It costs nothing to keep them as they will fat on sagebrush and greasewood, and the deserts which are so hard on horses & mules, are just what they thrive on.
**San Francisco Mining Press**

\* Jeff Davis, the horse, was the Civil War mount for General U.S. Grant.

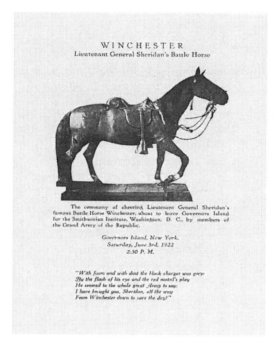

WINCHESTER
Lieutenant General Sheridan's Battle Horse

The ceremony of cheering Lieutenant General Sheridan's famous Battle Horse Winchester, about to leave Governors Island for the Smithsonian Institute, Washington, D. C., by members of the Grand Army of the Republic.

Governors Island, New York,
Saturday, June 3rd, 1922
2:30 P. M.

"With foam and with dust the black charger was grey;
By the flash of his eye and the red nostril's play
He seemed to the whole great Army to say:
I have brought you, Sheridan, all the way
From Winchester down to save the day!"

*General Philip Sheridan's war horse was famous for carrying the general on their "ride to the front." In 1862 the officers of the Second Michigan Cavalry presented a Morgan horse about 16 hands, to Sherman at Rienzi, Mississippi. For a time the horse was known as Rienzi. After their ride from Winchester to Cedar Creek, Va., General Sherman renamed his horse Winchester. The spirited gelding was wounded four times in battle. Winchester died in 1878 and was preserved by a taxidermist. His form now resides at the Smithsonian Institution in Washington, D.C.*
LOC

Many Civil War photos do not have details attached, however, the photo to the right is an exception. Thanks to the Charles Howard family, their relative Clark Kellison, a private in the West Virginia Cavalry, has been remembered. He served under General Averill in one of the first battles of the war in 1861, Philippi West Virginia, and Droop Mountain West Virginia

in 1861. He was discharged at Fort Kearney, Nebraska where this photo was taken. Private Kellison looked as regal as a general on his own horse, and later honored General Averill by naming his son P. Averill Kellison.

**FINAL STATEMENT** – documents
Soldiers Mustering out of the Union Army – Pay request
**#2** – If the soldier is entitled to pay for the use of his **horse**, the Company Commander will certify to that fact, and also to the time he has pay due for having been so mounted on his own horse.

**New York Times** – August 1863
Report from the front
.........the mules did their work nobly, as did also the men mounted upon them, and the success of the experiment was so great that the regiment have used their mules in all expeditions since.......

## 13  CIVIL WAR DRAFT AND DODGERS

*Many letters throughout this volume comment on the draft, bounties, and draft dodgers. Therefore news accounts, music and documents are included giving a glimpse into realities of the era.*

*Conscription into a fighting force has never been popular and the Great War of the Rebellion was no different in this respect. There were four major drafts for the Union army and constant recruiting. State quotas had to be met and bounties were offered to encourage volunteer enlistment. Recent immigrants to the United States were nearly "shanghaied" into being immediate patriots. In 1863 the US Congress issued orders to draft all mem between 20 and 40 years of age, with exemptions for those who could find substitutes or pay $300. July 1863, there were four days of draft riots by crowds of more than 50,000 in New York City.*

**August 11, 1864** – Stamford, Canada

Dear Madam, By request of your husband I write to you. On the second day of August Peter left our plase with the entintion of going home and told me if you or his Brother write to him to answer the letter and tell you off him. Peter was an excellent hand on the farm and I was sorry to part with him. But he got most terible Home-sic and made up his mind to make you a visit at all hazards, thinking he could do so in safety and if ABE should get him he would not keep

213

him long on account of the lameness in his hip.

If times seemed suitable he intended to work away as usual in some by place and dodge the **LINCOLN SPIES.** Peter done this thing with the best intention. He wanted to be nearer his family and command higher wages in order that he might be of service and help you to get along during this terible war. This is about all I can say. I hope he got home in safety for your sake.

His brother wrote him the Third of August advising Peter to stay in Canada by all means if he knew when he was safe. Tell John we got the letter and that hay is worth $15 dollars per ton, dry goods are ranging higher than usual. Calico for dressings or ladies dresses is worth from 15 to 25 cents per yard. Cotton shirting ranges from 20 to 30 a yard and so on. The WAR effects prices in Canada as much as at the same rate per cent as it does you, the only difference is the percentage on money. Tell Mr. Burger that Duke Bell got something like seven dollars from Peter.

PS I should like to have you answer this note that I may know if Peter is safe and sound. Yours Truly, Ralph Kuler

**New York Times** – August 20, 1862
**MILITARY Ads – Army Substitutes!**
United States Army Substitutes Association
No. 67 William St, corner of Cedar
The Association has completed arrangements for providing substitutes for persons who may be drafted into the Army of the United States under the recent orders of the Secretary of War. Books are now open at the office.
W. A. Greenleaf, Secretary

*The following words are from 1861, when the Confederacy was looking for suitable recruits and leaders to serve in the military. The thought is also relevant for today:*

**Southern Confederacy** Newspaper – March 1861
Spirit of the Times
…….the miserable plan of bringing up a child in the habit of dependence upon others now shows in all its blank absurdity. What is such a one worth in the current great crisis that has dawned upon our nation.

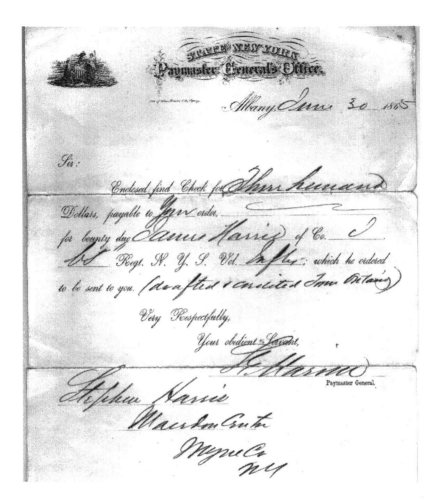

**Bounty Payment Certificate**
*Protests, Draft Riots in New York City, tricks, subterfuge and escape*
*to Canada were used to avoid the War Between the States. Legally*
*escaping conscription could also be accomplished by paying a*
*substitute to serve in lieu of a man, although the Union Provost*
*Marshall General soon had to establish a "Military Equivalent"*
*directive stating that a "negro is not the military equivalent of a*
*white man and cannot be substituted as such in the draft." Several*
*letters in this volume comment on those who "ran" or tried to do so.*

**Moore's Rural New-Yorker** – January 1862
An embalmer is being tried in Richmond for smuggling persons
liable to conscription, sending them North in coffins.

**The New York Times** – August 20, 1862
THE DRAFTS TO FILL THE FIRST AND SECOND
         Requisition of 600,000 MEN
The undersigned for $100 insures parties against drafts
in the State of New York. If drafted will furnish a substitute
according to law.        D. P. Webster, Insurance Broker
Office No. 212 Broadway, Room 6
ARMY SUBSTITUTES – US ARMY & NAVY BANKING &
SUBSTITUTE OFFICE
The undersigned has completed arrangements for providing
SUBSTITUTES for a limited number of persons who may be
drafted into the Army of the United States under the last order of
the Secretary of War. Advances made on Quartermasters' vouchers,
Contractors' and Recruiting Officers bills and Officers' pay roll.
RICHARDS KINGSLAND, Army and Navy agent, No. 4 Broad St.,
one door from Wall St. NY

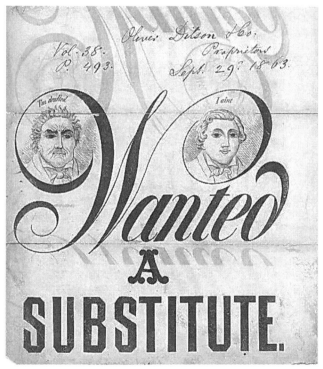

*Civil War music, "Wanted A Substitute," dated 1863, expresses the
dissatisfaction of draftees for the substitute System, whereby those
with cash could purchase their way out of serving in the war. The*

*drawings on the cover show an unhappy draftee "I'm drafted," and an obviously wealthy man proudly proclaiming, "I aint."*
LOC

**The New York Times** – August 1862
MILITARY – $20 A MAN!
TO Recruiting Officers – $20 apiece will be paid for the right kind of men to-day and to-morrow, Apply to Capt. ISAAC P. LOCKMAN (late first Lieutenant Co. H. Ninth Regiment NYS M) No. 78 Bowery, from 10 to 12 AM and at No. 83 Nassau from 1 to 3 PM

**ARMY SUBSTITUTE ASSOCIATION**
No. 168 Broadway – This association is prepared for the payment of $100 dollars to guarantee a substitute in case they are drafted; the money so paid to be deposited in the hands of some well-known banker with the stipulation from them that it is not to be used for a ny ot her pur pose. R eference of t he highest c haracter given. A.W. Platt for the Association

**The New Bounties** are NOW ALL PAID $90 in ADDITION to the regular pay. $20 OF IT IN CASH soon after the swearing in. $40 of it when the regiment is full. RELIEF TICKETS, worth $3 a week given immediately to families. Uniforms at once, and good quarters on Staten Island with fine bathing and fishing. $100 Bounty, or 160 acres of LAND at the end of the war, which will probably close within another year. $2 PAID DOWN to any one bringing in a recruit when he swears in.
Experienced officers and the best treatment guaranteed.
Apply at No. 183 Essex St. NY to Capt. WM. W Badger & Lieut. Charles Livingston

**The New York Times** – Wednesday, August 20, 1862
US QUARTERMASTER-GENERAL OFFICE
Three thousand dollars have been subscribed by the clerks in the United States Quarter-master General's office #6 State Street to encourage enlistments in the city. From this sum a reward of $30 each is offered to one hundred men volunteering into one or more of the regiments now in the field.

**The New York Times** – December 30, 1863
The US secretary of war has decided not to allow agents from the north to recruit colored soldiers in the District of Columbia. If any are obtained they will be credited on the quota of the district.

STATE OF NEW JERSEY,
EXECUTIVE DEPARTMENT,
Trenton, June 8th, 1864.

CIRCULAR.

It has been officially intimated that a call will soon be made for 300,000 additional men to serve for three years or during the war. I am informed that, in anticipation of this call, the enrollment lists of the several sub-districts are now being revised.

In many districts the former enrollment was imperfect, and injustice was done the people in the assignment of quotas upon such incorrect lists. In most instances errors were brought to the notice of the State authorities too late to procure the proper correction.

It is important that the municipal authorities of the several cities and townships should inspect the new enrollment before it is returned, and have all inaccuracies corrected.

The names of non-residents, aliens, persons deceased, those under or over the required ages, those exempt by reason of physical disability, and those now in the Army and Navy, should be erased from the lists.

JOEL PARKER.

**The New York Times** – August 1863 **JUMPING THE BOUNTY**
The thieves, petty gamblers and vagabonds, generally of this city, have been operating in those sections of this and adjoining states where the draft has been enforced, by offering themselves as substitutes, being accepted, they receive the three hundred dollars, are mustered in, and become part and parcel of the army.....this is no sooner done than they, in their own parlance, "jump the bounty"......pocketing the money and playing possum to Uncle Sam, and escaping from his service and custody forthwith.

**Moore's Rural New Yorker** – November 1862
The Stuben New York Courier says that one local man walked 40 miles to claim exemption from the draft on the grounds of inability to endure long marches and the hardships of camp life.

**The Philadelphia Inquirer** – August 1861
BOUNTY LAND WARRENTS TO BE GRANTED TO THE
SOLDIERS
Mr. Colfax (Ind.) gave notice of a bill to be offered at the opening of
the next session, granting to the soldiers of the present war bounty
land warrants on Government lands subject to entry at one dollar
and fifty cents per acre, and granting homesteads to actual settlers
on the alternate sections of land reserved from railroad grants, and
subject to entry at two dollars and fifty cents per acre.
Mr. Vallandigham (Ohio) from the Special Committee appointed
at the last session, reported a bill restricting the franking privilege.
The House then adjourned.

STATE OF NEW-YORK,
County of _____

## NOTICE OF ENROLLMENT.

Sir :—Take Notice, that you have been enrolled as liable to do Military duty in the
_____ Regimental District of this State. If you claim exemption for any
reason, you must file a written statement of such exemption, verified by affidavit, in the office
of the _____ Clerk of the _____ of _____
on or before the fifteenth day of August next.
Dated at _____ this ___ day of
_____ 1864.

_____
Enrolling Officer.

**New York Times** – December 30, 1863
NEWS OF THE REBELLION
.........**In the Rebel congress measures of a desperate nature**,
prompted by desperate necessity were being speedily framed
and adopted.  The house passed a bill to prohibit the circulation,
and trafficking United States currency; also a bill **abolishing the
system of substitutes in the army,** and compelling those who have
furnished substitutes to enter the army in person, at the same time
holding on to the substitute.

**Moore's Rural New Yorker** – CONGRESS
*(as usual)*This body has done as yet little that is worthy of note.
Notices of a number of bills have been given, among which is
one to abolish the $300 clause of the Conscription Act, which will

probably be passed, and the introduction and discussion of several resolutions. Congress will again adjourn from Thursday of this week to the 6th of July. (as if there were no war)

*The last six words and the first two were penciled on the article by the sender, and included in a letter.*

"LET THE STARS AND STRIPES BE WAVING O'ER THEIR GENEROUS SACRIFICE."

*Decoration Day was originated after the American Civil War when the Grand Army of the Republic set the date aside as a time for the nation to decorate the graves of the war dead. The last Monday in May is now known as Memorial Day and is a federal holiday. In the early part of the 1900's postcards such as the one above were sent to friends and relatives to honor the day of remembrance.*

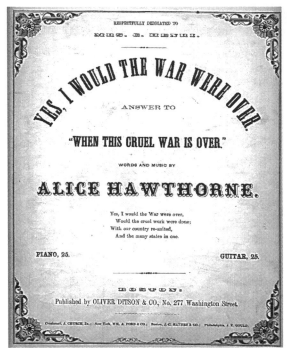

RESPECTFULLY DEDICATED TO

**YES, I WOULD THE WAR WERE OVER.**

ANSWER TO

**"WHEN THIS CRUEL WAR IS OVER."**

WORDS AND MUSIC BY

**ALICE HAWTHORNE.**

Yes, I would the War were over,
Would the cruel work were done;
With our country re-united,
And the many states in one.

PIANO, 25.                                    GUITAR, 25.

Published by OLIVER DITSON & CO., No. 277 Washington Street.

**March 22 –**
East Maine
Cousin Almeda it is
with pleasure that
I write you a few
lines it is Sunday
and we have no
meeting to day and
are all well we got
home safe    found
our folks well    we
have heard from
Enoch and Silas
they were well and
are not coming
home maybe never
I feel very lone
some for I was in
hopes that I should
see them this
Spring but I must give it up and think it is all for the best

**I do hope this wicked war will end** before long so our children
and friends can come home but we shant live to see that day but
may we all be prepared to meet whare we shall part no more in a
world where ther is no WAR nor troubles

About the school Mr. Barnum has inquired they are all engaged
and there are more teachers then schools    I am very sorry for I
should like to have you teach some where near us for I think you
would like it    Almeda you must come and see us    give my
respect to your folks tell them the cousin are all well    from your
friend Maria Barnum, PS  Write to me as often as you can and I will
answer    Direct East Main Broome Co NY
R N  Silsbee Meshoppen,  Wyoming Co  Penn.

**Moore's Rural New-Yorker** – March 12, 1864 – News in Brief:
*Wisconsin is enlisting Indians to fill her quota
*Nearly 90,000 veteran volunteers have re-enlisted
*The war costs about a hundred thousand dollars an hour
*Thirty-six Indiana regiments have re-enlisted as veterans
*The people of Chicago have organized a Fuel Saving Society

\*Some 400 soldiers leave Louisville Ky. Daily for Grant's army
\*There is about $80,000 now due the army of the Potomac
\*The Sanitary Fair at Buffalo is closed and has netted $30,000.
\*Coal is selling at Elmira, NY at six and three quarters a ton
\*The Mississippi Valley Sanitary Fair will commence on the 17th of May
\*General Pope, preparing an active spring campaign against the Indians in the North-West
\*About 200 freedmen a week are enlisting at Chattanooga. They come from Georgia, and Alabama in squads of from five to twenty

**December Sunday 21, 1863** – New Woodstock
My dear friend    at last I have found time to write a few lines to you to let you know that I am well and hope this will find you the same.  I don't know what to say for my long absence but I presume you will excuse me.  I have got through working out and am now at going to school    we have a very good school.  I like very much and I am leaning to I think. we have a lady teacher this term    I worked out all summer and liked it very much  Nelson has inlisted in the Army a gain and has gone in the cavlry and William Walker has inlisted in the Army  he is not gone yet but is a going soon    they are a going to get a large bounty  Nel has got some of his now and has sent it home    Billy Wood has been home on forlough    he came home through  Killowog on the cars    he has grown to be a nice young man and **a good soldier**  we was all very glad to see him all hated to have him go back to war a gain but what cant be cured must be indured.
We have all got to write compositions up to our school next week I don't like it very much    have written one and I think that was enough but she said we must  write them a gain    I guess we will have a spelling school this winter we have not had one yet  I was very sorry to hear that Ophelia was dead and Nettie must have felt very bad because they was both such good friends    Orson goes up to school this winter and Carrie goes and she is a learning very much at last she is very hard to learn and her eyes are so poor that it hurts her to read long but this teacher takes a great deal of pains with the little ones and with Carrie and don't have her read long so she learns faster than would of if was not for that  Our folks are all well all that is to home and ma sends her love to you she often says

what a good girl Amelda is, oh how I would like to see her  Nettie is
a going to be nother a pretty girl I think she is awful pretty  her hair
curls all over her head and she is just as charming as she can be  it
was a year ago last Sunday that Frank was war killed     it has been
a long year to us  we are so grateful glad you called your baby boy
Frankey but ma said she hopes he wont never have to go to war  Ma
dreadful hated to have Nel go to war  she didnt know he was a going
& never thought of such a thing until he inlisted and then it was to
late for her to do eny thing  Ma sends her love to all the folks and
says to tell Anne to "write to me when she can and then I will write
to her"  I would have written you be fore but I have not had time as
you know    I have to write for she cant and she wants often to write
the boys  I don't know as I can think of eny more  excuse all the
mistakes  my  pen is not very good  so I will close good by
From your loving friend   ...   Meliss Wood

**Uniforms, Citizens Attire & Accoutrements**
Music courtesy of A. Sweet

Some of the most elaborate and distinctive uniforms of the Civil War were worn by Zouave troops. Patriotic envelope with a Zouave waving the United States flag

**The New York Times** – August 1862
The Excelsior Brigade
The splendid new uniforms provided soldiers of Sickles veteran command have acted as a first-class advertisement for the brigade, and brought in shoals of recruits. The recruiting camp in the City Hall Park is crowded all day long, and all the organizations in the field, the Excelsior seems – next to Duryea's Zouaves – to be the most popular.

*The ideal uniform for Union soldiers was a distinctive blue so as not to be confused with the Rebel Gray. In reality soldiers wore an eclectic mixture of civilian and military garb.*

*UNKNOWN HEROES*

*Many photos of the Civil War era show well dressed women in wide hoop skirts and dashing, fully uniformed men. However, life for the average person was far different. There was a shortage of cash and fabric at home and in the military. Both North and South suffered, but a letter to Gov. Vance of North Carolina gives a poignant assessment of the situation:*

**October 11, 1862**
From: Lt. Col. S. H. Walkup (commanding)
48th Regt. N.C. Troops – Camp near Winchester, Va.
Govr. Z. B. Vance

I lay before you for your consideration the destitute condition of our regiment with the hope that you, who have experienced some of the severe trials of a soldiers life may hasten up the requisite relief. We have present six hundred & nineteen men rank & file in the 48th Regt. NC Troops. There of that number fifty one who are completely & absolutely barefoot & one hundred & ninety four who are nearly as bad off as barefoot & who will be altogether so in less than a month. There are but two hundred & ninety seven blankets in the Regt. Among the 619 men, which is less than one blanket to every two men.

In truth there is one Company (I) having 66 men & only eleven blankets in the whole company. The pants are generally ragged & out at the seats & there are less than three cooking utensils to each company. This sir is the condition of our Regt. Upon the eve of winter here among the mountains of Virginia, cut off from all supplies from home & worn down & thinned with incessant marchings, fighting & disease. Can anyone wonder that our Regt numbering over 1250 rank & file has more than half its number absent from camp & not much over one third, 499 of them fit for duty? The country is filled with Stragglers, deserters & sick men & hospitals are crowded from these exposures. A spirit of disaffection is rapidly engendering among the soldiers which threatens to show itself in general straggling & desertion if it does not lead to open mutiny.

Add to this that our surgeons have no medicines & do not even pretend to prescribe for the sick in camp, having no medicines & you have an outline of the sufferings & prospective trials & difficulties under which we labor.

We most pressingly need just now is our full supply of blankets, of shoes & of pants & socks. We need very much all our other clothing too, but we are in the greatest need of these indispensable articles & must have them, & have them now. Otherwise how can the Government blame the soldier for failing to render service when it fails to fulfil its stipulated & paid for contracts. A contract broken on one side is broken on all sides & void. The soldiers of the 48th NC & from all the State will patriotically suffer & bear their hardships & privations as long as those from any other state, or as far as human endurance can tolerate such privations, but it would not be wise to experiment to far in such times & under such circumstances as now surround us upon the extent of their endurance. With Lincolns proclamation promising freedom to the slaves, what might the suffering, exhausted, ragged, barefoot & dying Non slaveholders of the South, who are neglected by their government & whose suffering families at home are exposed to so many evils, begin to conclude? Would it not be dangerous to tempt them with too great trials?

Dear Sir, I feel the very earnest & solemn responsibility of my position as commander of this Regt. At this critical period & under these trying circumstances & wish to do all I can to remove the evils by seeking a speedy supply of blankets, shoes & clothing & therefore beg your earnest attention to the premises & I hope efficient aid to supply our necessities.

Your Excellencys most obt Servt.

S.H. Walkkup Lt. Col.    48th Regt. NC Troops

*Shortly after this letter was received by Governor Vance, he made public appeals to the citizens to help "clothe & shoe the soldiers," because the government could not do so alone.*

Brass buttons on both Union and Confederate jackets often indicated the solders home state and the unit in which they served.

**Southern Confederacy** – Atlanta, Georgia – March 12, 1861
**SHORT HAIR FOR LADIES** – Several Northern ladies have been advocating through Godey's Book the adoption of the fashion of short hair for ladies. We are sure no Southern lady will allow her head to be shorn of the glory of its fair length..........

*The photo came with a tattered letter fragment*: "I expect we will join the regiment soon; I am sick of being dogged around so much. We cant get enough to eat and what we do is not fit to eat. Those of us with money find victuals in the saloons. There is someone playing the violin in camp & it makes me think of home."

*Rebel attire often included **Secession Cockades**. Thousands of hand sewn rosettes were made by women in the south. The emblem was usually worn on a soldier's hat or jacket and each rebel state had its own version. Patriotism eventually led to putting the item on wagons, horses, walls and slaves.*

## Chicago Times – 1862
A woman attired without hoop skirts has been seen in E. Tennessee. She was a Seech.

## Moore's Rural New-Yorker – October 1862
The city Railway Company of Chicago proposes to tax the luxury of crinoline expansion.
*(To be fashionable by wearing huge hoop skirts it would cost extra to travel by rail.)*

## The Chicago Times – July 1862
A literary lady of New York says that Gen. Butler might have found a better way of reaching the rebel women of New Orleans than he employed. He should have taken with him a quantity of fashion magazines, and appealed to their tastes; the most savage specimen of female rebeldom would soften at the sight of a new hoop, the improved *tournure* of which, after being blockaded for a year and a half, she would be able at once to appreciate, and would wilt right down at the touch of a new French bonnet or mantilla.

*The Singer Manufacturing Company of Pittsburg, Pennsylvania, produced uniforms for the Union army. One of their slogans, seen on the Wagon above was: "We clothe the Union Armies while Grant is dressing the Rebels."*

**Moore's Rural New Yorker** – March 1862
So many frauds have been practiced by **clothing contractors** that Secretary Stanton has ordered their pay stopped

**Southern Confederacy**, Atlanta, Georgia – October 20, 1861
RAGS – save all your rags, cotton flax, hemp, &c., and send them to market where you can realize three cents a pound. The South wears out more such goods than two such Norths, yet the North saves double the quantity of rags for making paper. Let this be changed hereafter, save the rags to make paper and thereby make money.

Military invoice for overcoats and blankets dated 1862

**New York Times** – December 1863
**The Prisoners and Stolen Overcoats**
Yankee overcoats kept shady since the exposure of the large
extractions from the Yankee repository for the Yankee prisoners
in Richmond. Numbers of persons have purchased the coats from
someone exhibiting them for sale and were flattering themselves
they had obtained great bargains at from 40 to 60 dollars apiece,
when they were astounded by the intelligence that every person
found with a garment of this kind in his possession would be made
to account how and by whom he came by it. Yankee overcoats
became suddenly scarce, and there was not one in the market. The
dyers, we learn, are overrun with orders to dye them......changing
them from the hateful Yankee blue to the less suspicious black.

## CONVALESCENT SOL-
## DIERS.

WE publish on page 721 an illus-
tration of CONVALESCENT SOLDIERS
ON THEIR WAY TO JOIN THEIR
REGIMENTS, from a sketch by Mr.
J. A. Oertel. He writes:

"The subject struck me when I
saw it as one of interest in the present period. Washington just now
is very dry and dusty, as I have
indicated in the sketch. The soldiers were under escort. This is
military fashion. They were on
their way to the railway station near
the capital, and belonged to different regiments, representing nearly
all the States, and were in every
variety of garb. You will perceive
they are not in Broadway fashion.
The soldier who has seen service is
a different looking object from the
trim gent he was when he left
home."

The thinned regiments of the
Army of the Potomac which returned from the Peninsula in September last have been considerably
recruited by the arrival of convalescent soldiers from hospital. At
one time there were 20,000 soldiers
sick and wounded in the great military hospitals at Newport News
and Fortress Monroe—at least so
said the newspaper correspondents.
Now these hospitals are comparatively empty. Wounds have been
healed, and the bracing air of October has dispelled the fevers engendered by the Chickahominy malaria.

**Harper's Weekly** – September 1862
## THE FIRST VIRGINIA CAVALRY

We publish on page 612 a fine picture of the First Virginia Cavalry one of the crack regiments of the rebel service. Mr. Waud writes: "Being detained within the enemy lines, an opportunity occurred to make a sketch of one of the two crack regiments of the Confederate service. They seemed to be of considerable social standing, that is, most of them – F.F.V.'s so to speak, and not irreverently; for they were not only as a body handsome, athletic men, but generally polite and agreeable in manner. With the exception of the officers, there was little else but homespun among them, light drab-gray or butternut color, the drab predominating; although there were so many varieties of dress, half-citizen, half-military, that they could scarcely be said to have a uniform. Light jackets and trousers with black facings, and slouched hats, appeared to be (in those cases where the wearer could obtain it) the court costume of the regiment. Their horses were good; in many cases, they told me, they provided their own. Their arms were the United States cavalry sabre, Sharp's carbine, and pistols. Some few of them had old swords of the Revolution, curved, and in broad heavy scabbards.

"Their carbines, they said, were mostly captured from our own cavalry, for whom they expressed utter contempt—a feeling unfortunately shared by our own army. Finally, they bragged of having their own horses, and, in many cases, of having drawn no pay from the Government, not needing the paltry remuneration of a private. The flag represented in the picture is the battle-flag. White border, red ground, blue cross, and white stars."

## 15  SPECIE CONCERNS

*During an era of war soldiers, government and citizens at home all had to survive on reduced access to funds.*

*TAX – to help pay for the War of the Rebellion the United States instituted the first income tax in American history. A total of 3% was charged on all incomes over $8,000.*

*In 1862 the government issued greenbacks and "shinplasters" as coin of the realm. The Shinplasters were paper fractional currency of low denomination. Metal currency was slowly withdrawn from circulation and the metal used to produce war implements.*

*In December of 1862 the Union government suspended all SPECIE payments so there was no ability to exchange paper money for gold or silver. The ban lasted until 1879.*

*The Confederate states began to produce "Graybacks" before the first shots were fired. However, this currency was not guaranteed by the solid worth of precious metals. Eventually this resulted in massive inflation. The South also had difficulty printing their notes as quality printers and engravers were scarce. Nearly all the southern currency stated it could not be redeemed until "after the ratification of a treaty of peace between the Confederate States and the United States."*

*Sutlers were quick to capitalize on the reduced cash situation by coining their own non official government coins. These "tokens"*

*were privately minted specific to each sutler and could only be used at that sutler shanty. Die cutters were in great demand to produce the nearly worthless coins, usually valued about one cent in trade. All tokens could be used as currency. Not only were there sutler coins,* but patriotic *and store coins proliferated.* And still in *circulation were the copper* "Underground *Railroad" tokens.* **Civil War Patriotic token, dated 1863**

*By 1864 the Union government passed legislation making it illegal for private persons to issue any form of cash.*

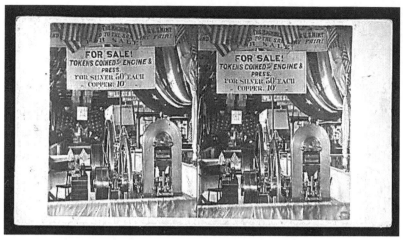

*A Sanitary Fair raised funds for their charitable support of the soldiers by charging for a TOKEN to be produced, offered in both silver and copper. LOC*

**Moore's Rural New-Yorker** – April 19, 1862
*The ship Northern Light brings $1,000,000 of specie from California
*Quarters have been provided at Chicago for 3,000 additional prisoners by orders of General Halleck
*The new Rebel Secretary of War, General George W. Randolph, is a grandson of Thomas Jefferson
*The Richmond Examiner says there are 250 whiskey distilleries in two districts alone in South Carolina
*The manufacture of rifle muskets at the US armory in Springfield continues steadily to increase and has now reached 12,000 per month
*The amount of bulk meat confiscated and seized by the government on the Cumberland River was very large. Amounting to 3,000,000 pounds

**New York Times article** – January 1862 – **regarding sutlers**
HOW THE EXPENSES OF WAR ARE TO BE MET
A PROPOSED TAX OF ONE HUNDRED AND FIFTY
MILLIONS  **Washington – January 7,** The Committee of Ways and Means have concluded to provide by taxation for a hundred and fifty millions during the current year.

The Committee of Ways and Means should not fail to impose

a monthly Tax on those who perform the office of **sutlers** to our armies. It is an exclusive privilege and a very valuable one. Merchants in civil life always pay a license. Those who sell in the camps should do likewise, and the funds go into the government treasury. The average value of a sutlership to a regiment is said to be $6,000. a year. If we have 600 regiments in service, the furnishing of sutler's goods to them yields a profit of nearly four millions annually. Why should not a fair per cent of this sum go to the government that furnishes the customers and the money they buy with?

Senator Hale's bill to protect the government treasury from swindling contracts comes none too soon. Its introduction today was marked by a severe speech from the senator.

**Harper's Weekly** – May 1865
OUR DEBT AND SPECIE PAYMENTS
The second series of the Seven-Thirty loan has been exhausted – in other words, the people of the United States have subscribed, in forty-five days, including holidays and Sundays, three hundred millions of dollars in support of their government. History may be ransacked in vain for a parallel. England stood aghast with amazement when the French nation, stirred by all the appliances of imperial menace and bureaucratic intrigue, offered the Emperor 750,000,000 francs, or $150,000,000 for the war in Italy. A bagatelle of $150,000,000 has been lent our government half a score of times since our war began; and now we are tendering $30,000,000 a day. ..........................Our national debt it is now pretty safe to estimate at three thousand millions of dollars. This is, of course, a very large sum of money. It may be said to amount to $100 a head for every man, woman and child in the country; the annual interest at $5 a head. .....................A question closely connected with the settlement of the national debt, and scarcely less important is, how soon can specie payments be resumed?

**The Vincennes Western Sun**, Vincennes, Indiana – August 3, 1861 – The Direct Tax Bill
This bill is now before the Senate; as passed by the House, it adds three per cent income tax, and **five Cents per gallon for distilled and two cents for fermented liquors**. The income tax is on all salaries, profits, interest, &c, over six hundred dollars per annum. All Democrats and Southern Americans voted against the bill, which passed by the small majority of seventeen.

**The New York Herald** – August 3, 1861

The Situation.......Congress has taken another bold step in the prosecution of the war. The Tariff and Direct Tax bill passed both houses yesterday, providing for a direct tax of twenty millions. The bill imposes a tax of three per cent on incomes over $800 per annum. The duty on sugar is fixed at two cents a pound, on coffee at three and a half cents, and on tea at fifteen cents.

Rebel "shinplasters" 1863

Confederate States of America – $5.00 – 1863
This bond would be paid to bearer, "two years after the ratification of a treaty of peace between the Confederate States and the United States"

Treasury note issued by the state of Virginia in 1862

Arkansas Treasury Warrant – Issued in 1862 – War Bond

*The Confederate States had monetary and supply problems due to inflation. Thus the TAX IN KIND policy was to be honored by all southern farmers; 10% of all a farmer produced was to be given to the Confederacy by act of their congress in 1863.*

**Moore's Rural New-Yorker** – February 8, 1862
Large amounts **of counterfeit money** is in circulation about the camp on the Potomac.

**Richmond Daily Dispatch** – December 30, 1863 – Eggnog Frolic
...... Eggnog Frolics have been exceedingly numerous this season not withstanding the exorbitant prices asked for all the articles used in compounding the beverage.  One half the money thus thrown away would have made glad the hearts of hundreds of sorrowing widows and orphans and added happiness to the givers.  How few remember the poor!

**Confederate loan, redeemable in 1868**

## NEWS

In 1867 a New York broker bought one million worth of confederate bonds. Many others had thousands of dollars in bonds but were not willing to part with them. The only reason given for this situation is that the Confederate government during the war deposited $7 million in England that was never reclaimed. If the bonds could be redeemed in England it would probably entitle the holder to the cash. *(From a news clipping with no attribution)*

**The New York Herald** – August 6, 1861
The income tax, as in England, may be unpopular, but its simplicity is certainly a strong recommendation in its favor as a measure of expediency at the present time. **That it will have anything like a permanent existence among us, however, is by no means likely.** The tax on watches may easily be borne, as it will fall on the wealthier portion of the community, although we do not doubt

that it will lead many of those now in the habit of wearing them to discontinue the practice. The general effect of the new schedule will be to induce the practice of domestic economy. Already, indeed, the reduction of incomes, caused by the stagnation of trade and the depreciation of property, has put an end to many of the extravagances which were before common to us. It is well for us as a nation that this salutary social change has been inaugurated, and that people who have been accustomed only to squander should find it necessary to practice the virtue of thrift.

*The money crisis in the south resulted in auctions of gold pieces.*

**Harper's Weekly** – 1861
Suspension of Specie payments in Kentucky. The legislature of Kentucky adjourned on the 24th by laws just enacted the courts of the State are suspended until 1st of Jan. next, and the banks are allowed to suspend specie payments.

1861 confederate note was scanned from a glass negative and Louisiana Bond.

Union Fractional Currency & Postage Currency dated 1862 & 1863

**The London Times** of Saturday – 1862
Published; an editorial expiating on the diminutive paper currency in America.

**Union News** – 1862
The first delivery of postage currency was made yesterday in exchange for coin.  Parties offering coin in exchange will have preference at the Treasury Department.

**MOORE'S Rural New-Yorker** – October 1862
The question has been raised whether the shinplasters and fractional notes circulated as money are not libel to stamp duty under the new tax law.

**New York Times** – 1864 – THE DEFICIENCY BILL

The following are among the amendments made to-day, by the Senate, to the Deficiency Appropriation Bill, at the suggestion of the Secretary of War: For deficiency in arms and ordnance, $7,700,000; for the manufacture of arms at the National Armory, $700,000; sick soldiers in private hospitals, $7,000; subsistence of soldiers, $5,824,000; Quartermaster's Incidentals, Quartermaster's Department, $2,000,000; clothing, camp and garrison equipage $7,000,000. Other items embraced, making an aggregate of $80,000,000 as a deficiency.

Courtesy of Lolita and Hal White

 Confederate Postage stamps

Brown, Farmville, Va.

C. H. SWANSKI, PHOTOGRAPHER FARMVILLE, VA.

Both these Confederate soldiers were from Farmville, Virginia. The photo on the left is Henry Stuart. The soldier in the right photo served in the 4th Virginia Infantry Regiment, fighting in the Stonewall Brigade with the Army of North Virginia. When the unit surrendered 7 officers were left alive and only 38 men, of those only 17 were armed.

Their hometown of Farmville was the site of the battles of High Bridge. During the last large battle in the area, near Sayler's Creek, General Lee retreated through the town of Farmville, finally surrendering at Appomattox Court House on April 9, 1865.

Confederate uniform button

Confederate Loan Coupons – redeemable 1867

*Abraham and Mary Lincoln*

*Postcard of the house where President Abraham Lincoln died. Located near Fords Theater in Washington, D.C.*

*President Lincoln was killed in 1865, just five days after the surrender of General Lee to General U. S. Grant. Along with the mourning came the craze for collecting Lincoln photos and memorabilia and images of the war.*

**New York Times** – 1865

New York Times – 1865

*Advertisements in the NEW YORK TIMES – 1865 – selling the
assassination memorabilia along with whisker unguent and
memorial medals.*

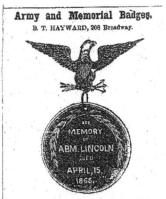

Hucksters throughout the centuries have capitalized on grief, death and disasters to promote products.

This Lincoln/ Washington memorial photo was scanned from a glass negative.

**City Point, Va.** – April 16, 1865
My dear Sister. As I have received your kind letter I will try to answer it as well as I can. I am pretty well at this present time. I was glad to get a letter from a dear Sis that I love so well. Dear Sister this war is a coming to a close very fast. Richmond has fallen, General Lee is captured and his army. Peace will soon be declared. We will give God all the praise and thank him for this great and Glorious Victory. I suppose you have seen it in the papers

before this time. God knows what is before us and he will do all things well. But my dear Sis, I want to tell you about my Jesus for he is all in all to me. **My Dear Sister, while I am a writing to you the news has come that Our Dear President is dead. He was Asasinated by a man by the name of George Booth I believe. I do not know the particulars about it.** you will see it in the papers before this letter reaches you I guess. I could not but help weeping when I heard of it, the best president we have had since Washington's time it is sad to think of it but it may be all for the best, God only knows, I trust he was a Christian. My Dear Sis I love you but I love my Jesus better, I love him better than any earthly friend that I have got. Dear Sis I believe that My Blessed Jesus has Sanctified me by his blessed truth. I feel to say here I blessed Jesus.....thinkest best. I feel all given up to his Holy and blessed will, my soul is filled with his Glory a great deal of the time I know in whose all fullness dwells that he will give this poor unworthy worm of the dust his Devine Presence. My Dear Sister do you not think it is the will of God even your Sanctification. I do. if you will seek for it in earnest nothing doubting. Dear Sis if it was God's will, and I could be at home now and take you by the hand and talk with you about Jesus. Oh! We should get both our souls blest. Oh! Sister will you be wholy his. You love him I trust, but you must love him more. Oh! Neel down and say, here I am blessed Jesus do whatsoever thou wilt with me. Dear Sis I will tell you what goes through my mind..."Blessed One"?? Holiness. Purity. Dear Sis you wanted me to write about my sickness. I have not room to write much about it, it is but a little consequence about myself. I feel for the souls of others. I speak to them when I feel it my duty by God's grace a helping me. But I will tell you that My Jesus was with me in all of my sickness, I may tell you about it sometime. Oh! My prayer is that my Dear Brothers might find Salvation. **Dear Sis the report is now that our President is not dead. there is so many story's about it we cannot tell yet.** Sis you wanted to know if I got a letter sometime ago from you. I did I believe. We have Glorious Meetings here now, night and day souls are Converted. God is with us. bless his Holy Name. all of you write as often as you can. I must close now so good By. May God Bless you all is my prayer from your unworthy Brother Benjamin P. Hunt      9th Corps Hospital City Point Va.

Letter Courtesy of R. Katchuk

Music courtesy of Allen Sweet

ORDNANCE OFFICE,

*WAR DEPARTMENT,*

*Washington, D. C. May 21st 1864.*

*Sir:*

*Your return of Ordnance and Ordnance Stores pertaining to Co. I. 56th Pennsylvania Volunteer Infantry for the fourth quarter of 1862 has been examined in this office, and referred to the Second Auditor for settlement.*

*Respectfully, your obedient servant,*

*By order:*

Geo. F. Balch

Captain of Ordnance.

*Lieut. Samuel Healy*
*Co. I. 56th Pennsylvania Volunteer Infantry,*

property return referred to above has passed the administrative scrutiny of the
and correct. IT SHOULD BE CAREFULLY PRESERVED BY THE RECEIVER.

Those discharged with disabilities, plus widows, and orphans filed claims for pensions. Thus continuing the cost of war on human lives.

# Discharge by Disbandment.

## TO ALL WHOM IT MAY CONCERN.

**Know Ye,** That *Benjamin F Cady* a *Sergeant* of Company *E* of the *One Hundred & Fifty* Regiment *Infantry* National Guard of the State of New York, who was enrolled on the *Second* day of *September* one thousand eight hundred and *Sixty Three* to serve for seven years; (Sections 22 and 135 Military Code,) is hereby **Discharged** from service in the Active Militia of the State of New York, this *Twenty Ninth* day of *June* one thousand eight hundred and *Sixty Eight* at *Canastota* by reason of the disbandment of his *Regiment* under orders of the Commander-in-Chief.

This Discharge does not exempt the said *Benjamin F Cady* from military duty in the Reserve Militia, nor entitle him to any other exemptions under provisions of the Military Code. If he shall hereafter enroll himself in any organization of the National Guard, the Commanding Officer of such organization is authorized and directed to enter upon the enlistment papers and muster-rolls the term of service as appears by this certificate, which term shall be credited and allowed upon the entire and completetion of seven years, in the same manner as if rendered continuously in one organization. And the said Commanding Officer is directed to take up this certificate and file it with the records of his Company or Regiment.

Given at *Canastota* this *29th* day of *June* 1868.

*Theo. F. Pern*

Brigad. Inspector
And Mustering Officer.

*Charles B Crouse*
Commanding 105 Regiment

Enclosed you will receive a certificate, No. *61126* for $124,00 payable to you as *Widow* of *deceased* or to your order, by any Paymaster of the U. S. Army, being for pay due *George P. White* a late *Corporal* in Captain *Morrison's* Company *B*, 3° Regiment of *New York Artillery* for services from the *14th* day of *August* 1861, when *Enrolled* to the *28th* day of *November* 1862, time of his *death* and the $*100* Bounty allowed by Act July 22, 1861,

Very respectfully,

Your obedient servant,

*E. B. French*

Second Auditor.

*Helen C. White,*
*Cover to*
*Amos H. White,*
*Washington*
*D.C.*

B.F.F.

Widow payment for Union soldier killed 1862

## DIRECTIONS FOR THE EXECUTION OF APPLICATIONS FOR CLAIMS.

Applications for Pensions must in all cases be sworn to before the Clerk of a Court of Record, or other person having the custody of the seal of the Court, and the seal should be affixed. The title of the Clerk or other officer should be inserted in the blank at the commencement of the application.

Applications for Bounty, &c., may be executed as in the case of Pensions, or before a Justice of the Peace. If executed before a Justice of the Peace, the certificate of the Secretary of State, or of a Clerk of a Court of Record, must be attached, showing that the magistrate is duly commissioned and qualified to administer oaths, &c.

☞ If there are any blanks, as to the age of the applicant, letter of company or number of regiment of which the soldier was a member, or any date, &c., such blank should be filled before execution.

Two credible witnesses who are acquainted with the applicant, and who were also acquainted with the deceased soldier, and with his social relations, should subscribe and swear to the second part of the application prepared for that purpose, and at the same time as the applicant.

Boston June 22nd '64

Mr Taylor,

I send the papers to be filled the blanks as to date of death, marriage &c has better be written in pencil so that when you return the papers to me I can fill them in my hand writing. She watches Mr Howard will have to write for herself. They mite any money might to be sent to her by the Col of the Regt. The back Pay I can get for her, but I cant get any of her husband's personal effects. She would better write to the Adjutant General of the U. States at Washington in regard to them.

W. T.

The Cost of War

## 18 GRAND ARMY OF THE REPUBLIC (GAR) –
## Memorabilia – 50th Anniversary of Gettysburg Invitation

*As the American Civil War reached its conclusion entrepreneurs began campaigns to sell souvenirs, publishing books and building memorials.....to celebrate, commemorate, to heal. Veteran organizations were formed in every state of the Union, both North and South. The GAR (The Grand Army of The Republic) was among the most prominent. The United Confederate Veterans (UCV) was formed in 1888 and their final reunion was in 1951. There was respect for each other between the men of both organizations.*

Major General.........
Member of the Grand Army
of the Republic, wearing
reunion ribbons

These tickets were to
a GAR event

GAR SHIELD in recognition of Sergeant George W. Clark – Post # 31 – Department of New Jersey. 12th Regiment New Jersey volunteers.

This shield is a work of art, each section is hand painted, lettered and cut with precision and pieced together to form the whole. The three orange color arms contain the history of the unit.

Courtesy of the Bruce Stuart Clark family who also had relatives serving in the Confederacy.

258

Remembrances in honor to those who served our country

GAR saber holder, tag from hall 42 and souvenir badges

The last reunion of the North & South Soldiers at Gettysburg was in 1938. An eternal light was dedicated:

"PEACE ETERNAL IN A NATION UNITED"

A member of the GAR wearing a medal from the 1899 convention and a ribbon from the 20th reunion of the 89th NY, Veterans Association event, 1909 Memorial Day postcard, and medals of GAR and Sons of Union Veterans

**COMMISSIONERS**

MAJOR-GEN'L DANIEL E. SICKLES, U. S. A.
BVT. BRIG.-GEN'L ANSON G. McCOOK
COL. LEWIS R. STEGMAN

COL. CLINTON BECKWITH
BVT. COL. HORATIO C. KING

BREVET COLONEL HORATIO C. KING
CHAIRMAN

BVT. MAJOR THOMAS W. BRADLEY
BRIG.-GEN'L HENRY D. HAMILTON, ADJ.-GEN'L S. N. Y.

A. J. ZABRISKIE
ENGINEER AND SECRETARY

# NEW YORK COMMISSION
### FOR THE
## BATTLEFIELDS OF GETTYSBURG AND CHATTANOOGA

APPOINTED A COMMISSION TO PLAN AND CONDUCT A PUBLIC CELEBRATION OF
THE 50th ANNIVERSARY OF THE BATTLE OF GETTYSBURG, JULY 1, 2, 3, 4, 1913

TELEPHONE, 62 GRAMERCY

1 EAST 9th STREET, NEW YORK CITY

Dear Sir and Comrade:—

Answering your favor just received, I beg to call your attention to the marked sections of the following circular.

Fraternally yours,

*Horatio C. King*

Chairman.

1. Congress has limited the attendance to 40,000 Union and Confederate veterans from all the States as the officials of the railroads entering Gettysburg have decided that they cannot provide transportation for a greater number.

2. At a meeting of the General Commission having in charge the arrangements for the Fiftieth Anniversary Celebration, held in Philadelphia, January 23–25, 1913, the number of veterans allotted to the State of New York was 10,000. In view of this action the New York Commission at a meeting held January 27, 1913, decided to grant a preference:

    (a) to surviving soldiers now residing in this State who served in regiments or other commands that participated in the Battle of Gettysburg.

    (b) to those veterans of the War of the Rebellion now residing in this State not connected as above, who had the longest term of service.

3. No provision is made by law for the transportation of families of veterans, nor for shelter and subsistence for them by the Federal Government.

4. Veterans will be quartered under canvas, eight to a tent, and provided with rations by companies, practically as issued in the time of the Civil War. To each veteran will be given blankets, a tin plate, cup, knife and fork and two spoons, and he will take his meals at a table contiguous to the open air kitchen.

5. There will be a general hospital for the sick and several infirmaries in the camp.

6. The camp is located about one-eighth of a mile north of the clump of trees known as "The High Water Mark." It is expected that the railroad trains will be run into this camp and arriving veterans will be detrained there.

7. Veterans arriving as Posts or in special groups will be assigned to tents together; all others will be assigned to tents set apart for New York veterans.

8. The passenger association of the trunk lines has announced that *Gettysburg terminal lines will not park any cars.*

9. It is expected that the Federal Government will provide an abundance of spring wagons and ambulances for the transportation of veterans over the field.

10. Public exercises to be announced later, will be held on each day from July 1 to 4, inclusive.

11. The State of New York will hold special ceremonies in the National Cemetery near the New York State Monument, at which Rev. Newell Dwight Hillis, D.D., Pastor of Plymouth Church, Brooklyn, N. Y., will be the orator. The full program will be issued at a later date.

262

# NEW YORK MONUMENTS COMMISSION.

NEW YORK, June 20th, 1913.

Dear Comrade:

Enclosed find transportation order for ticket to Gettysburg and return; also identification card and identification tag, together with New York State badge. These documents are of particular value to you and should be carefully preserved during your trip.

*Advice:* Carry sufficient provisions with you, to Gettysburg and returning, to cover the meals you need. You cannot depend upon dining cars or restaurants on the routes, many of which are quite long.

Every man will need some money for personal use. Each man must protect this himself.

Remember that no women or children are furnished with quarters in the general camp. Only veterans are accommodated.

Persons receiving a transportation order, or holding an unused ticket, and being unable from any cause to use same, shall return it immediately to A. J. Zabriskie, Engineer and Secretary, 116 Nassau Street, New York City. Misuse is liable to fine and imprisonment.

Boy Scouts will be on hand to conduct veterans to quarters.

Fraternally yours,
NEW YORK MONUMENTS COMMISSION.

No. *6248*   **STATE OF NEW YORK**

*Office of* NEW YORK COMMISSION *on the* GETTYSBURG CELEBRATION
116 Nassau Street - - - New York City
*New York Identification Credential—NOT TRANSFERABLE*

This Certifies that *Hiram Stout*

late of *Co E 148ª Regiment*

as *Private* is entitled to quarters and rations
and all the courtesies of the camp during the Reunion Celebration at Gettysburg, July 1 to 4, 1913.

Age *79* years; height *5* ft. *9½* inches; weight *180* lbs.

Transportation Order No. *7472*

LEWIS R. STEGMAN,
CHAIRMAN

Signature of Applicant *Hiram Stout*

If signed by mark then one witness _____

**Notice to the Veteran and to the Railroad Ticket Agent**

This identification card is intended to identify the veteran at the camp in Gettysburg and must be stamped by the ticket agent when the railroad ticket is issued and be given with it to him and be presented by him to the commandant on arrival at Gettysburg camp

263

Memorial citation for First Lieutenant R.Q.M. Leroy Larrabee

This is a typical remembrance for those whose lives were lost in our Civil War.

Memorial roster for Binghamton Fountain Hose Fire Company
No. 4
Photo scanned from a glass negative

Certificate of Recognition for the American Civil War service of
Private Peter Benninger presented to his family as a reminder of his
extreme patriotism.

Peter Benninger at the age of 20, enlisted in the United States
service at Laceyville, Pennsylvania, March 8, 1862, serving as a
private of Company F, 107th Regiment, Pennsylvania Volunteer

Infantry for three years. As part of the Army of the Potomac he participated in the battles of Cedar Mountain, the Second Bull Run, Chantilly, Fredericksburg, Gettysburg, Mine Run, Spotsylvania, North Anna, Petersburg, Weldon Raiload, Prebles Farm, Hatchers Run, · Boydton Road, Five Forks and Appomattox. He was wounded at South Mountain when a minie ball passed through both thighs. After recovering in the hospital he rejoined his unit until discharged in 1865. He was an active member of the Whitney Point GAR and became a successful, fourth generation, blacksmith. He lived to be 93 years old, proud of his service to community & country.

Courtesy of Pearl Webb

**Harper's Weekly** – December 10, 1864
FOR THE SOLDIER'S CHILD

The New York State Volunteer Institute was established about eighteen months since at Suspension Bridge, Niagara County, New York, to furnish a home for and to educate the sons and daughters of dead or disabled officers and soldiers, and if funds enough can be raised it will be made a National instead of a State institution. It is a military school, but it proposes to fit the cadets for any honorable pursuit.

The appeals to the public charity for projects connected with the war have been so many, and the applications for the advantages of the Institute have so largely increased, that the proprietors now propose to relieve those who wish to aid the institution by changing a donation into a purchase. That they may furnish shelter, food, clothing and a liberal education to the children under their charge they ask fifty thousand subscriptions at two dollars each, for which every subscriber will receive a fine large steel plate portrait of the

President, General Grant, or any corps commander, and also a
certificate representing a share in the distribution of real estate in
and near the city of New York to be made on Washington's birthday,
February 22, 1865, the profits to be devoted to the benefit of the
Volunteer Institute.
We are informed that the institution has the approval of General
Hooker, Governor Seymour, the late General Wadsworth, and Mr.
Rice, Superintendent of Public Instruction, the President is Colonel
W. H. Young, and the Treasurer Captain H.R. Randall, PO Box
4262, New York City.


The Southern States also made efforts to serve women left in need
by war…..a postcard view of the Confederate Women's Home in
Richmond, Virginia

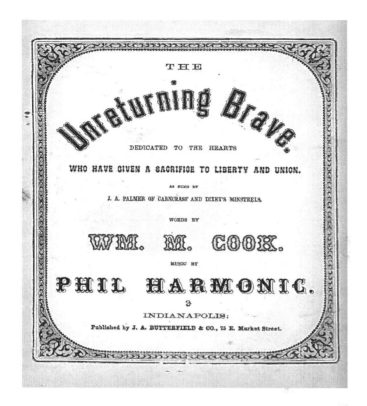

THE

**Unreturning Brave.**

DEDICATED TO THE HEARTS

WHO HAVE GIVEN A SACRIFICE TO LIBERTY AND UNION.

AS SUNG BY

J. A. PALMER OF CARNCRASS' AND DIXEY'S MINSTRELS.

WORDS BY

**WM. M. COOK.**

MUSIC BY

**PHIL HARMONIC.**

3

INDIANAPOLIS:

Published by J. A. BUTTERFIELD & CO., 75 E. Market Street.

IN MEMORIAM
They died to keep our nation one.
For North, for south, their work was done,
And done so well that now we stand
A great and undivided land
Whose strength is union and whose good
Is sealed in lasting brotherhood.
Taps!
Lights Out!
Asleep!
One flag, one country,
Shall forever keep
And on the sod which covers them
Shall set a blossoming diadem
W. J. LAMPTON

*Marketing practices never change. Post Civil War, depictions of heroes were used as just another ploy to sell goods.*

*Abe selling candy*

*Books concerning the American Civil War were written before, during and after hostilities ended. New information continues to be found in letters, diaries, photographs and forgotten manuscripts. Battles are still discussed, debated and reenacted.....and, perhaps humans are learning the true cost of war..........from the echo of words from those who lived and died during a supreme era of conflict in the United States of America*

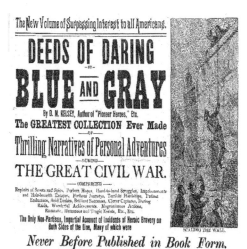

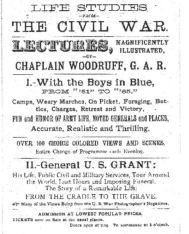

A tourist destination, The Casino in Endicott, NY, 1900

## 19  PERHAPS
*Both North and South complained bitterly about "uncivilized warfare" being perpetrated by the other...............*

**Harper's Weekly** – May 1864
….."Confederate Atrocities Go Beyond the Pale of Civilized War"….

**Richmond Daily Dispatch**
April 7, 1864 – Atrocities of the enemy in North Alabama
The darkest chapter in the history of this cruel war, if not in any other war, will record the atrocities of the Yankees wherever in the Confederate states they have been permitted to march their thieving, brutal hordes. Their deeds, so in violation of all the rules of civilized or humane war fare, entitle them to a place in history with the Goths and Vandals…………….

*PERHAPS*
*Perhaps the attitudes of people like Dr. Muir have evolved...or not....*

**Moore's Rural New-Yorker** – October 18, 1862 –
THE FIGHTING AT ANTITAM
The Rochester Democrat has been permitted to make the following extract from a private letter:
Dr. Muir, Surgeon-General of the English Army for Canada, was present at the battle of Antietam, and told a friend of mine in this city, that he had been in India, the Crimea and in Cuba and was present at Solferino and that **he had never before seen such fighting as at Antietam, and that he felt proud of the fact that the men on both sides were of his own race.**

**New York Times** – August, Sunday 1863
A most "civil" war………. "there has been but two or three shots fired today (near Sumter) as both parties are observing the Sabbath day."

**Illustrated London News** – 1862
From a speech by Rev. S. Cox.......... "E Pluribus Unum," many
states united in one, each state a sovereign – all these sovereigns
united in one country, which neither Slavery nor rebellion can put
down..........."

"As freemen war but to establish peace
The deadliest vengeance speediest will cease"

**The Richmond Dispatch** – August 1863
"There is no hope of a humane observance of the code of civilized
warfare by the Yankees."

**PERHAPS**
**Perhaps mankind creates hell**
**By believing any war civilized**

*Battlefields baptized in blood became lasting memorials....*

## REFERENCES:

Tribute Book – by Frank B. Goodrich – 1865
Tales of The Civil War –Sutler article by Waldo Campbell Hibbs
The New York Times – newspapers of the Civil War Years
The Chicago Times – 1862
The Richmond Dispatch – Civil War era
Moore's Rural New Yorker – 1861 – 1865
Illustrated London News – 1862 – 1865
Evening Post weekly
The Philadelphia Inquirer
Harper's Weekly
Frank Leslie's Illustrated
The Library of Congress
The American Conflict – A history of The Great Rebellion – by
Horace Greeley – 1866
McClellan's Own Story – by George B. McClellan – 1887
Under Both Flags – a Panorama of the Great Civil War – C. R.
Graham – 1896
The History of the Civil War in America – by John S. C. Abbott –
1863
A History of the Civil War – by Benson J. Lossing, L.L.D. – 1912
The Civil War Through The Camera – by Henry W. Elson – 1912
The New York Herald
The Civil War at Charleston – 1966 a Post Courier Booklet
Southern Confederacy Newspaper, Atlanta Georgia

## CIVIL WAR – "Where Liberty Dwells" – NAME LIST

Jud Allen
Mr. Arnold
Miss Barnes
Mr. George Bacon – D 1862
Charley Barager
Mrs. Horace Booth – D Aug. 1862
Miss L. Bacon
Elouise Bacon
Mr. Baff – did Musical show at Trusdalls Hall
Miss Ella Benedict
George Barager – soldier, attorney, Town Supervisor
Peter Brink and Lady
Mr. Barber
Freman Booth
Miss Butler (Teacher at Albany Normal School – 1861)
Miller Belknap
Arnold Bunnal
Mr. Berger
Duke Bell
Mr. Brown
Maria Barnum (East Maine, Broome Co.)
Peter Benninger
Sammy Brooks – seen on Army steamer Oct. 1864
Richard (Dick) Clark
Charlie Clark
Henry Clark – cousin of F. A. Keeler
George W. Clark, Sergeant, NJ 12th Regt.
Henry Cornell
Mrs. Richard Cornell
Ida Carlow
Mr. Covwn (tends mill)
Leon Chidsey (married in Binghamton 1862)
Capt. Caryl – missing 1862
Sam Chidsey
Mr. Cross
Professor Cochran (Albany Normal School)
Capt. E. H. Converse
Mr. Chamberlain

Dalton Doolittle
Abe Daniels
Sol Darling
Mrs. Dodge (Alice Merrill) – lost child, Oct. 1862
George DeBoyce
James Dickinson
Mr. Dunbar (Ithaca)
Rev. Ellis – Methodist Minister, Candor
Curtis Flanders – dead in war, April 1862
Mr. Fortner
Bill Gridley
Selea Gridley
Seth Gridley
William Cadwell Gridley
Mr. Gleason
Edwin Gile
Miss Goodwin
Sarah Henry
Miss Haywood
Lucia Hart
Julia Hart
Jennie Hart
Kelsey Hart
E. Harder – died 1862 – 26th Regt.
Rev. Haywood
Miss Tempie E. Hamilton
Joseph Porter Hamilton
David Dickerson Hamilton, 7th Tenn. Regt. Archer's Brigade
Eleazer Hamilton & Wife Emily Perry Hamilton – Nashville, Tenn.
Eleazer Dent Hamilton
John Hall Hamilton
Margaret Amanda Page Hamilton
Mrs. Holcum
Capt. James Hope, Soldier, Artist
Mrs. Hubbard & two daughters from Conn.
Benjamin P. Hunt
Joshua T. Hunt
(Cousin) Will H. Hunt
Charlie Hunt
Walter Hunt (Uncle of F. A. Keeler)

Lieut. Leroy Hewith – Died 1862, buried from Candor Methodist Church
E. Hans (of Spencer)
Jerry Hitt
Truing Hitt
Capt. James Hope (artist)
Hattie Hall (or Hull) of Oxford
Lieut. Harder
Mr. Hummerston (house burned 1862, Candor)
Miss Johnson (student Albany Normal School)
Miss Annie Jamison
Fred Joslyn
Mary Joslyn (or Josslyn)
Frank Josslyn
William Josslyn (uncle of Frank, both went to Michigan)
Joe Judson
Clark Kellison
George King (from Chenango Forks)
Mr. Ketchum
Sarah Kesley
M. E. Kesley
Mary Kesley
Ward Kesley (cousins of William Cadwell Gridley)
Sarah Keeler (student at Albany normal school & sister of F. A. Keeler)
Ira Keeler – candy salesman – father of Frances A. Keeler
Mary Keeler – sister of Augusta – 2nd wife of W. C. Gridley
Harrison Keeler (Owego)
David Keeler (27th Regt., wounded 1862) cousin of F. A. Keeler
F. P. Kerr
Cam Kerr, 169th Regt. Co. C. Va.
Milt Knox – had mumps in camp Stevenson, Al.
Capt. Krom
Ralph Kuler (Canada)
Leroy E. Larrabee
Mrs. Joe Lyttel (Eloise Bacon)
Eliza E. Lumbold (Brooklyn, Michigan)
Doc McKeys (dentist)
Mary Marshall
Sue Marshall (married in Binghamton 1862)

William Newby – married _____ Preston, in army & ok 1864
Mr. Norton, Ohio
Truman S. North (Co. C, 109th Regt. NYV)
Mr. J. North
Lieut. Oakley – unit going to Texas
Fred Pampily
Mrs. Parmalee
Edison Parker
Alexander Philps
Charles Phelps
John Preston
O. B. Preston
Frank Preston
Charles Peters
John Powell
Capt. Roberts
Elicity Rogers
Mr. & Mrs. Joel Robinson
Susan Richardson (from Ottawa, Illinois, aunt of F. A. Keeler)
Maggie Richardson (died in 1860 – cousin of F. A. Keeler)
Fernando Runge – killed 1864
Lon Robinson
Lou Robinson Married Bodintha S., Abe Daniels Niece)
Alb Robinson – 109th of Candor, NY
C. R. Sackett (Cousin of F. A. Keeler)
Asa Sackett
Fannie Sackett
Hiram Scott
Henry Smith (engaged to Rosa Way)
W. G. Sterling
B. S. Sanders
O. W. Smith
Nant Smith
Sarah Sullivan
Phoebe E. Smith
Joseph S. Smith (Co. E, 114th Regt. NYV – 19th Army Corps, New
Orleans, Louisiana – wounded in head June 1864
Dick Seaborn
Hiram Stout
W. R. Sturgess (sutler)

George Sturgess (sutler)
Susan Sturgess
Eugene Smith
Mary Smith (niece of George Barager)
Henry Stuart (Virginia)
Hiram Stout
Tom Swan
R. N. Silsbee (Wyoming Co. Pa.)
Mr. Thurston (quartermaster)
Mr. Tompkins
Professor Towner (brought musical convention to Candor Baptist Church 1862)
John Trusdall
Ella Trusdal
Mr. Turner (brother of Mary)
Rob Turner (may be above)
Sate Van Kleek
John V. – Camp near Bellfoken
William Walker
Mary Ward – married Rev. Bose, Methodist Minister
Hiram Ward (father of Mary)
Mrs. Waller
Miss Ina Ward
Lau Ward
Rosa Way (engaged to Henry Smith 1862)
Rowena Way
Lau Williams
John Winner
Mrs. Jacob Wilbey
Roswell Woodbridge – died 1864
Mrs. John Woodford
George Woodford
Julia A Wood
Billy Wood
Melissa Wood (New Woodstock)
Annette Wuring
Miss Eliza Wood
Mr. & Mrs. Whiton (from Conn) – relatives of W.C. Gridley
Peter Young
Theodore Yarington
Edward Yessy

*NOTE: The names are spelled exactly as written in the original letters. Often a name was spelled different in the same letter. Military, census records and deeds could also list the same person with various spellings.*

Families predominantly mentioned in this volume:

IRA KEELER – Born in 1810 –
Sarah Warren Sackett Keeler – born in 1812 – Died 1886 – married Ira in Candor in 1836

> Her Parents were Nathaniel and Sarah Warren Sackett

Children: **Frances Augusta Keeler** – Born 1840 – died 1876
> George LeGrange Keeler – Born 1842 – died 1906
> Sarah Warren Keeler – Born 1844 – died 1899
> Mary A. Keeler – born 1848
> Rosabella Keeler – born 1850
> Laura R. Keeler – born 1853 – died 1881

**William Cadwell Gridley** – Born 1840 – died 1900
Frances Augusta Keeler – born 1840 – died 1876

**Children of William C. Gridley & Frances Augusta Keeler**
> Charles LeGrand Gridley – 1864
> John T. Gridley – born 1867
> Samuel Sackett Gridley – born 1874

When Frances Augusta Keeler Gridley died in 1876 her sister Mary A. Keeler moved to the Gridley homestead to care for the children and keep house, as listed in the 1880 census. In 1885 Mary & Will Gridley were married. By the 1892 census they had a 1 year old son. William was listed as a farmer.

**LOCAL RECORD**
**Owego** – Saturday, September 5, 1885
Mr. William C. Gridley and Miss Mary Keeler were married at the residence of the bride's mother last Tuesday evening. C.C. Johnson officiating

*The following letter to Wm. C. Gridley was from his second wife
Mary, dated 1889. She was obviously as in love with Gridley as was
her deceased sister Augusta.*

**New York** – Thursday, May 9, 1899
Darling Cad, I am going to start for Scranton Friday morning and
expect to get to Candor Saturday night. I hope you will meet me.
Do not say anything to anyone that I am coming. If I am not there
Saturday I shall be there Monday night. I received your lengthy
letter Tuesday morning & was glad to hear that all was going well.
Rosa and I went to the theater last night seen Black Crook. It is the
most leggy show in NY. Wont you be glad when I get home, I shall.
Friday, I guess I will stop in Binghamton a day or two so you need
not meet me Saturday. I will write you again.
Ever your loving, Mary

William C. Gridley continued to farm, and provide produce to
relatives in other states for their businesses. Below is a letter head
from one such business.....Gridley Brothers, in Amboy, Illinois

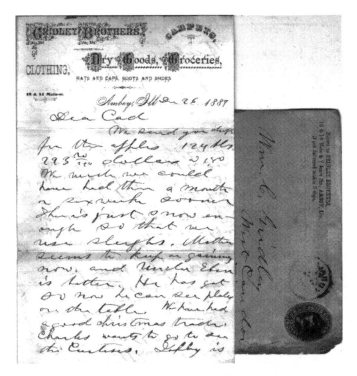

34622754R00167

Made in the USA
Middletown, DE
30 August 2016